Palgrave Macmillan Studies in Banking and Financial Institutions

Series Editor: **Professor Philip Molyneux**

The Palgrave Macmillan Studies in Banking and Financial Institutions are international in orientation and include studies of banking within particular countries or regions, and studies of particular themes such as Corporate Banking, Risk Management, Mergers and Acquisitions, etc. The books' focus is on research and practice, and they include up-to-date and innovative studies on contemporary topics in banking that will have global impact and influence.

Titles include:

Yener Altunbaş, Alper Kara and Öslem Olgu
TURKISH BANKING
Banking under Political Instability and Chronic High Inflation

Paola Bongini, Stefano Chiarlone and Giovanni Ferri *(editors)*
EMERGING BANKING SYSTEMS

Vittorio Boscia, Alessandro Carretta and Paola Schwizer
COOPERATIVE BANKING: INNOVATIONS AND DEVELOPMENTS

Vittorio Boscia, Alessandro Carretta and Paola Schwizer
COOPERATIVE BANKING IN EUROPE: CASE STUDIES

Roberto Bottiglia, Elisabetta Gualandri and Gian Nereo Mazzocco *(editors)*
CONSOLIDATION IN THE EUROPEAN FINANCIAL INDUSTRY

Alessandro Carretta, Franco Fiordelisi and Gianluca Mattarocci *(editors)*
NEW DRIVERS OF PERFORMANCE IN A CHANGING FINANCIAL WORLD

Dimitris N. Chorafas
CAPITALISM WITHOUT CAPITAL

Dimitris N. Chorafas
FINANCIAL BOOM AND GLOOM
The Credit and Banking Crisis of 2007–2009 and Beyond

Vincenzo D'Apice and Giovanni Ferri
FINANCIAL INSTABILITY
Toolkit for Interpreting Boom and Bust Cycles

Peter Falush and Robert L. Carter OBE
THE BRITISH INSURANCE INDUSTRY SINCE 1900
The Era of Transformation

Franco Fiordelisi
MERGERS AND ACQUISITIONS IN EUROPEAN BANKING

Franco Fiordelisi, Philip Molyneux and Daniele Previati *(editors)*
NEW ISSUES IN FINANCIAL AND CREDIT MARKETS

Franco Fiordelisi, Philip Molyneux and Daniele Previati *(editors)*
NEW ISSUES IN FINANCIAL INSTITUTIONS MANAGEMENT

Hans Genberg and Cho-Hoi Hui
THE BANKING SECTOR IN HONG KONG
Competition, Efficiency, Performance and Risk

Carlo Gola and Alessandro Roselli
THE UK BANKING SYSTEM AND ITS REGULATORY AND SUPERVISORY FRAMEWORK

Elisabetta Gualandri and Valeria Venturelli *(editors)*
BRIDGING THE EQUITY GAP FOR INNOVATIVE SMEs

Kim Hawtrey
AFFORDABLE HOUSING FINANCE

Otto Hieronymi *(editor)*
GLOBALIZATION AND THE REFORM OF THE INTERNATIONAL BANKING AND MONETARY SYSTEM

Sven Janssen
BRITISH AND GERMAN BANKING STRATEGIES

M. Mansoor Khan and M. Ishaq Bhatti
DEVELOPMENTS IN ISLAMIC BANKING
The Case of Pakistan

Anders Ögren *(editor)*
THE SWEDISH FINANCIAL REVOLUTION

Dominique Rambure and Alec Nacamuli
PAYMENT SYSTEMS
From the Salt Mines to the Board Room

Catherine Schenk *(editor)*
HONG KONG SAR's MONETARY AND EXCHANGE RATE CHALLENGES
Historical Perspectives

Noël K. Tshiani
BUILDING CREDIBLE CENTRAL BANKS
Policy Lessons for Emerging Economies

The full list of titles available is on the website:
www.palgrave.com/finance/sbfi.asp

Palgrave Macmillan Studies in Banking and Financial Institutions
Series Standing Order ISBN 978–1–4039–4872–4

You can receive future titles in this series as they are published by placing a standing order. Please contact your bookseller or, in case of difficulty, write to us at the address below with your name and address, the title of the series and the ISBN quoted above.

Customer Services Department, Macmillan Distribution Ltd, Houndmills, Basingstoke, Hampshire RG21 6XS, England

---

New Issues in Financial and Credit Markets

Edited by

Franco Fiordelisi
Professor of Banking and Finance, University of Rome III, Italy;
Bangor Business School, Bangor University, UK and
Essex Finance Centre, Essex University, UK

Philip Molyneux
Professor of Banking and Finance, Bangor Business School,
Bangor University, UK

and

Daniele Previati
Professor of Banking and Finance, University of Rome III, Italy

palgrave
macmillan

First published 2010 by
PALGRAVE MACMILLAN

Palgrave Macmillan in the UK is an imprint of Macmillan Publishers Limited, registered in England, company number 785998, of Houndmills, Basingstoke, Hampshire RG21 6XS.

Palgrave Macmillan in the US is a division of St Martin's Press LLC, 175 Fifth Avenue, New York, NY 10010.

Palgrave Macmillan is the global academic imprint of the above companies and has companies and representatives throughout the world.

Palgrave® and Macmillan® are registered trademarks in the United States, the United Kingdom, Europe and other countries.

ISBN: 978–0–230–27544–7 hardback

This book is printed on paper suitable for recycling and made from fully managed and sustained forest sources. Logging, pulping and manufacturing processes are expected to conform to the environmental regulations of the country of origin.

A catalogue record for this book is available from the British Library.

Library of Congress Cataloging-in-Publication Data

New issues in financial and credit markets / edited by Franco Fiordelisi, Philip Molyneux, Daniele Previati.
p. cm.—(Palgrave Macmillan studies in banking and financial institutions)
Includes bibliographical references and index.
ISBN 978–0–230–27544–7
1. Banks and banking. 2. Finance. 3. Credit. 4. Financial crises. I. Fiordelisi, Franco, 1972– II. Molyneux, Philip. III. Previati, Daniele.

HG1601.N495 2010
332.1—dc22 2010027504

10 9 8 7 6 5 4 3 2 1
19 18 17 16 15 14 13 12 11 10

Printed and bound in Great Britain by
CPI Antony Rowe, Chippenham and Eastbourne

Contents

Tables and Figures

Tables

Figures

Contributors

Pablo de Andrés Alonso (PhD in Business Administration, 1995) is Professor of Finance at the Universidad de Valladolid, Spain. His research interests range between corporate governance, corporate finance and real options. He has published his research in such journals as the *Journal of Banking and Finance*, *Journal of Business Finance and Accounting*, *Corporate Governance*, *Universia Business Review* and *Investigaciones Económicas*. He is in charge of the doctoral programme New Trends in Business Administration and he is Executive Editor of the *Spanish Journal of Finance and Accounting*. He was a Visiting Researcher at Harvard University in 2009–10.

Francesca Arnaboldi is Assistant Professor at the Università di Milano, Italy and Visiting Fellow at the Cass Business School, City University, London. Her main areas of interest are banking, corporate governance and financial innovation. She has presented her work at several international conferences and published various chapters in referred books and articles.

Elena Beccalli is currently Associate Professor in Banking and Finance at the Università Cattolica del Sacro Cuore, Italy, and Visiting Senior Fellow in Accounting at the London School of Economics (LSE), UK. She has written books and articles in national and international academic journals in the area of the economics of financial institutions. Her research interests include stochastic efficiency measurement, technology and performance, mergers and acquisitions and analyst forecasts.

Marcello Bianchi is the Chairman of the OECD Corporate Governance Committee. He is also Head of the Regulation Impact Assessment Unit at Consob (the Italian Financial Markets Authority) where he has worked since 1990. At Consob, he has directed several research and regulatory activities concerning corporate governance issues, namely major shareholdings, pyramiding, related party transactions, take-overs and board structure.

Miguel Boucinha has been an economist at the Economic Research Department at the Banco de Portugal since 2007, working in the Financial Stability Division. He has a Licenciatura and an MSc from the Universidade Nova de Lisboa and is currently working on his PhD at the same institution. His main fields of interest are industrial economics, regulation and banking.

Fatima Cardias Williams holds degrees from Brazil (BSc), the United States (MSc) and the United Kingdom (PhD). Formerly at the Instituto Nacional de Pesquisas da Amazonia – INPA, Manaus, Brazil, Dr Cardias Williams is a scientist at European Plant Science, Bangor, UK. A contributor on several Pan-European and Latin American projects, Dr Cardias Williams publishes scientific and financial papers. Her current research includes discrete choice modelling of banking sector consolidation.

Alessandro Carretta is Full Professor of Economics and Management of Financial Intermediaries at the University of Rome Tor Vergata and Director of the PhD programme in Banking & Finance. His current research interests relate to banking management, asset based lending and corporate culture in financial institutions.

Dimitris Chronopoulos is a Lecturer in Finance at the University of St Andrews School of Management. He completed his PhD in Accounting and Finance from the University of Essex in 2009. His research interests lie in the area of performance measurement in banking and finance, with particular focus on financial conglomeration and mergers and acquisitions.

Angela Ciavarella is an Economist at the Department of Economic Studies of Consob (the Italian Financial Markets Authority). She holds a PhD in Economics from the Università di Napoli "Federico II" and a Master's in Mathematical Economics and Econometrics from the Université de Toulouse. Her research interests comprehend corporate governance, regulatory impact assessment and institutional economics.

Marta de la Cuesta González has a PhD in Economics and Business Management. She is Senior Lecturer at the Department of Applied Economics of the Universidad Nacional de Educación a Distancia, UNED, Madrid. She was Vice-chancellor of Economic Affairs at UNED from 2005 to 2009. Her main research interests are in the area of banking and finance, corporate social responsibility and socially responsible investments. She is teacher at undergraduate and postgraduate levels, and she is responsible for delivering modules in the areas of banking, financial systems and sustainable finance.

Vincenzo Farina is Assistant Professor of Economics and Management of Financial Intermediaries at the Università di Roma "Tor Vergata". His current research interests relate to banking management, focusing on strategy, corporate governance, culture and organizational change.

Franco Fiordelisi is Professor of Finance and Banking in the Faculty of Economics at the Università di Roma III, Italy. He is also Visiting Research Fellow at Bangor Business School, Bangor University, UK, and the Essex Finance Centre of Essex University, UK. His recent books include *Shareholder Value in European Banking* (Palgrave Macmillan, 2006), *New Drivers of Performance in a Changing Financial World* (Palgrave Macmillan, 2008) and *Mergers and Acquisitions in European Banking* (Palgrave Macmillan, 2008). He has published various articles in national and international academic journals in the area of the economics of financial institutions.

Josanco Floreani is a Lecturer in Banking and Finance at the Faculty of Economics of the Università di Udine, Italy, from which he graduated in Economics and received a PhD in Business Sciences. His main research interests are related to the economics and governance of the securities industry and the regulation of financial markets.

Pascal Frantz has an MSc in applied physics (ENSPG, Grenoble), an MBA (LBS) and a PhD in Accounting and Finance (LBS). He is currently a Lecturer in Accounting and Finance at the London School of Economics. His research interests include economic analysis in the areas of accounting, corporate governance and mergers and acquisitions.

Gimede Gigante has a PhD in Banking and Finance from the Università di Romà "Tor Vergata," Italy. He also has an ITP (International Teachers Program) qualification from SDA Bocconi in 2008. He has been a Visiting Scholar at NYU's Stern School of Business and Visiting Researcher in Finance at Columbia Business School, New York. He is currently a Research Fellow at the Università di Roma III, Italy. His research interests lie in the area of intellectual capital in the banking sector.

Claudia Girardone is Reader in Finance at the Essex Business School, Essex University. Her research focus is on modelling bank efficiency and productivity and competition issues in banking. Her recent work includes a textbook entitled *Introduction to Banking* (FT Prentice Hall, 2006) and articles on efficiency, integration and market power in banking markets. She has published widely in these areas, and her recent publications appear in *Review of Development Economics, Economics Letters, Journal of Business, Finance and Accounting* and the *Journal of Banking and Finance*.

Rebecca de Juan is Lecturer in Economics at the Universidad Nacional de Educación a Distancia (UNED), Madrid. A graduate of UNED in 1993, she has a PhD in Economics from UNED and a Master's in Economics Analysis from the Escuela de Hacienda Pública. She received a Young Economists' Essay Competition Award in the 26th EARIE. Her research interests are industrial organization, banking and micro-econometrics. She has published several papers in the *International Journal of Industrial Organization, Review of Industrial Organization, The Economic and Social Review* and *Revista de Economía Aplicada*.

Karligash Kenjegalieva is a Lecturer in Economics at the Department of Economics of Loughborough University. She previously worked in capacity of Cost Effectiveness Modeller at the University of Sheffield and as a Research Associate at Loughborough University. Her main research interests and publication record cover a range of topics on efficiency and productivity analysis; banking and transition economics; parametric, semi-parametric and non-parametric econometrics and bootstrapping, Markov chain and Monte-Carlo simulations.

Duccio Martelli obtained a PhD in Banking and Finance from the Università di Roma "Tor Vergata", Italy. His research interests relate to real estate, corporate culture and asset management.

Ewa Miklaszewska is Professor of Finance and Banking at the Uniwersytet Ekonomiczny w Krakowie and Associate Professor of Economics in the Department of Management and Public Communication at the Uniwersytet Jagielloński. She has held several visiting positions in Polish and foreign universities and Polish regulatory bodies. She specializes in strategic developments in the global banking industry.

Katarzyna Mikolajczyk is Assistant Professor of Finance at the Uniwersytet Ekonomiczny w Krakowie. She has published heavily on the outcomes of privatization programmes in transition countries and on the impact of structural changes in the banking industry (including mergers and acquisitions) on bank efficiency.

Phil Molyneux is currently Head of Bangor Business School and Professor of Banking and Finance. His main area of research is on the structure and efficiency of banking markets and he has published widely in this area. He has also published a variety of texts on banking areas and has acted as a consultant to a wide range of organizations including the European Commission, UK Treasury, Citibank Private Bank, McKinsey & Co, Credit Suisse and various other international banks and consulting firms.

John Nankervis is Professor in Finance and Research Director at the Essex Business School, Essex University. His research interests are primarily in the area of financial econometrics and, in particular, autocorrelation testing and bootstrap methods in time series. He has published in leading journals such as *Econometrica, Journal of Econometrics, Econometric Theory, Journal of the American Statistical Association, Journal of Business and Economic Statistics* and *International Economic Review.*

Valerio Novembre is an Economist at the Department of Economic Studies of Consob (the Italian Financial Markets Authority). He holds a PhD in Economics, Markets and Institutions from the IMT Institute for Advanced Studies in Lucca and an MSc in Finance and Regulation from the London School of Economics. His research interests cover financial regulation, regulatory impact assessment and institutional economics.

Maurizio Polato is an Associate Professor in Banking and Finance at the Faculty of Economics of the Università di Udine, where he teaches Securities Exchange Economics. He graduated in Economics from Università di Venezia 'Ca' Foscari and received a PhD in Business Economics from the same university. His main research interests are related to the economics and governance of the securities industry, banking economics and risk management.

Daniele Previati is Professor of Banking and Finance in the Faculty of Economics at the Università di Roma III, Italy. He has widely published in a large number of academic journals. His research focuses on stakeholder management in banking and other financial institutions.

Nemanja Radić (PhD) is Lecturer in Banking and Finance at the London Metropolitan Business School. His key teaching areas are Domestic and International Banking, International Corporate Finance, Introduction to Financial Services, Policy Issues in Financial Services (dissertation supervision), International Banking (dissertation supervision) and International Banking and Finance (dissertation supervision). His specialist area focuses on efficiency, risks and competition in banking.

Geetha Ravishankar is Research Associate at Loughborough University, UK. Her current research interests focus on efficiency and productivity analysis using Data Envelopment Analysis and econometric methodologies, as applied to the banking and financial services industry.

Nuno Ribeiro works in the Economic Research Department of the Banco de Portugal in capital markets, financial systems and financial stability issues. Currently, he is the head of the Financial Stability Division. His main fields of interest are financial stability, banking, industrial organization and corporate finance.

Elena Romero-Merino is Professor of Finance at the Universidad Europea Miguel de Cervantes (Spain). Born in Palencia in 1978, she obtained her Bachelor's degree in Economics and Business and her PhD in Business Administration at the Universidad de Valladolid. Her academic research focuses on corporate governance, non-profit organizations and financial institutions. She has published her research in such journals as the *British Journal of Management, Universia Business Review* and *Nonprofit and Voluntary Sector Quarterly.*

Bruno Rossignoli is Professor of Banking and Finance at Università di Milano, Italy and member of CEFIN, Centro Studi di Banca e Finanza, Università di Modena e Reggio Emilia, Italy. He is author, co-author and editor of numerous books and articles. His main research interest is in the area of credit and banking.

Cristina Ruza y Paz-Curbera is an economist and graduate with a Master's degree in Banking and Finance from the University of Bangor, and in Public Finance and Taxation from the Centro Colegio de Economistas de Madrid and Escuela de Hacienda Pública (Instituto de Estudios Fiscales) y Universidad de Alcalá de Henares, both with distinction grade, and she was awarded PhD in 2004 by the Universidad Nacional de Educación a Distancia (UNED). Nowadays she is a PhD lecturer in the Applied Economics Department (UNED) at undergraduate and postgraduate levels, and she also participates in a master module in the areas of banking and sustainable finance.

Marcos Santamaría-Mariscal is Professor of Finance at the Universidad de Burgos, Spain. Born in Burgos (1975), he obtained his Bachelor's degree in Economics and Business from the Universidad Nacional de Educación a Distancia (UNED), Spain and his PhD in Business Administration at the Universidad de Burgos. His academic research focuses on corporate governance, corporate finance and financial institutions. He has published his research in such journals as *Corporate Governance* and *Universia Business Review.*

Paola Schwizer is Full Professor of Economics and Management of Financial Intermediaries at the Università de Parma. Her current research interests relate to banking strategies and organization, corporate governance and internal control systems, Basel 2 and risk management.

Rossella Signoretti is an Economist at the Department of Economic Studies of Consob (the Italian Financial Markets Authority). She holds a PhD in Banking and Finance from the Università di Roma "Tor Vergata". Before joining Consob, she was research assistant in finance at the Università di Roma III. Her research interests cover corporate governance, regulatory impact assessment and institutional economics.

Giuseppe Torluccio (MbA, PhD) is Professor in Banking and Finance at the Faculty of Economics of the Università di Bologna, Italy where he is also coordinator of the Banking and Finance PhD programme. He has been Visiting Researcher at the State University of Arizona and that Olin Business School, Washington University, St Louis. His research interests are related to financial institutions, focusing on credit risk, SME financing, ICT and research and development.

Eleuterio Vallelado-González is Professor of Finance at the Universidad de Valladolid. Born in Laguna de Duero (Spain), he obtained his Bachelor's degree in Economics and Business, his PhD at the Universidad de Valladolid and an MBA from New York University. He is author of several books, and his articles can be found in the *Journal of Banking and Finance, Applied Economics, Financial Review, Abante,* the *Spanish Review of Finance and Accounting* and *Cuadernos de Economía y Dirección de Empresas,* among others. His research interests include corporate finance, corporate governance in banks and behavioral finance.

Thomas Weyman-Jones has been Professor of Industrial Economics at Loughborough University in the UK since 1995. His research interests include efficiency and productivity analysis and applied micro-econometrics, and how these techniques can be used to inform regulatory policy. His published research work has examined the economic performance of European and Asian banking systems, and has also been applied to European airlines, energy and water supply networks and climate change.

Zhi Shen has completed his PhD at the Department of Economics at Loughborough University. His research interests are mainly on efficiency and productivity analysis in banking industries. His work on cost efficiency analysis in Asian banking industries has been published in the *Journal of Chinese Economic and Business Studies* and presented at several international conferences including the fifth North American Productivity Workshop, 2008.

Jonathan Williams is Professor in Banking and Finance at Bangor University, UK. His research interest focuses on banking sector deregulation. He has written on bank privatization, foreign banks, governance, efficiency and productivity, competition and risk, market power, management behaviour and mergers and acquisitions. His recent empirical work includes discrete choice modelling of bank failure and consolidation in Latin American banking sectors.

Introduction

Franco Fiordelisi, Philip Molyneux and Daniele Previati

This text comprises a selection of papers that focus on recent developments in financial institutions and markets which were presented at the European Association of University Teachers of Banking and Finance Conference (otherwise known as the Wolpertinger Conference) held at the University of Rome III, Italy, in September 2009. The text is divided into three topical themes that cover financial crises, lending business, and finally capital markets and risk management.

Part I Financial crises

Since the onset of the global financial crisis in the summer of 2007, the eventual collapse of Lehman's, and other major bank and financial firm bailouts during 2008 (particularly in September 2008), much has been written about the causes and consequences of the crisis. Section one of this text contributes to this debate with a range of topical chapters that examine effects of the crisis.

Chapter 1 by Rene van der Linden (INHOLLAND University of Applied Sciences Amsterdam/Diemen, the Netherlands) examines the impact of the crisis on the Chinese economy and financial system. He finds that the banking sector has been less affected by the crises than in other countries, and notes that the economic slowdown was relatively short-lived. In recent years Chinese banks have become more healthy and competitive, and several gradual reforms have put banks on a more stable footing to negotiate the global economic downturn. The progress of the banking industry has been driven mainly by government-led reforms and support. While the Chinese banking sector has not been unscathed by the global crisis, it is performing better than most other sectors of the Chinese economy. Further reforms should be geared to improving corporate governance, and further strengthening of the regulatory and supervisory framework. The ability and willingness of the government to support the banking sector is high, but as long as the state remains a large controlling shareholder, conflicts of interests and interference are likely to prevail which might reduce the soundness and competitiveness of banks.

One of the key features of the crisis was the problems faced in the inter-bank market. This was because banks stopped lending to each other when they could not evaluate the credit risk of bank counterparts. **Chapter 2** by Claudio Porzio (University of Napoli Parthenope, Italy), Antonio Meles (University of Napoli Parthenope, Italy), Francesca Battaglia (University of Napoli Parthenope, Italy) and Maria Grazia Starita (University of Napoli Parthenope, Italy) examines this issue by focusing on the liquidity features of e-MID (the only electronic market for inter-bank deposits in the Euro area and the US). The chapter looks at volumes that would have been recorded in the absence of the financial turmoil in the post-shock window, and compares these with volumes actually transacted. They find that an increase in the e-MID/Eonia spread caused a decrease in the sell-initiated transactions and an increase in the buy-initiated transactions over the crisis period.

Chapter 3 by Joaquín Maudos (Universitat de València and Instituto Valenciano de Investigaciones Económicas (IVIE), Spain) and Juan Fernández de Guevara (Universitat de València and Instituto Valenciano de Investigaciones Económicas (IVIE), Spain) provides a broader perspective by analyzing the impact of both financial development and integration on the economic growth of the Euro area since the introduction of the Euro and the implementation of the FSAP in 1999, quantifying the differential impact of the financial crisis in 2008. The results reveal that both financial development and integration have been fundamental in driving the recent growth in European economies. Specifically, from 1999 to 2008, the economic impact of progress in the degree of financial development has contributed to an average 4.7 % economic growth. However, financial development fell on average some 9.4 % in the Eurozone from 2007 to 2008, which explains a decrease of 0.75% in annual GDP growth. Taking into account that the Eurozone GDP fell by 1.3 % in 2008, the reduction resulting from the crisis demonstrates the importance of the financial crisis as a trigger for problems in the real sector.

One area much debated post-crisis has been the institutional arrangements for bank supervision. In particular, is it best for the central bank to be the supervisor? In **Chapter 4** Elena Seghezza (Università di Genova, Italy) and Giovanni B. Pittaluga (Università di Genova, Italy) evaluate these issues and focus on the role of central bank independence. In the past various arguments have been used against attributing supervisory and regulatory functions to central banks. The most important of these arguments is that of the conflict of interests that arises between managing monetary policy and conserving financial stability. This position has been strongly argued above all in the literature based on the time-inconsistency hypothesis. The authors note that in reality a goal-independent central bank is a political player which, equipped with supervisory functions, can seek the support of commercial banks and offer them favorable regulatory measures. The commercial banks offer their support to the central bank by exercising pressure on government in return for regulations in their favor. In this way there is a political exchange between commercial banks and the central bank. This leads the authors to conclude that supervisory and regulatory functions, instead of damaging a central bank's anti-inflationary credibility, may actually increase it.

The influence of the booming housing market on bank credit extension, and the crisis that ensued, is analyzed in **Chapter 5** by José Manuel Pastor (Universitat de València and Instituto Valenciano de Investigaciones Económicas (IVIE)), Javier Quesada (Universitat de València and Instituto Valenciano de Investigaciones Económicas (IVIE)), and Lorenzo Serrano (Universitat de València and Instituto Valenciano de Investigaciones Económicas (IVIE)). They investigate whether the tightening of the credit market has been more severe in those countries that had formerly experienced a housing-price bubble. They hypothesize that the countries with higher mortgage lending in the balance sheets of their commercial and savings banks should expect a more severe credit tightening after the housing prices stopped rising and started moving down. Overall they find positive evidence regarding the relative size of the housing sector in relation to the intensity of the credit crunch. Countries which experienced the highest housing-price hikes are those where the credit deceleration has been more intense. The size of housing loans relative to banks' portfolios, together with a much higher correspondent risk in the inter-bank markets, has probably been the main cause of the liquidity crisis that ensued from 2008 onwards.

In **Chapter 6** Gianfranco A. Vento (Università Telematica G. Marconi, Italy) and Pasquale La Ganga (Banca d'Italia, Italy) examine inter-bank market and liquidity distribution during the financial crisis. They complement the analysis reported in Chapter 2 by again examining the experiences of e-MID. In particular they investigate the operative solutions recently adopted by the e-MID inter-bank market for unsecured inter-bank transactions. The chapter analyzes the inter-bank transactions within the euro area since the current financial crisis started, both in the e-MID and in the over-the-counter inter-bank markets, discussing whether the introduction of an anonymous and collateralized segment in the e-MID market since February 2009 is a viable solution to improve liquidity distribution within the euro area.

A key policy response of governments to the crisis has been to undertake major fiscal expansions in order to stave off recession. In **Chapter 7** Frans H. Brinkhuis (INHOLLAND University of Applied Sciences Amsterdam/Diemen, the Netherlands) investigates the consequences of the quantitative easing strategy for the American economy, specifically the effect on the yield curve and on possible future inflation. He also compares the strategy of the US authorities with the quantitative easing approach adopted by the Bank of Japan (BOJ) between 2001 and 2006. Empirical evidence on the quantitative easing strategy in Japan suggests that the commitment of the BOJ to maintain zero interest rates led to a substantial lowering of the yield curve. Bank reserves and purchases of government bonds appeared to have had no clear relationship with the yield curve. As the Fed did not have the clear-cut commitment of the BOJ, it is vital for the Fed to communicate its strategy in a clear way to the public and financial market. Only then can credit easing have consequences for the yield curve. The author argues that it could well be that over the short run the Fed policy will not result in extra lending by banks and will not lead to a fall in yield curve. Over the longer term, inflationary pressures resulting from credit easing policy can only be conquered if the Fed is able to let its balance sheets shrink at the appropriate pace.

The final chapter in this section on the crisis looks at the link between reforms, competition, and risk-taking in banking. **Chapter 8** by Barbara Casu (Cass Business School, City University, London, UK), Alessandra Ferrari (University of Reading, UK) and Tianshu Zhao (Stirling University, UK) investigates these relationships in the wake of the recent financial turmoil, from the viewpoint of banks and regulators. They note that most of the legislation following the 1930s financial crisis was based on the assumption that competition makes banks more risk-prone, and it should therefore be restrained to preserve stability. During the 1990s this view was questioned and fundamental programmes of liberalization were carried out by many governments. Deregulation was however often accompanied by prudential re-regulation to ensure (in theory at least) that bankers took only "prudent" risks. Research on the effects of financial reforms on banks' competitive conduct, risk taking, and production performance has important policy implications for improving the supervision and regulation of banking. This chapter adds to the debate by providing an insightful review of the theoretical and empirical literature on the effects of financial reforms on competition and risk.

Part II The lending business: markets and instruments

Over the last decade or so credit markets have changed dramatically, characterized by the emergence of new institutions. **Chapter 9** by Federica Poli (Università Cattolica del Sacro Cuore Milano, Italy) and Erika Teordora Uberti (Università Cattolica del Sacro Cuore Milano, Italy) investigate the emergence of credit brokers in Italy. Some estimates maintain that about 25% of residential mortgage loans are intermediated by the credit broking sector. In this chapter the authors empirically investigate the diffusion of credit brokers across Italian provinces. The results show that the geographical presence of credit broking firms is related to various socioeconomic and banking features of the territory where they are located. There is also evidence of a "herding effect" which the authors put down to the relatively unregulated nature of the sector.

Chapter 10 by Vincenzo Capizzi (Università del Piemonte Orientale, Italy), Renato Giovannini Università Telematica G. Marconi, Italy) and Valerio Pesic (Università di Roma "La Sapienza", Italy) examines the effects of venture capital and private equity investments on Italian small and medium-sized enterprises (SMEs). The study shows that venture capitalists are more likely to finance firms that are younger, smaller, and more endowed with intangible assets than the average. Additionally, the findings imply that such financing is greater when asymmetric information problems are greater. They also confirm that venture capital and private equity financing act as certifying parties. The certification effect enables SMEs to raise funds from other sources.

The pricing of consumer credit has long been a controversial issue as financial firms often provide relatively complicated mechanisms to price their products, and often this information is complex and/or confusing for consumers. In **Chapter 11** Massimo Caratelli (Universita' Di Roma Tre, Italy) undertakes an experiment to examine how consumers view the role of the Annual Percentage Rate (APR) in choosing various installment credit agreements. In Italy and other countries financial firms have to stipulate the APR on all consumer credit products. The chapter illustrates that consumers find it difficult to understand the use of APR and make irrational choices based on APR information. It is concluded that to improve disclosure, alternative borrowing cost measures should be included in consumer credit advertisements.

Part III Capital markets and risk management

Chapter 12 by Giuseppe Torluccio (Università di Bologna, Italy) and Mario Toscano (Università di Bologna, Italy) investigate momentum and reversal trends in capital markets. There is an extensive literature that seeks to investigate future fluctuations of stock prices to model how portfolios allow investors to increase profits and returns.

A number of studies have found momentum and reversal patterns in various markets. This study investigates the performance of the DJ Euro Stoxx industries, and finds strong evidence of short-term momentum and long-term reversal patterns. Similar momentum results are found when the industries are weighted, for both price and profitability, although reversal patterns change as a consequence.

The mangement of interest rate risk has been an important element of bank risk management for many decades. **Chapter 13** by Göran Bergendahl (Göteborgs Universitet, Sweden) and Ted Lindblom (Göteborgs Universitet, Sweden) reassesses the role of duration analysis in firm asset and libaility mangement. Duration techniques have been used widely by banks to manage interest rate risk, and the main objective has been to protect the balance sheet. This chapter provides an overview of the key issues related to duration analysis. It also demonstrates how methods of this kind may be applied to risk management in different sectors, with emphasis on the banking, insurance and energy sectors.

Chapter 14 by Caterina Lucarelli (Università Politecnica delle Marche, Italy) and Gianni Brighetti (Università degli Studi di Bologna, Italy) presents an interesting insight into how individual attitudes to risk – risk tolerance – can be evaluated. The authors investigate the emotional side to risk-taking behaviour, focusing on various subjective obstacles that may restrict individuals' ability to take conscious investment and debt decisions. Using an empirical cross-disciplinary approach, they mix financial competences with others derived from psychology and affective neuroscience. The authors use a variety of tests on a sample of 176 individuals with different levels of financial education/competence including traders, bankers, and bank customers. Overall they find that individuals who have a stronger knowledge of financial products tend to have greater self-evaluated risk tolerance.

The measurement of bank risk has become one of the most topical areas of banking research, especially post-crisis. In **Chapter 15** Ted Lindblom (Göteborgs Universitet, Sweden) and Magnus Willesson (Linnaeus University, Växjö), Sweden examine the measures of bank operational risk and look at the implications for bank capital. The new Basel Accord forces the banks to develop and design internal risk information models and systems. This seems to have a major impact on the risk management of banks in general, and on their assessment of operational risk exposures in particular. This chapter generates empirical findings about the adaptation of Swedish banks to the new regulations, especially by evaluating how operational risk measurement is related to the measurement of other types of risk exposure. The authors find that there is a strong relationship between bank size and the choice of regulatory approach for measuring operational risk, and that there is a spillover effect within banks from their credit risk to their operational risk measurement. It is also concluded, however, that the capital incentives to adopt more sophisticated operational risk approaches appear to be small.

Part I

Financial Crises

1

China's Macro-policy and Regulatory Framework of the Financial Sector to be Tested by the Global Economic Slowdown

René W. H. van der Linden

1.1 Introduction

Aside from GDP growth figures, by any measure, China is acquiring all the hallmarks of a developed nation in terms of internet-usage, auto sales figures, and Starbucks- and KFC-density. China increasingly influences global economic activities and amidst the global recession 2008/09, China's stability has become crucial to containing the global financial crisis. In contrast to the Asian financial crisis of 1997/98, the global financial crisis of 2007/09 has adversely affected the growth of GDP, net exports and employment, even though it took a cautious approach to capital liberalization and the degree of integration into global financial markets was low compared to the EU and the USA. However, currently China is more resilient to external shocks than it was a decade ago. After years of prudent economic policy-making, the country has achieved remarkable fiscal consolidation and a strong external position. The soundness of the banking system, and the limited direct exposure of banks to sub-prime and related securitized financial products, have helped China to face the financial turmoil with confidence. In November 2008, the policy-makers responded with a proactive fiscal stimulus package combined with a rise in short-term credit to stimulate growth. These expansionary policy measures can be perfectly transformed into ready-for-use infrastructure projects without the risk that part of the stimulus package will leak away.

The global financial crisis places a heavy burden on financial market regulators worldwide. It calls the effectiveness of existing regulatory and supervisory provisions into question and demands a review of supervisory practices and requirements for additional new rules and directives. Given the extent and speed of contagion as it spreads across financial markets around the world, it is questionable whether the commitment of future market opening on the part of the Chinese authorities can prevail. Although the Chinese banking industry is not averse to opening up more, the impact of the global recession on it has been less significant, since Chinese banks still focus mainly on the domestic market and their exposure to overseas capital markets is rather limited.

The aim of this chapter is to investigate the following research questions:

- What has been the impact of the global financial crisis (2007–2009) on the Chinese real economy and financial business industry?
- To what extent are the counter-crisis policy measures able to sustain economic growth and prevent an asset bubble?
- How will the regulatory and supervisory framework of the financial sector be reviewed in the light of the current global economic slowdown?
- What are the costs and benefits of implementing an amended Basel II capital framework on the Chinese banking sector?

This chapter describes the impact of the global financial crisis on the real economy of China (section 1.1.1), the Chinese banking sector reforms in the face of a global economic slowdown (section 1.1.2), the broadening of the range of banking products in different sectors (section 1.1.3), potential fears for an asset bubble in the light of the economic recovery momentum (section 1.1.4), the broadening of the foreign investment base to create a more level playing field of competition (section 1.1.5), the opening-up of the Chinese banking industry to more effective supervision (section 1.1.6), and the costs and benefits of implementation of an amended Basel II framework on the Chinese banking industry (section 1.1.7).

1.1.1 The impact of the global financial crisis on the real economy of China

As the global financial crisis spread from developed countries to emerging economies in 2008 and spilled over from the financial sector to the

Table 1.1 Key macro-economic indicators: China (2006–2010)

	2006	2007	2008	2009 (forecast)	2010 (forecast)
Real GDP Growth (% yoy)	11.6	13.0	9.0	8.4	8.8
Industrial production (% yoy)	15.4	18.5	12.9	9.5	8.6
Gross fixed investment (% yoy)	14.9	12.3	10.0	6.9	8.3
Gross fixed investment (% GDP)	40.7	40.1	41.1	43.7	41.2
CPI (% yoy) eop	2.8	6.5	1.2	1.4	2.8
Exports (% yoy)	27.2	25.8	17.6	–18.0	13.0
Imports (% yoy)	19.7	20.3	18.7	–7.3	17.0
Current account (% GDP)	9.0	10.7	9.6	4.9	3.2

Source: Deutsche Bank Research, Country Infobase China, 2 December 2009.

real economy, two widely shared assumptions about China collapsed: Firstly, that China would not be affected by a recession in the West, and secondly, that it was immune from financial turmoil with its relatively closed capital account and insulated banking sector relying primarily on deposits, and not exposed to risky financial products.

Table 1.1 shows that many selected key macro-economic indicators have dropped significantly since 2007. The real GDP growth figures decelerated rapidly from 13% in 2007 to around 8.4% in 2009, which marks the sharpest contraction of China's real economy in 20 years. Industrial production figures show an even stronger contraction in the same period. Net exports and the current account have fallen significantly, but partly due to the stimulus package net exports gradually increased again during 2009. The combination of an export- and fixed-investment-led growth model encouraged the existence of overcapacity and led to downward pressure on prices in 2008/09. However, China's price changes have an increasing correlation with international market prices and since the central banks have supplied huge amounts of money to the market, more inflationary pressure is to be expected in the mid to long term.[1]

Since 2009, there are serious fears that the robust GDP growth of around 8% may not be sustainable and is too one-sided, since it relies too much on government-injected fixed investments in the infrastructure as well as tax rebates for suffering industries (Schmidt, 2009). As short-term credits fall due, they will have to be refinanced, and much of this refinancing may have to be done by taking out longer-term loans, which might raise the banks' non-performing loans (NPLs) and threaten the stability of the financial system. Government-driven policies to promote consumption, such as tax rebates for household appliances, have helped to sustain the consumer demand, but with the risk of overcapacity (Wang, 2009b). However, since most of the stimulus package is used to improve the infrastructure it is debatable whether overcapacity will be a threat in the long run. Overcapacity exists in China's industrial sector, but the majority of the fiscal stimulus package went into infrastructure, property, and auto and white goods consumption. Considering that infrastructure is still a key bottleneck in many areas, it is not very likely that this will lead to overinvestment.[2]

While capital inflows could add to base money supply if not fully sterilized (set off) by the People's Bank of China (PBC), it is the credit expansion that has fuelled the liquidity and asset market boom. Since late 2008, the PBC has not only reduced its sterilization operation, but also cut the reserve requirement ratio (RRR) and its interest rate several times in order to counter the faster-than-expected economic slowdown. This policy response reflects the shifting concern of the PBC from controlling excess liquidity to providing sufficient liquidity with the risk of rising property prices (Anderson, 2009; Wang et al., 2009). Although RRR and interest rate are not considered as two effective tools to fine-tune the real economy, the lowered RRR and interest rate helped to reduce the borrowing costs payable by the government, and China's huge money supply helped to provide financing for a large number of industrial capital expenses followed by rapid recovery of private-sector fixed assets investments (FAIs). The result is that China's GDP growth bottomed at the end of 2008, and the rebound has begun since then. While external demand remained very weak in 2008 and 2009, net exports gradually became less of a drag on growth as expected. For 2010, two opposing driving forces will offset each other: net exports and consumption will take over the very volatile FAI growth (Liu et al., 2009).

1.1.2 Chinese banking sector reforms facing a global economic slowdown

The state-owned commercial banks (SOBs) or so-called Big Five[3] have extraordinarily high savings deposits at their disposal (almost 50% of disposable income). Despite their reserves, Chinese banks are risk-averse and lend money only very restrictively. Aside from strict state regulations, Chinese banks are burdened with a moderate amount of NPLs. Consequently, bank and debt restructuring have been major issues in the Chinese financial system. Technically, Chinese banks were almost bankrupt before the banking sector reforms started, but during the gradual reforms a downward trend in the 'bad debts' has been driven by the transfer of impaired assets to state-owned asset management companies (AMCs) and strong loan growth.[4]

The banking sector reforms can be divided into four stages, namely the specialization (1978–1993), commercialization (1994–2002), ownership restructuring (since 2003), and public listings (since 2005). In the stage of specialization the banking sector suffered from huge NPLs and low efficiency. The banking industry was dominated by the Big Four (without the Bank of Communications), and the NPLs were largely affected by the so-called 'financial dependency triangle' between the state council, SOBs, and state-owned enterprises (SOEs). The high involvement of the state council in monetary policy activities also explains the limited independence of the PBC (van der Linden, 2008). In the second stage the Big Four were commercialized through the establishment of three policy banks[5] to undertake policy loans previously granted by the Big Four. Banks were also allowed to compete with each other in almost all businesses. For instance, prior to 2001, the Bank of China (BoC) was the only bank that was allowed to conduct foreign exchange (FX) business, but since deregulation in 2001 other banks were enabled to compete for FX business against each other. The stage of ownership restructuring, meaning the dilution of state ownership with private stakes, was initially meant to reform SOEs in the late 1990s. In 2003, the banking sector adopted a similar strategy, starting with rural cooperatives and then spreading to SOBs. Since 1998, this reform started with the disposal of NPLs and capital injections to fix the balance sheets excluding the cost of reforming the most troubled SOB in terms of bad loans, namely the Agricultural Bank of China (ABC). However, progress has also been made in recapitalizing and restructuring the ABC and this is one of the government's top priorities. Its reform plan may look different from the other Big Five banks, as ABC's function as a key lender to the rural population cannot be weakened, but the goal of commercial independence will be the same. In addition to the ABC reform, the consolidation process (including mergers) of the rural-sector banks and cooperatives will take place to improve overall rural-sector efficiency.

Since 2005, the China Construction Bank (CCB) became the first Hong Kong-listed Chinese bank through a successful Initial Public

Table 1.2 Capital adequacy ratio (CAR) of commercial Chinese banks (2003–2008)

	2003	2004	2005	2006	2007	2008
Number of banks meeting CAR requirements	8	30	53	100	161	204
Share in total banking assets	0.6%	47.5%	75.1%	77.4%	79.0%	99.9%

Source: China Banking Regulatory Commission (CBRC, 2009b), 31 July 2009.

Offering (IPO) on 27 October 2005. The BoC and Industrial and Commercial Bank of China (ICBC) followed CCB and successfully finished their listings in 2006 and 2007 respectively. ABC's IPO is expected to be done in 2010. All of China's five key SOBs were listed either at home or overseas, or both. The IPO of China's SOBs effectively helped to improve their corporate governance and introduce modern banking practices. After these gradual reforms the performance of Chinese banks has improved significantly. However, the positive effects of these reforms are likely to be reduced by the global recession.

As Table 1.2 shows, the number of banks meeting the 8-per-cent capital adequacy ratio (CAR) has risen through the years and together these commercial banks account for more than 80% of total banking assets since 2007. Since almost all key banks are better capitalized and able to offload the bulk of NPLs from their balance sheets, years of strong loan growth has ensued as these banks lent aggressively and grew their balance sheets again. The CBRC, as the main supervisory authority in the banking industry since 2003, focuses more on tightening the CAR calculation and making future sub-debt issuance more difficult. The CBRC proposes to reduce banking system leverage, as banks, particularly small and medium-sized banks, have been issuing sub-debts to each other to prop up their capital base for growth. These cross-holdings of sub-debts inflated the banking system's capital base, and increased the system's leverage and risk (Lin and Wu, 2009).

1.1.3 Broadening banking products: different sector activities

China's booming real economy has been accompanied by a fast-growing banking sector with an average annual growth rate of total assets of 17.7% from 2003 to 2008. However, a significant number of Chinese banks still rely on corporate lending, and net-interest income still represents the largest portion of the Chinese banking sector's total profit (62.9% in 2007 and 61.2% in 2008). Other sources of income are the return on investment (mainly through establishment and operation of Sino-foreign joint-venture mutual fund companies, 27.4% in 2007 and 24.5% in 2008) and net-fee-based income (mainly through distribution of mutual funds, investment, and wholesale and personal banking business). The market consensus is that the PBC is likely to increase the interest rate in 2010 to avoid potential overheating, while keeping the saving rate relatively stable to promote consumption. Therefore, the net-interest margin is likely to increase in the near future. Fee-based income from credit cards and wealth management products has been growing, but still makes up only a small portion of banks' overall earnings (9.4% in 2007 and 9.7% in 2008) (CBRC, 2009b).

The share of consumer loans in total loans is estimated to have approached 20% in 2007. The largest component of consumer loans is mortgage loans (around 80%). Although consumer lending has seen a strong growth in recent years, the corporate sector claims the largest share of bank loans, estimated at around 80% of the total. Within the corporate sector, the majority of loans go to government-led infrastructure projects, while banks are very cautious about lending to the private sector and small and medium-sized enterprises (SMEs). Companies with good creditworthiness are not keen to borrow, as demand recovery is still slow, and will be more inclined to invest in capital expenses to acquire or upgrade physical assets such as buildings and machinery. As a result, the emerging SMEs have not had their financing needs served sufficiently. Traditionally, Chinese banks prefer to provide loans to a large corporation, and to SOEs rather than SMEs, for several reasons: Firstly, SMEs normally don't have many fixed assets as deposits; secondly, SMEs normally don't have sufficient credit history or records; thirdly, as the approval process is basically the same, banks prefer to provide loans to a large corporate sector which often has governmental support; fourthly, banks consider the default rate of large corporations and SOEs will be low; and fifthly, China is not applying a market rate to the interest rate, therefore banks have little incentive to provide loans to SMEs.[6] Many SMEs do not have the critical mass to achieve the necessary economies of scale and scope to remain cost-competitive, which offers numerous acquisition opportunities for foreign players. These SMEs have been relying on retained earnings and informal lending for funding needs. Therefore the PBC has become increasingly concerned that the SME sector is underserved. In this regard, two areas need to be addressed simultaneously. Firstly, SMEs have to improve their financial reporting if they want to access bank financing. Secondly, banks also have to develop expertise in SME credit assessment. If China wants to develop successfully into a market-driven economy, the SME sector should have proper access to bank funding.

Since the outbreak of the global financial crisis, consumption-related financial products are more encouraged by the authorities, and consumer banking has been identified as having a very high potential and is not much affected by political influence compared to corporate banking. Consumer banking is still at an early stage of development, and high dependency on loans makes the industry especially vulnerable to price fluctuations in the real-estate market, which would pose an increasing risk for banks. Household credit products such as loans for cars, LCD TVs, and other home appliances, remain relatively small but are encouraged by the government. Major players in consumer banking in China are the Big Five, thanks to their large branch networks. However, competition has been heating up as income from consumer banking, especially mortgage products, is seen as a generator of more steady long-term income, which is less cyclical than income from corporate banking. Twelve joint-stock commercial banks[7] have put more emphasis on increasing their market share in consumer loans. For example, the Minsheng Bank focuses on trade finance services, and China Merchants Bank puts more emphasis on retail banking services and has issued more than 10 million credit cards. Although the credit card business does have a bright potential it accounts for less than 3% of consumer lending: the number of debit cards is much bigger, since Chinese customers are still cautious about spending on personal credit (Pang, 2009). Mortgage lending has the potential to become the new market for Chinese banks, with a lower default rate than other consumer loans.

Foreign banks have also joined in the competition by capitalizing on the internationally recognized brand names. Many of the 32 foreign banks issue co-brand cards with their local partners to combine the international brand with local relationships. As more banks are intent on gaining market share via quality of service, competitive pressures have kept fee charges low. Big local banks enjoy the advantage of existing relationships with large local companies, which opens the door to offering their employees card products. Foreign banks on the other hand have focused more on wealthy customers in the big cities, and enjoy advantages over local banks due to their international network and established brand names. The global financial crisis could erode these advantages and the regulatory authorities are likely to adopt a cautious approach to new product developments (Hansakul, 2009).

1.1.4 Fears for asset bubble in the light of economic recovery momentum

The global economic slowdown 2007/09 marks a policy reversal from monetary tightening to monetary easing. It remains to be seen how long these counter-crisis policy measures are sustainable. The question about the sustainability of growth often arises from different angles: growth recovery has been driven by government stimulus and not by private demand. The sustainability of domestic demand growth lies importantly with the development of the real-estate sector, where the government faces a policy dilemma (Wang, 2009a). On the one hand, a brake must be placed on soaring property prices due to massive lending growth and ease of credit. On the other hand, if a major correction happens in the market, the economic consequences can be much graver, because a dramatic fall in property prices may bring down many commercial banks which might lead to a banking crisis. This is one reason why the government issued a series of policies, including tax reductions, to stabilize real-estate prices (Pang, 2009).

If policy-makers focus on pursuing further economic growth by diverting more money into the growth of domestic consumption, there is not much to worry about with China's recovery momentum (Qiwen, 2009). This does not mean that the problems in the banking industry have been solved. Non-market-inspired lending practices and state intervention will continue, and a large number of NPLs in the banking sector will not be resolved. In addition, the real-estate sector remains a politically sensitive sector for the authorities, taking into consideration the widening gap between the growth of money supply and GDP with the risk of fluctuations in asset prices (Hongbin and Xiaoping, 2009).

The central government acknowledges that a reasonably vibrant property market is crucial for its efforts to boost consumption. However, from the experiences of Japan, the USA, and other Asian countries, it is also well aware of the serious negative consequences of letting an asset bubble grow to a full-blown stage and collapse under its own weight. Local governments have an even bigger stake in the health and buoyancy of the property markets, given that land sales are an important source of income for many local governments. The key risk is whether and when local governments' aggressive spending in 2009 will lead to the rise of NPLs and asset inflation (Soss et al., 2009). The ideal situation for both central and local governments is property and land sales remaining buoyant, and at the same time property prices remaining stable or rising slightly.

In 2009 the three key themes of the central authorities have been stated as: 'stabilize economic growth, structural adjustment and promote consumption'. Compared with the economic focus prior to 2009 on 'ensuring economic growth, expanding domestic demand and improving people's livelihood', the new focus has clearly put less emphasis on growth, and has rather highlighted the risk for the need for some kind of tightening, although the overall stance on monetary policy has not been changed. Boosting consumption is probably the only consensus among China's political leaders right now. This somewhat ambiguous stance of the Chinese government is understandable considering the status of the Chinese economy: the growth momentum has been lifted by the stabilization of global growth, although the sustainability of the global recovery is not clear. The government has clearly observed that some asset bubbles have already emerged in the Chinese property market, so it will be difficult for the authorities to ignore them.

1.1.5 Broadening of the foreign participant's base to create a more level playing field

The Chinese government's strategy to gradually transform a bank-based into a market-based financial system has included a gradual opening-up of the domestic financial industry to the international financial markets. This strategy has been based on the insight that a transfer of expertise as well as stronger competition can impose substantial positive effects on the domestic market. That is why the authorities embarked on a step-by-step admission of foreign banks and foreign portfolio investors to the domestic markets. Foreign banks can enter the Chinese market in three ways, namely through an application for a banking license, taking a minority stake in a domestic bank (with several restrictions), or a joint-venture agreement with domestic banks. A foreign investor can apply to the China Securities Regulatory Commission for the status of a qualified foreign institutional investor, which is also subject to strict conditions. The obstacles to foreign participation in Chinese markets consist of both direct restrictions on foreign direct investments (FDIs) and indirect entry barriers through financial market regulation. The FDI restrictions are based on national security and protection of critical industries (for example regulations on mergers and acquisitions of domestic firms by foreign investors), while the entry barriers refer to licensing requirements (for example limited minority stakes in China-based banks) and additional regulatory requirements with regard to higher capital, limitations on branch network expansion, and so on.

The process of opening up Chinese financial markets to the outside world has clearly been characterized by a great deal of cautiousness and circumspection. As global financial markets grew significantly in the last two decades, and the variety and complexity of financial products increased sharply, the Chinese policy-makers largely limited market entry by foreign firms to wholesale investment and commercial banking services. Access conditions have remained strict, and the regulatory requirements placed on foreign firms have remained substantially more than those applied to domestic financial companies, all of which have retained a substantial share of public ownership. Complex financial instruments, such as derivatives or difficult financing structures, have remained highly regulated for all market participants, and the regulatory authorities have been keen to maintain close control of market activities. While respecting the country's cautious approach to market opening, especially at a time of global financial crisis, foreign market participants have identified a number of regulatory burdens. In the area of banking regulation, the following key practical improvements could be made for foreign strategic investors in order to create a more level playing field for competition:

- Co-ordinated regulation and supervision through efficient, consistent licensing and reporting;
- Foreign debt lending by alleviating limits on banks to borrow overseas;
- Clarification of legal and regulatory status of foreign banks' ownership rules;
- Branch network expansion through alleviating reporting requirements;
- Clarification of application requirements for bank-card issuance;
- Abolition or alleviation of additional capital and deposit requirements;
- Abolition of additional qualification criteria for RMB licenses (Dyck and Kern, 2009).

Although foreign participants are subject to restrictions and have limited access to their financial markets, Chinese authorities' efforts in deregulating and liberalizing the financial sector have continued, despite the global economic slowdown. Licensed foreign institutions (for example HSBC and Citibank) can provide a full range of corporate banking services to both foreign and domestic enterprises such as account services (including both foreign currency and RMB accounts);

lending services (including revolving and syndicated loans); trade services (including letters of credit and forfaiting); payments and cash management (including accounts services, receivables, and liquidity management); and electronic banking and global market services such as FX derivatives business.[8]

1.1.6 Opening-up process of the Chinese banking industry to more effective supervision

Gradually the Chinese authorities have shown that they are progressively moving towards supervision based on legal and market principles, and away from administrative controls (providing more prudential and effective supervision). The institutional changes to the regulatory framework of the Chinese financial sector were complemented by an overhaul of the existing legal structure and the adoption of a series of new laws and administrative measures governing the banking and securities industries. In doing so, the authorities were also keen to respond to a number of lessons learned in advanced industrialized economies about the governance of financial markets, including the need to run the central bank as a separate, independent institution, as well as the benefits of mandating separate, dedicated authorities with the regulation and oversight of the banking, securities, and insurance markets.

Since the opening-up process of the Chinese banking industry has encountered different financial risks, the authorities have realized the necessity to enhance overall supervisory capacity and use more systemic, diversified, and specialized supervisory methods to ensure the safety and soundness of the Chinese banking system. The opening-up process has to be supported by strict prudential supervision benchmarked with international standards and best practices. The basic principle of China's banking supervision is to 'practice consolidated supervision, manage financial risks, improve internal controls and raise transparency' while the focus is placed on monitoring the major risks in commercial banks and the systemic risks in the entire banking system. This approach aims to enhance commercial banks' own risk-management and control systems, and requires a higher degree of transparency in order to impose market discipline on the banks. Pushed forward by the global financial crisis, China will raise the professional standards of supervision and its effectiveness in various ways. Efforts will be made to accelerate the pace in unifying the supervisory standards for the domestic and foreign banks, in order to create a level playing field for competition and to benchmark the Chinese regulatory and supervisory practices with international rules and standards. In this respect, China is in the process of applying the *Core Principles for Effective Banking Supervision* issued by the Basle Committee on Banking Supervision, with the objective of raising the effectiveness and transparency of supervision. Last but not least, the implementation of international financial reporting standards in China will be pushed forward to create a better external environment for sound banking supervision.[9]

1.1.7 Costs and benefits of implementing an amended Basel II framework

China's banking system is mainly regulated by *Commercial Banking Law* (1995) which has made banks more responsible for their own profitability, liquidity, and risk management in line with the Basel II framework. At the same time the state council may direct banks to conduct their loans according to the needs of the national economy and social development. This means that this law sends out conflicting signals: be profitable, but at the same time, make effective policy loans, even though three policy banks have been established for this purpose (Hefferman, 2005; Pang, 2009). For a long time the Basel II framework had a low priority for the Chinese banking system, since they had more pressing issues to solve such as bad-quality loan portfolios and poor governance standards, but the Chinese regulatory bodies have gradually taken over more elements of this framework. Currently the big listed banks such as the Big Five have already fully implemented Basel II in their corporate banking business, and many other Chinese banks are already gauging the impact of the implementation of Basel II.[10] The contrast between Chinese risk-management standards and international best practices has become smaller, although it has not yet disappeared. Chinese banks have now cleaned up their balance sheets, and improved their internal structures and governance standards. The challenges that Basel II brings to Chinese banks are numerous, including capital and risk management as well as organizational structures, incentive compatibility between banks and regulators, market-oriented effective off-site and on-site supervision, and the fostering of financial innovation. There are numerous other direct benefits which Chinese banks gain when they adopt Basel II: Firstly, freed capital due to lower capital reserves can be used to expand into new areas of business. Secondly, Chinese banks adopt global best practices since the Basel Committee works closely with banks of member countries in identifying business issues, providing solutions based on global best practices, and stimulating closer cooperation with foreign financial institutions. Thirdly, the banks will strengthen core competencies by adopting advanced methods to identify and measure risks in a quantifiable manner. Banks will manage risks better, and reduce losses due to current risk exposure.

Although the impact of the Basel II framework on the Chinese banking system will likely contribute to increased systemic safety and soundness, the implementation still faces some problems. In particular, pillar 3 about disclosure and transparency could be seen as insufficient. Market discipline is mostly inefficient since creditors have few incentives to monitor banks because of the central and supportive role of the state, and inadequate bankruptcy laws. Overall, disclosure and corporate governance are, from a legal perspective, more or less in line with international standards, but the enforcement remains difficult. The weakest points, however, concern human resources as well as the availability of required historical data. In fact, bankers and regulators alike lack the relevant banking and modelling experience, and the data collection has only just started. Another shortcoming with regard to pillar 1 (minimum capital requirements) is a lack of data on default risk for constructing internal rating models, which may lead to improper capital requirements. Taking the current stage of development of the Chinese banking industry into consideration, it will be preferable to strengthen the implementation of the Basel II Accord and put the emphasis on what the Chinese banks currently lack most, namely corporate governance and structures that support the development of risk management. Potentially, one of the most profound implications of Basel II is the change of mindset in the credit culture, something that Chinese banks have completely lacked before. At the same time, incentives for staff will be greater to analyze creditworthiness based on cash flows rather than on provided collateral, and to grant loans according to needs. As a result, the internal control functions and monitoring are likely to be strengthened and the creation of NPLs could be reduced (Cousin, 2007).

1.2 Conclusions and recommendations

The global financial crisis of 2007/09 has adversely affected China's real economy through a reduction of GDP growth, a fall of net exports, and a rise in unemployment. The authorities have responded rapidly and vigorously with expansionary fiscal and monetary policy measures. This response has served to mitigate the economic downturn and facilitate a recovery during the course of 2009. Overall, China faced a faster-than-expected slowdown, but also a stronger than expected growth recovery.

The global recovery momentum will make it much harder for global demand to absorb increased production capacity from China. China has come to depend too much on export and investment for growth. However, the authorities have taken steps to encourage an economic rebalancing, so that domestic consumption and capital expenses contribute more to expansion. This transition would help both China and the global economy by easing China's massive current account surpluses. Given the low level of China's public debt, the policy-makers saw further room for a fiscal stimulus package plus monetary easing to combat the economic slowdown with a focus on infrastructure development, generating employment, and promoting social stability. So far strong economic growth has allowed the Chinese authorities to use widely available public funds to support its financial system. Without the need to tackle the root causes of the global recession, the sustainability of this situation is questionable. In addition, the risk is that too much liquidity may lead to a bigger asset bubble in the equity and/or the real-estate markets, followed by a sharp policy tightening.

Although the banking sector has become more healthy and competitive, and several gradual reforms have put banks on a more stable footing to negotiate the global economic downturn, the progress of the banking industry has been driven mainly by government-led reforms and support. It would be unrealistic to expect China's banking sector to be unscathed by the global recession. The key to survival in this environment will lie in the improvement of financial expertise and corporate governance, and further strengthening of the regulatory and supervisory framework. The ability and willingness of the government to support the banking sector is high, but as long as the state remains a large controlling shareholder, conflicts of interests and interference are likely to prevail which might reduce the soundness and competitiveness of banks. The consolidation process of the banking industry may be accelerated by the economic downturn, where the weakness of less financially sound banks will be exposed. In the long term, Chinese banks should continue to strive for prudent risk management which, as the experience of foreign banks indicates, is a crucial determinant of winners and losers. The future of China's banking sector is promising, considering the economy's growth potential and the still low penetration rate in terms of consumer (comparing to corporate) banking activities.

The global financial crisis has placed a heavy burden on financial market regulators worldwide. It requires a review of the effectiveness of existing regulatory and supervisory practices. Given the extent and speed of contagion as it spread across financial markets around the world, doubts about the benefits of deregulation and liberalization of domestic financial markets, and integrating them into the global economy, are voiced repeatedly. China is being hit hard by the global financial crisis, even though it had taken a cautious approach to financial liberalization and its degree of integration into global financial markets had been comparatively low. The benefits of liberal and open financial markets are especially evident in China, where unprecedented economic success over the past decades is largely attributable to improved financing conditions that were created in the process. Therefore it is important to avoid a protectionist 'buy Chinese' procurement-policy reaction to the global recession. It is all the more reassuring that China remains committed to its policy to open markets, which implies that it gradually has to get rid of remaining investment barriers over time and even out additional regulatory burdens on foreign-funded market participants. The current policy-makers has made a strong commitment to maintain and intensify international cooperation through the country's constructive role on different international platforms. In addition to crisis resolution, the growing importance of the Chinese financial markets that can be expected for the coming years suggests that far-reaching convergence of Chinese and international regulatory standards will be highly beneficial. The overall regulatory and supervisory framework did not change significantly, but the authorities are applying stricter measures to evaluate the systemic risks of China's financial sector, and closely monitor the performance of financial institutions. It is very likely that the post-crisis regulatory environment will be characterized by a much stronger convergence of regulatory standards and supervisory practices globally than was observed in the past. This will include a more intense imposition of the Basel II framework on Chinese banks, which will, despite the high implementation costs, improve their financial systemic safety and soundness. In the long run the implementation of an amended Basel II framework will give Chinese banks more possibilities to manage their own varying risk exposure, and the ability to withstand the meddling of authorities. Bringing risk and capital in line with one another will ensure that banks refrain from lending recklessly, and keep on asking for improvements of the regulatory environment.

Acknowledgement

I gratefully acknowledge comments and assistance from Robin Zhao Liang, analyst at NM Rothschild and Sons, Hong Kong.

Notes

1. Partly based on comments from Robin Zhao, analyst at Rothschild Hong Kong, 15 December 2009, and Hongbin and Xiaoping (2009).
2. Based on comments from Robin Zhao, analyst at Rothschild Hong Kong, 15 December 2009.
3. Agricultural Bank of China (ABC), Bank of China (BoC), China Construction Bank (CCB), Industrial and Commercial Bank of China (ICBC), and the Bank of Communications (BOCOM). Starting from 2007, the China Banking Regulatory Commission (CBRC) added BOCOM to this segment as a state-owned commercial bank, while this bank was segmented as a joint state-commercial bank prior to 2007.
4. An AMC is an investment company that buys outstanding debts and then manages and resells these debts in order to recover (some of) the funds. For each of the major state-owned commercial banks there is one AMC which is funded by the MoF (10 billion RMB for each) and a loan by the PBC (a total of roughly 563 billion RMB). AMCs exchange bonds with the respective banks for NPLs. See Schneider, 2009.
5. The policy banks include the Agricultural Development Bank, the Export-Import Bank of China, and the China Development Bank.
6. Based on comments from Robin Zhao, analyst at Rothschild Hong Kong, 15 December 2009.
7. The non-state-owned joint-stock or joint-stake commercial banks include CITIC Industrial Bank, Everbright Bank of China, Huaxia Bank, Guangdong Development Bank, Shenzhen Development Bank, China Merchants Bank, Shanghai Pudong Development Bank, Industrial Bank, China Minsheng Banking Co., Evergrowing Bank, China Zheshang Bank, and China Bohai Bank.
8. Based on comments from Robin Zhao, analyst at Rothschild Hong Kong, 18 August 2009.
9. All companies registered in China must meet the same accounting standard, which is called Chinese GAAP (General Accepted Accounting Principles).
10. Based on comments from Daisy Wu, analyst at Credit Suisse Shanghai, 18 August 2009.

References

Anderson J. (2009). UBS investment research, emerging economic focus. *How Scary is a 'W'?*. 22 July.

China Banking Regulatory Commission (CBRC). (2009b). *Annual Report 2009*, 31 July.

Cousin V. (2007). *Banking in China*. Palgrave Macmillan, pp. 175–190.

Deutsche Bank Research. (2009). *Country Infobase China*, 2 December.

Dyck S. and Kern S. (2009). China's financial markets in the global context. *Deutsche Bank Research*, Brussels, 30 March, pp. 23–25.

Hansakul S. (2009). China's financial markets: a future global force?. *Deutsche Bank Research*, 16 March, pp. 12–16.

Hefferman S. (2005). *Modern Banking, Banking in Emerging Economies, China*. City University UK, pp. 305–316.

Hongbin Q. and Xiaoping M. (2009). From the Horse's mouth. *HSBC Global Research*, 8 July, p. 2.

Lin S and Wu D. (2009). *China Banks Sector, Proposed Regulatory Changes*. Credit Suisse, 26 August.

Liu L., Baig M., Ma J. and Tan D. (2009). *Global Market Research: China Outlook 2010*. Deutsche Bank Hong Kong, 18 December.

Pang C. (2009). Give credit where credit is due: granting loans still generates most income for Chinese Banks. *Business Forum*, China Issue 2, March–April, pp. 52–53.

Qiwen Z. (2009). Growing worries about recovery momentum. *China Daily*, 3 August, p. 4.

Schmidt D. (2009). For better or for worse: the long-term impact of the economic crisis on china could lead to very different scenarios. *Business Forum*, China Issue 2, March–April, pp. 36–37.

Schneider F. (2009). *Politics and Economics of Modern China: A 'Happy' 60th Birthday?*. University of Leiden, 30 September, pp. 73–75.

Soss N., Feldman J and Mo H. (2009). *Global Economy: Monthly Review*, Credit Suisse, 16 December, pp. 18–19.

van der Linden R. (2008). Deepening banking reforms in china. In Molyneux P and Vallelado E (eds), *Frontiers of Banks in a Global Economy*. Palgrave Macmillan, p. 188.

Wang T. (2009a). What is driving china's recovery?. *UBS Investment Research*, China Economic Comment, 12 June, pp. 2–3.

Wang T. (2009b). Strong recovery may lead to change in macro policy. *USB Investment Research*, China Economic Comment, 16 July, pp. 1–2.

Wang Q., Zhang S., Tai K. and Stanley M. (2009). *China Economics Chartbook*. July.

2

Financial Turmoil and Asymmetric Information Theory: Evidence from the e-Mid Platform

Claudio Porzio, Francesca Battaglia, Antonio Meles and Maria Grazia Starita

2.1 Introduction

The industrial countries have been severely affected by the financial crisis because of the high degree of financial engineering of their economies. In order to understand the transmission effect of sub-prime mortgage default on the financial system and, consequently, on the economic system, it is necessary to retrace some key stages (as in Cassola et al., 2008b).

The years prior to 2007 were characterized by low interest rates and stock price volatility, a reduced risk premium, and large liquidity availability. The coexistence of these factors has triggered a frantic search for investments with high returns, and thus an excessive use of products arising from securitization. Therefore, the asset-backed securities were included in the portfolios of institutional and retail investors: this situation implies a complex and opaque mechanism of risk-sharing. The weak link, which caused the securitization mechanism to fail, has been identified in the sub-prime mortgage default. The fall of prices on the real-estate market and the weakness of the US economy resulted in an increase in credit default. This situation led to a rapid downgrading of mortgage-backed securities and a rapid increase in banks' credit default swaps, which were forced to grant ample liquidity lines to the vehicles. The re-intermediation caused by the diffusion of the 'originate to distribute' model, and direct exposure to sub-prime mortgages, created a climate of suspicion about the exposure of different banks to the crisis, which inevitably infected both the inter-bank market, where banks exchange liquidity, and the real economies.[1]

We find evidence of asymmetric information due to an unfair distribution of information about the exposure of banks to financial instruments linked to sub-prime mortgages.

The aim of this paper is to evaluate the effect of the financial crisis on the monetary market through evidence from the e-MID platform, which currently represents the more transparent and liquid money-market segment. To be precise, the overnight segment incorporates only two types of information: information relating to the liquidity system, and information about the borrowers' quality, but not about the behaviour of the European Central Bank.

We analyze the volumes of the e-MID overnight segment, by using two variables: the normal volume and the abnormal one. Specifically, the first variable represents the volumes that would have been recorded in the absence of the financial turmoil, in the post-shock window. In particular, we assume that the normal volumes at *t* time depend on the volumes recorded in the *t-n* previous periods and on the interest rates of the other money-market segments, while the actual volumes recorded during the crisis incorporate the asymmetric information related to the real exposure of banks to US sub-prime mortgage products.

Analysis of the e-MID volumes drivers and study of the signs of abnormal volumes allow us to identify the behaviour of lenders through buy-initiated volumes and the behaviour of buyers through sell-initiated volumes.[2] We expect that the difficulty of buyers' assessing the creditworthiness of lenders would cause a lack of supply, leading to a decrease of buy-initiated transactions, an increase from normal volumes and a sign change of the abnormal ones

With reference to the lenders' actual exposure to 'toxic' assets, we expect a lack of demand, which should correspond to an increase in interest rates.

The remainder of the paper is organized as follows: in section 2.2 we analyze the related literature, while in section 2.3 we illustrate the empirical analysis. The paper ends with some final considerations.

2.2 Literature review

In order to manage their assets and liabilities and to maximize their profits, banks are subjected to two constraints: the first one related to liquidity, and the second to solvency. In fact, on one hand, they must realize in the short term a sustainable match between inflows and outflows, and, on the other hand, they have to honour, at all times, both their obligations undertaken in respect of depositors and the promise of funds allocation related to the lending activity (Mottura, 2008).

In this context, the money market traditionally assumes a crucial function within the banking system in order to face unexpected liquidity needs (Bini Smaghi, 2008). Especially in the bank-oriented financial systems, money-market rates represent the marginal cost of the funding activity: through their monitoring, the monetary authorities keep monetary rates close to the official ones and influence medium to long-term interest rates on which lending rates depend. Consequently, the literature focuses on the money market's structural features and its key function of transmitting monetary policy.

The literature reviewed in support of the empirical analysis carried out in this paper can be divided into three groups: the first one concentrates on the money market functions for banks and the financial system as a whole; the second focuses on the effects of the recent financial crisis on the money market; finally, the third one analyzes the information asymmetries and their effects on the money market during the financial crisis.

The first group of studies focuses on two of the most important functions played by the money market in the banking system: the *endogenous* one, that is the rebalancing of the existing mismatch between inflows and outflows in different time periods (Bhattacharya and Gale, 1987), and the *exogenous* one, that is the exchange of liquidity among banks which represents the basic mechanism of monetary policy transmission affecting interest rates charged by banks to their customers (ECB, 2008).

Except for the paper written by Flannery (1996), the second group of studies is fairly recent: in fact, it includes studies that analyze the effects of the financial crisis on the money market and the 'contamination' effects on bank rates. This research can be mainly found in the scientific output of the monetary authorities and strictly relates to the banking system, who were worried about the economic slowdown due to the financial crisis (Buiter, 2008; ECB, 2008; Ewerhart and Tapking, 2008; Linzert and Schmidt, 2008; Michaud and Upper, 2008; ECB, 2009; Eisenschmidt and Tapking, 2009). This type of analysis can be useful to adjust forecasting models, in order to consider events usually not taken into consideration because of their expected low frequency. The values of the parameters, recorded during the financial crisis and among which the most significant are the Euribor rate and the transaction volumes on the overnight market, can also be used for the stress testing of existing liquidity and treasury management models (as in the ICAAP process). Consequently, it is necessary to identify and analyze the drivers of 'normal' and the 'stressed' transaction volumes and the interest rates.

Finally, the third group includes studies that, starting from Akerlof's contribution (1970), extend the asymmetric information approach both to the credit (Stiglitz and Weiss, 1981) and the inter-bank (Flannery, 1996) markets; other studies consider information asymmetry as the main rationale of the 'contagion' in the money market and its subsequent paralysis (Cassola et al., 2008b). This group also includes studies modelling the banks' behaviour in the inter-bank market, with a particular focus on their information set and on their portfolios' quality (Heider et al., 2009; Eisenschmidt and Tapking, 2009). Another paper (Heider et al., 2009) analyzes the same behaviour, but in a different way. Here the authors identify in the life cycle of the inter-bank market three different phases, determined by the counterpart risk and the use of resources provided by the monetary authorities. In particular, in the first phase, volumes and inter-bank interest rates are under control: in this context, there are no liquidity shocks and banks generally do not make deposits at the central bank, because it offers an interest rate lower than the one developed by the money market. In the second phase, the lowering of credit quality produces both an increase in the spread of interest rates referring to different maturities, and the subsequent departure of the best lenders from the inter-bank market. During this period, the increasing use of marginal deposits can be seen as the first unambiguous sign of the lenders' flight from the inter-bank market. The third phase is characterized by a dramatic increase in the spread between the marginal lending rate and the marginal deposit rate and by an extensive use of marginal deposits, which culminates in the collapse of the overall inter-bank market: only the worst borrowers continue to operate in this market (a supply vacuum), while lenders withdraw from transactions, by depositing liquidity at the monetary authority (a demand vacuum).

From the analysis of the above-mentioned literature, we can see the absence of a model to directly link the banks' behaviour in the inter-bank market to the typical descriptive parameters of market function.

2.3 The empirical analysis

2.3.1 Methodology

Before explaining the adopted methodology, we have to specify that the analyzed period was divided into two temporal windows, one referring to the pre-crisis period and the other referring to the financial crisis period.

The choice of 9 August 2007 as a watershed date between the two above-mentioned periods is not random: in fact, the selection of that date is supported not only by the marginal lending facility of the ECB discussed previously, but also by two other important elements. First, as demonstrated by analysis of the buy-initiated daily average volumes (that is, transactions started on the initiative of those banks which needed liquidity) by Cassola et al. (2008a), it is clear that by grouping the daily volumes in intervals of half an hour on that date, volumes gradually reduced until they completely reset between 13.00–13.30 and 13.30–14.00. Moreover, statistical analysis of timing of the overnight volumes reveals a structural break on the same date. We investigate that break through the implementation of one an *ad hoc* method.[3] As we have a probable date, we use the Chow test (Chow, 1960), which tests the null hypothesis of lack of breaks.

With reference to the first research question (the drivers of e-MID volumes), we use two autoregressive models with multiple predictors: one for the buy-side and another for the sell-side, in which we include the lagged values of the dependent variable and other regressors.[4] In particular, the independent variables we use for the creation of a buy-side model (1) and a sell-side model (2) are the following:

$$
\begin{aligned}
&Vol_{buy,t} = \beta_0 + \beta_1 Vol_{buy,t-1} + \beta_2 Vol_{buy,t-2} + \beta_3 Vol_{buy,t-3} + \beta_4 Vol_{buy,t-4} + \\
&\beta_5 spread_{(e-MidO/N\_rate-Eonia\_rate),t} + \beta_6 spread_{(marginal\_lending\_rate-Eonia\_rate),t} + \\
&\beta_7 spread_{(Eurepot/n\_rate-Eonia\_rate),t} + \beta_8 spread_{(Eurepo1w\_rate-Eonia\_rate),t} + \\
&\beta_9 spread_{(Ois1w\_rate-Eonia\_rate),t} + \beta_{10} spread_{(Euribor1w\_rate-Ois1w\_rate),t} + \\
&\beta_{11} shock
\end{aligned}
\qquad (1)
$$

$$
\begin{aligned}
&Vol_{sell,t} = \beta_0 + \beta_1 Vol_{sell,t-1} + \beta_2 Vol_{sell,t-2} + \beta_{23} Vol_{sell,t-3} + \beta_4 Vol_{sell,t-4} + \\
&\beta_5 spread_{(e-MidO/N\_rate-Eonia\_rate),t} + \beta_6 spread_{(Eonia\_rate-depositfacility\_rate),t} + \\
&\beta_7 spread_{(Eurepot/n\_rate-Eonia\_rate),t} + \beta_8 spread_{(Eurepo1w\_rate-Eonia\_rate),t} + \\
&\beta_9 spread_{(Ois1w\_rate-Eonia\_rate),t} + \beta_{10} spread_{(tax\_Euribor1w-Ois1w\_rate),t} + \beta_{11} shock
\end{aligned}
\qquad (2)
$$

The use of the two models is, therefore, instrumental in the identification of those variables that can explain the evolution of the volumes recorded during pre- and post-shock periods.

In order to answer the second research question (the turmoil effects on the e-MID volumes), we estimate the abnormal volumes as the difference between the 'normal' (or expected) and the actual ones. The normal volumes are the volumes that would have been expected from August 2007 to December 2008 (the financial crisis temporal window) if the credit market turmoil had not arisen; while the expected daily volumes for the post-shock period were obtained by using only the significant regressors, so the abnormal volumes, calculated as the difference between the normal and the actual ones, are statistically significant. By definition, positive abnormal volumes give evidence for the existence of effective trading volumes lower than the expected ones, that is the volumes that would be recorded in the same temporal window without the shock. But negative abnormal volumes provide evidence for the outperformance of the effective trading volumes compared to the normal ones.

The creation of these new variables is crucial not only for the second research question, but also for verifying the possible presence of asymmetric information.

2.3.2 Data and variables used in the buy-side and sell-side models

The data, relating to transactions occurring on the e-MID platform, refer to the period from 2 January 2007 to 31 December 2008, consisting of 1537 working days. The data contains information for each standard transaction. In order to verify the presence of asymmetric information, we remove from the dataset the days corresponding to the first and last day of the reserve maintenance period, and those in which the ECB carried out open-market operations.

For the purposes of this analysis, we take into account only overnight transactions in euros, which currently represents about 85 % of all exchanges taking place on the market.

With reference to the variables used in the creation of the two models, we need to clarify that the estimate of normal volumes, finalized to verify the existence of imperfect information, takes into account the descriptive parameters of the banks' behaviour in the overnight submarket. In particular, the modus operandi of these intermediaries can be approximated by the response of the e-MID volumes to the changes of reference rates of the other segments of the money market.

There follows that a summary of the variables used in the construction of the buy-side and sell-side models:

- lagged volumes (Vt-p): literature (ECB, 2009) suggests that volumes at *t* time are strongly related to volumes recorded in the previous days. Specifically, we exclude from the two models, as not significant, lags after the fourth day;
- spread between e-MID O/N rate/Eonia rate: the base hypothesis that justifies the inclusion of such a regressor, depending on the weight taken by the e-MID (overnight unsecured market) referring to the unsecured money markets (Banca d'Italia, 2002), is that the pattern of volumes is strongly connected with the price of liquidity (ECB, 2009);
- spread between marginal lending rate/Eonia rate: this variable is an indicator of the opportunity-cost of last resort rather than the unsecured money market;
- spread between Eonia rate/deposit rate: the regressor is a proxy of the opportunity-cost of investing in ECB risk-free deposits rather than in the unsecured money market;
- spread between Eurepo *t/n* rate or Eurepo one-week rate/e-MID rate: this differential represents the ratio between the unsecured overnight market and the secured market segment (ECB, 2009). The choice of these maturities is determined by their proximity to the segment facility;
- spread between Ois one-week rate/e-MID O/N rate: the use of this variable is justified by its assumed alternative function referring to e-MID segment, and its supposed complementary referring to the Eurepo segment;
- spread between Euribor one-week rate/Ois one-week rate: the differential is an expression of the money market's tensions;
- shock: the inclusion of the dummy variable, which takes value 0 before the crisis and value 1 during the turmoil, captures the effect of the financial turbulence on average daily volumes.

2.3.3 Results

This section summarizes results obtained with respect to the research questions we have highlighted previously. In particular, Tables 2.1 and 2.2 show the significant regressors of the two models.

From Table 2.1 it is clear that the buy-initiated volumes recorded during *t* time depend in a significant and positive way on those

Table 2.1 Coefficients and *p*-value of the buy-side model significant regressors

Variable	Coefficient	*p*-value
Constant	3450.812	0.000
$Volume_{t-1}$	0.4329	0.000
$Volume_{t-2}$	0.1189	0.001
$Volume_{t-3}$	0.1639	0.000
$Volume_{t-4}$	0.0754	0.024
$Spread_{(\text{e-MID O/N rate/Eonia rate}),t}$	7796.081	0.002
$Spread_{(\text{Eurepo } t/n \text{ rate/Eonia are}),t}$	3573.723	0.038
Shock	−836.0938	0.001
R^2	0.5982	
Adjusted R^2	0.5946	

Source: Our elaborations on the e-MID data.

Table 2.2 Coefficients and *p*-value of the sell-side model significant regressors

Variable	Coefficient	*p*-value
Constant	1473.184	0.000
$Volume_{t-1}$	0.2704	0.000
$Volume_{t-2}$	0.1256	0.001
$Volume_{t-3}$	0.0760	0.004
$Volume_{t-4}$	0.0965	0.000
$Spread_{(\text{e-MID O/N rate/Eonia rate}),t}$	−3999.9	0.002
$Spread_{(\text{Eonia rate/ deposit\_facility rate}),t}$	655.2479	0.000
$Spread_{(\text{Eurepo } t/n \text{ rate/Eonia are}),t}$	−981.1193	0.004
Shock	0.5982	0.000
R^2	0.3919	
Adjusted R^2	0.3887	

Source: Our elaborations on the e-MID data.

registered until the fourth previous day. The significant and positive relationship between the e-MID O/N rate and the Eonia rate seems to show that on one hand buyers, in order to raise funds, are willing to pay a higher rate, becoming price-takers; on the other hand, sellers remain in place by becoming 'aggressors' towards the buyers' proposals, if they consider the offered rate appropriate to the risk of the operation.

With reference to the spread between the Eurepo T/N and the Eonia rates, the significant and positive relationship demonstrates that borrowers consider the secured segment as an alternative source of liquidity.

Table 2.2 shows clearly that the sell-initiated volumes, recorded during *t* time, depend in a significant and positive way on those registered until the fourth previous day.

These volumes are negatively correlated with the spread between the e-MID and the Eonia rates, and with the differential between the e-MID and the Eurepo *t/n* rates. In particular, the decrease in sell-initiated transactions is due to the lenders' behaviour during money market tensions: on one hand, they become price-takers and, on the other hand, they have to leave the O/N segment in search of alternative and safer liquidity investments (Eurepo *t/n* segment). This behaviour is consistent with the dynamics of money market function as described in the literature (Cassola et al., 2008a, 2008b); Heider et al., 2008; Eisenschmidt and Tapking, 2009).

Another sign of the lenders' behaviour is the relationship with the floor of the corridor rates: the relationship between the e-MID volumes, the spread between the e-MID O/N, and the marginal deposit rates is positive, indicating that the more the money rate outperforms the deposit rate, the more sales increase overnight (Heider et al., 2008).

In both models, the relationship with the dummy variable is significant and negative: in the post-shock window the buy-initiated and sell-initiated volumes fall sharply.

With reference to the second aim of the research, the abnormal buy-initiated volumes are, in absolute terms, higher than those estimated for sell-initiated transactions. In particular, buy-side volumes show a significant decrease from August 2007 and move in this direction for the entire post-shock period (this provides evidence for the fortunate availability of supply); but sell-initiated transactions begin to decline and abnormal volumes become positive only from the last two months of 2007 (this gives evidence for the fortunate availability of demand).

2.4 Summary and conclusions

Analysis of the drivers of e-MID volume shows unexpected behaviour by the overnight segment's operators: the increase in the e-MID/ Eonia spread causes a decrease in the sell-initiated transactions and an increase in the buy-initiated ones.

This is consistent with the money market's characteristics: on one hand, the increasing interest rate spread pushes lenders to leave the unsecured overnight market and to move to more secure segments (general collateral, for example), consistent with the their risk-tolerance; on the other hand, it pushes borrowers to accept the higher cost of funding, in order to meet their urgent need for liquidity. The abnormal volumes analysis shows a change in the evidence for this differential from August 2007.

At any rate, the decrease in buy-initiated transactions is not accompanied by a decline in the borrowers' liquidity needs or by inaction relating to possible cuts in the money cost imposed by the financial authorities.

As all this information is available to the banking system, the only factor that can affect trading volumes is the unfair distribution of information relating to the borrowers' risk exposure. In this scenario, lenders confront two sets of problems: the assessment of the borrowers' creditworthiness, because of the associated risk on the unsecured overnight market, and the self-assessment of their risk of possible exposure to a shock. Because of the difficulty of assessing both their own and borrowers' creditworthiness, lenders leave the market, causing a lack of supply (buy-initiated volumes begin to decrease from August 2007) (Cassola et al., 2008a; Cassola et al., 2008b; Heider et al., 2008; Eisenschmidt and Tapking, 2009). As a consequence, 'good' borrowers, following the lenders' behaviour, decide to leave the market: liquidity rationing and interest rate increase reduce demand (Akerlof, 1970; Stiglitz and Weiss, 1981; Flannery, 1996).

Therefore the money market collapses, because only bad borrowers remain in the market. In this scenario, the ECB tries to restore the basic inter-bank market function of release and absorption of intra-day liquidity (Bini Smaghi, 2008; Cassola et al., 2008a; Cassola et al., 2008b; Heider et al., 2008; Eisenschmidt and Tapking, 2009).

Acknowledgements

The authors would like to thank Alessia Naccarato, Daniele Perla, Ornella Ricci, and Giuseppe Squeo for their useful suggestions, and Sandro Rivo and Andrea Zappa from e-MID Sim for providing statistical data.

Notes

1. If we consider that in the bank-oriented systems, there is a close relationship among money-market rates, bank rates, and the action of monetary authority, the step from the inter-bank market to the real economics is very short.
2. The buy-initiated transactions refer to transactions started on the initiative of a borrower; the sell-initiated transactions are the transactions started on the initiative of a lender.
3. Generally, these techniques test the presence of changes in the regressions' coefficients through the use of the F statistic.
4. The lagged values of these regressors are not significant.

References

Akerlof G. (1970). The market for lemons: qualitative uncertainty and the market mechanism. *Quarterly Journal of Economics* 84, 488–500.

Banca d'Italia. (2002). Relazione annuale, Roma.

Bhattacharya S. and Gale G. (1987). Preference shocks, liquidity, and central bank policy. In Burnett WA and Singleton DJ (eds.), *New Approaches to Monetary Economics*. Cambridge: Cambridge University Press, pp. 69–88.

Bini Smaghi L. (2008). Restarting a market – the case of the interbank market. BIS Review 154/2008.

Buiter W.H. (2008). Lessons from the North Atlantic financial crisis. Paper prepared for presentation at the conference "The Role of Money Markets" organized by Columbia Business School and Federal Reserve Bank of New York on 29–30 May.

Cassola N., Drehmann M., Hartmann P., Lo Duca M. and Scheicher M. (2008a). A research perspective on the propagation of the credit market turmoil. ECB Research Bulletin, no. 7, June.

Cassola N., Houlthausen C. and Lo Duca M. (2008b). The 2007/2009 Turmoil: A Challenge for the Integration of the Euro Area Money Market? ECB Workshop on "Challenges to monetary policy implementation beyond the financial market turbulence".

Chow G. (1960). Tests of equality between sets of coefficients in two linear regressions. *Econometrica* 28(3), 591–605.

Eisenschmidt J. and Tapking J. (2009). Liquidity risk premia in unsecured interbank money markets. ECB working paper, no 1025, March.

European Central Bank (ECB). (2008). *Financial Stability Review*, Frankfurt.

European Central Bank (ECB). (2009). *Euro Money Market Study*, Frankfurt.

Ewerhart C. and Tapking J. (2008). Repo markets, counterparty risk, and 2007/2008 liquidity crisis. ECB working paper, no 909, June.

Flannery M.K. (1996). Financial crises, payment system problems, and discount window lending. *Journal of Money, Credit and Banking* 28(4–2), 801–824.

Heider F., Hoerova M. and Holthausen C. (2009). *Liquidity Hoarding and Interbank Market Spreads: The Role of Counterparty Risk*. ECB Working Paper.

Linzert T. and Schmidt S. (2008). What explains the spread between the euro overnight rate and the ECB's policy rate?. ECB working paper, no 983, December.

Michaud F. and Upper C. (2008). What drives interbank rates? Evidence from the Libor Panel. *BIS Quarterly Review,* March.

Mottura P. (2008). La Northern Rock e la sua crisi di liquidità. Bancaria, no. 6.

Stiglitz J.E. and Weiss A. (1981). Credit rationing in markets with imperfect information. *American Economic Review* 71(3), 393–410.

3
The Impact of European Financial Integration on Economic Growth

Juan Fernández de Guevara and Joaquín Maudos

3.1 Introduction

The international financial crisis that started in the summer of 2007 with the sub-prime crisis in the US, and became more widespread in the summer of 2008, triggered a dramatic decline in financial market activity. Once the financial turmoil exploded, it spread rapidly to the rest of the economy, having a virulent impact. Many of the economies around the world are witnessing one of the worst recessions since the 1929 crash and the Great Depression of the 1930s.

European authorities have been aware of the importance of both financial development and integration for economic performance, for one reason: financial integration contributes to the development of the financial system by increasing competition, expanding markets, and increasing the efficiency of financial intermediaries. The result is lower intermediation costs and a more efficient allocation of capital. In addition, financial integration increases the depth and liquidity of financial markets, and consequently enhances the resilience of the European financial system. It also offers greater scope for geographical risk diversification, promoting consumption and income risk-sharing.

It was precisely for these reasons that the integration process of financial markets started in the mid 1980s in the EU, with the objective of achieving a single perfectly integrated internal market. In general, the studies available illustrate that the integration process has indeed advanced, with a positive effect on economic growth (see European Central Bank, 2009; European Commission, 2009, among others).

But it is not only the degree of financial development that has been affected by the financial turmoil. A report by the European Central Bank in May 2009 (and also a report by the European Commission, 2009) noted a slowdown and even a reversal of the financial integration process. One of the reasons for this decline is the protectionist measures implemented by some countries as a reaction to the turmoil, along with a preference for national institutions ('home bias'), given the lack of trust in international markets.

There is a vast amount of literature analyzing the relationship between economic growth and financial development (Goldsmith, 1969; King and Levine, 1993a, 1993b; Levine, 1993, 2005; Levine and Zervos, 1998; Levine et al., 2000; Loayza and Rancière, 2006, among others) with the general conclusion that a positive relationship exists between them. But it is the work of Rajan and Zingales (1998) that explains the mechanism through which financial development promotes economic growth, that is, the level of dependence of firms on external funds.They proposed a causality test which corrects for both country and industry effects; it also considers that firms which are more dependent on external funds will grow more in financially developed countries. This methodology has been applied in several papers (Cetorelli and Gambera, 2001; Claessens and Laeven, 2005; Maudos and Fernández de Guevara, 2006; Fernández de Guevara and Maudos, 2009).

In order to evaluate the contribution of integration to EU economic growth, the European Commission has supported some studies (London Economics, PricewaterhouseCoopers and Oxford Economic Forecasting, 2002 and Guiso et al., 2004). The studies carried out until now are limited, given that they quantify the potential benefit of financial integration in a scenario of full integration corresponding to a single European market (which does not reflect reality, especially in retail markets). However, the economic impact related to the effective advance of integration has not been estimated yet. The contribution of our work is therefore to evaluate the economic impact of the progress achieved to date in the degree of financial integration.

The aim of our work is to analyze the impact of both financial development and integration on the economic growth of the Euro area since the introduction of the euro and the implementation of the FSAP in 1999, quantifying the differential impact of the financial crisis in 2008. In order to achieve this, our work evaluates the part of financial development growth which is attributable to financial integration over the period analyzed, so as to isolate its contribution to economic growth. Thus, we decompose the observed financial development into a component related to financial integration and into another component which could be considered 'pure' financial development. Moreover, unlike previous papers (Guiso et al., 2004), the estimated impacts cover the total economy, including not only the manufacturing sector but all sectors of the economy.

This chapter is structured as follows. Section 2 outlines the methodology used to measure the impact of financial development and integration on economic growth. It also describes how total financial development is decomposed into the parts attributable to financial integration and to what we call pure financial development. The results of the decomposition of financial development and its effects on growth are evaluated in section 3, while a summary and conclusion is presented in the last section.

3.2 Methodology: financial development, integration, and growth

The basic framework for analyzing the effect of financial development and integration on economic growth is the specification adopted by Rajan and Zingales (1998). The intuition of the test is simple, and is based on testing whether the sectors most dependent on external finance present higher growth rates in countries with a higher level of financial development, once the characteristics of the different sectors and countries have been controlled for. The novelty of the specification is to introduce the interaction between a country characteristic (financial development) and an industry characteristic (financial dependence), thereby avoiding some problems of identification present in the cross-country regressions common in the literature on economic growth.

Specifically, the estimated model is the following:

$$\begin{aligned} Growth_{j,k} = {} & Constant + \psi_1 Sector\ dummies_j + \psi_2 Country\ Dummies_k + \\ & \psi_3 \left[\frac{Value\ added_{j,k}}{Value\ added_k}\right] + \psi_4 Financial\ dependence_j * \\ & Financial\ development_k + \epsilon_{j,k} \end{aligned} \tag{1}$$

where j = sector, k = country, *Growth* = annual real value-added growth rate of sector j in country k, and *Financial development* is a variable that approximates the degree of efficiency in financial intermediation (measured by the total capitalization/GDP). The *sector* and *coun-*

try dummies capture the influence of specific effects of each sector or country, respectively. The weight of each sector in the value-added total of each country in the initial year captures the possible effect of convergence at the industry level. According to this effect, sectors that initially have a higher weight in total production tend to grow at a slower rate, so a negative ψ_3 can be expected.

Since the objective of this work is to analyze the effects of financial development and integration on growth, and particularly to quantify the effects of the current financial crisis, we will use the results obtained by Maudos and Fernández de Guevara (2006). This work applies the methodology of Rajan and Zingales (1998), and quantifies the effect of financial development on economic growth using a sample of 53 sectors in 21 countries over the period 1993–2003. The main advantage of this paper is that they extend the sector coverage of the sample including the services sectors, whereas previously the Rajan and Zingales methodology has been tested in several papers only for the manufacturing sector (for example Rajan and Zingales, 1998; Cetorelli and Gambera, 2001; Claessens and Laeven, 2005). Furthermore, this paper updates the financial dependence indicator, calculating it for a more recent period (mid-1990s to early 2000s) instead of the original indicator calculated for the 1980s by Rajan and Zingales (1998), and used in most of the papers that apply this methodology.

Maudos and Fernández de Guevara's (2006) results show that the sectors most dependent on external finance grow faster in countries with more developed financial markets, irrespective of the indicator of financial development used (stock market capitalization/GDP, credit/GDP, or total capitalization/GDP). Specifically, the economic impact of going from a situation of low financial development to another of higher development translates into approximately 0.50 percentage points of growth of the more financially dependent sectors. Consequently, in line with prior studies by Rajan and Zingales (1998), Cetorelli and Gambera (2001), Guiso et al. (2004), and others, Maudos and Fernández de Guevara (2006) obtain evidence supporting the hypothesis that financial development facilitates economic growth. The following section uses this elasticity to calculate the effect of both financial development and financial integration on economic growth.

To achieve our purpose, we need to compute total capitalization (financial development) for each country. Total capitalization is defined as the sum of outstanding debt (domestic and issued abroad), stock market capitalization, and bank credit to the non-financial sector. Data is taken from different sources[1]: European Central Bank, BIS, IMF, World

Table 3.1 Decomposing the growth of financial development: pure financial development vs. financial integration: 1999–2008

		Observed financial development			Financial development in a scenario of no integration		
		1999–2007	1999–2008	2007–2008	1999–2007	1999–2008	2007–2008
C^{D}_{t-i}/C_{t-i}	[1]	79.0	79.0	72.2	79.0	79.0	72.2
$(C^{D}_{t}-C^{D}_{t-i})/C^{D}_{t-i}$	[2]	14.5	9.0	–4.9	14.5	9.0	–4.9
C^{EU}_{t-i}/C_{t-i}	[3]	12.2	12.2	19.9	12.2	12.2	19.9
$(C^{EU}_{t}-C^{EU}_{t-i})/C^{EU}_{t-i}$	[4]	104.3	60.8	–21.3	11.7	–11.4	–20.6
(C^{RW}_{t-i}/C_{t-i})	[5]	8.8	8.8	7.8	8.8	8.8	7.8
$(C^{RW}_{t}-C^{RW}_{t-i})/C^{RW}_{t-i}$	[6]	11.7	–11.4	–20.6	11.7	–11.4	–20.6
$(C_{t}-C_{t-i})/C_{t-i}$	[7]=[1]×[2]+[3]×[4]+[5]×[6]	25.3	13.5	–9.4	13.9	4.7	–9.2
Difference of growth EU-15-RW	[4]–[6]	92.6	72.1	–0.7	11.3	8.8	–0.1

Eurozone accumulated variation (percentages).
C^{D}_{t} = domestic capitalization in year *t*; C^{EU}_{t} = capitalization from other EU-15 countries in year *t*; C^{RW}_{t} = capitalization from the rest of the world in year *t*.
Source: Eurostat, IMF, BIS and own elaboration.

Federation of Exchanges, EURONEXT, OMX, and World Development Indicators (The World Bank). Total capitalization is calculated at the country level and aggregated for the Eurozone. The growth of total capitalization (C) is shown in line 7 of Table 3.1.

Given that this work aims to assess both the impact of financial development on growth, and how European integration has acted as a catalyst for financial development, we need to isolate the part of progress in financial development attributable to integration. On the basis of the assumptions described below, we decompose the growth of total financial development into two parts: one part attributable to financial integration, and the other part that we call 'pure' financial development. To do this, we decompose total financial development into the effects of domestic capitalization, capitalization coming from EU countries, and capitalization coming from the rest of the world. That is, the accumulated variation of total financial development (as percentage of GDP) between years t and $t\text{-}i$ is decomposed into a weighted sum of the variations in domestic capitalization (C^D), capitalization from other EU-15 countries (C^{EU}), and capitalization from the rest of the world (C^{RW}). The weighting factors correspond to the percentage each source of funding represents in the total in the initial year. By decomposing the growth of total financial assets we can assume what would have been the growth of total capitalization if financial integration had not advanced. To this end, we assume that if the degree of integration had not advanced, the growth of funds received by each European country from other EU-15 countries would have been equal to the growth in funding obtained from the rest of the world. In fact, since 1999 growth in funding from other countries in the EU-15 (as % of GDP) has been higher than the growth of financial liabilities with the rest of the world (outside Europe). The simulation exercise therefore estimates the level of financial development (total funding collected as a percentage of GDP) that would have been reached in 2008 if the growth of funds received from EU-15 countries (excluding domestic finance) had been equal to the growth of funding from non-European countries.[2]

3.3 Financial development, financial integration and growth: results

Using the approach and assumptions discussed earlier, Table 3.1 contains the observed values of growth in total capitalization (financial development indicator) and their decomposition in the contribution of domestic funding, funding from other EU-15 countries, and funding from elsewhere during 1999–2007, 1999–2008 and 2007–2008. In the first period, the total capitalization increased on average by 25.3% for Eurozone countries,[3] with a significant contribution of capital from the EU-15. That is to say, 50% growth in total funding (provided as % of GDP) can be explained by the financial contribution of the EU-15, with domestic financing being lower (45.5%), and especially that obtained from other countries (4%).

Table 3.1 also shows the results of what would have been the growth in total capitalization if the change in funding obtained from other EU-15 countries was equal to that of the rest of the world. It is clear that funding from the EU-15 increased more quickly than from the rest of the world from 1999 to 2007, as has already been proven. It is for this reason that the hypothetical scenario means reducing capitalization growth and, therefore, the level of financial development achieved. To be specific, instead of financial development increasing by 25.3%, non-integration would have meant a growth of 13.9%, and therefore 11.4% less financial development.

Results referring to period 2007–2008 show that the financial turmoil has caused a reduction of 9.4% of the total financial development in the Euro area. Even more interesting is that if we compare this reduction of financial development with what we would have observed if financial integration had not taken place, the reduction of financial development would be almost identical (9.2%). This fact indicates that the crisis is of a global nature and that although the process of financial integration has come to a halt because of the crisis, there has been a reduction in financial transactions with the rest of the world of almost the same percentage.

In order to examine the impact of financial development (and integration) on growth, Table 3.2 decomposes the growth of total capitalization into its 'pure' component (calculated as the difference between the observed growth of total capitalization and the effect of financial integration) and the effect of integration over the periods 1999–2007, 1999–2008, and 2007–2008. The results illustrate that integration accounts for 44.8% of financial development growth in Eurozone countries until 2007. If we extend the decomposition to 2008, the contribution of integration increases to 65.2%, since the difference in the growth of funding from the EU-15 and elsewhere increases its influence on the variation in total capitalization. In 2008, the regression in integration accounts for only 1.4% of the drop in financial development with respect to 2007, explaining its low impact on economic growth, as we shall see later.

Table 3.2 Decomposition of total capitalization and effect on GDP growth

	Increase of financial development		Effect on growth (pp. and percentage)			Effect on growth/ GDP growth
		Percentage distribution		Percentage distribution	GDP growth	Percentage distribution
1999–2007					2.07%	
Total financial development	25.2%	100.0%	0.195	100.0%		9.4%
Pure	13.9%	55.2%	0.162	83.1%		7.8%
Effect of integration	11.3%	44.8%	0.033	16.9%		1.6%
1999–2008					1.69%	
Total financial development	13.5%	100.0%	0.090	100.0%		5.3%
Pure	4.7%	34.8%	0.069	77.0%		4.1%
Effect of integration	8.8%	65.2%	0.021	23.0%		1.2%
2007–2008					–1.3%	
Total financial development	–9.4%	100.0%	–0.751	100.0%		57.8%
Pure	–9.2%	98.6%	–0.723	96.3%		55.6%
Effect of integration	–0.1%	1.4%	–0.028	3.7%		2.1%

Source: Eurostat, IMF, BIS and own elaboration.

In this section we also quantify the economic growth brought about by financial development in the EU-15 since 1999. This estimate is simply the product, at the sector and country level, of the estimated elasticity times the increase in the level of financial capitalization (as a percentage of GDP) in the period 1999–2008, taking into account the degree of financial dependence of each sector.

Table 3.2 illustrates the annual contribution (in percentage points) of financial development to GDP growth in the Euro area from 1999 to 2008. On average, the annual contribution was 0.09 pp., accounting for a 5.3% increase in GDP. Table 3.2 also shows the effect of financial development on growth during the periods 1999–2007 and 2007–2008. It is obvious that the decline in financial development in 2008 meant that financial development had less of an impact on growth. Thus, the crisis of 2008 reduced GDP growth by 0.751 pp. That is, 57.8% of the 1.3% fall in the Euro area's GDP in 2008 is due to the fall in financial development, demonstrating the magnitude of the financial crisis.

The results obtained thus far quantify the contribution of financial development to economic growth, and the impact of the financial crisis in 2008. However, progress in financial development is not only because the financial integration process has advanced, but could also be influenced by other factors.

By applying these simulated values of a lower level of financial development in the absence of advances in financial integration, and following Rajan and Zingales' (1998) approach, we can quantify the impact of financial integration on economic growth. As Table 3.2 illustrates, financial integration's contribution to growth is lower. Specifically, the table reports the percentage point reduction in the GDP annual growth rate in a scenario in which the degree of financial integration has not advanced. On average, the progress made in financial integration following the adoption of the FSAP and the introduction of the euro contributed 0.021 pp. to GDP growth in the Euro area until 2008, with financial integration explaining 1.2% of annual GDP growth.

Finally, because the decline in the degree of financial integration in 2008 explains only a small percentage of the fall in the value of total capitalization (1.4%), its impact on growth is modest. Specifically, the decline in the level of financial integration explains 2.1% of the decline in the Euro area's GDP in 2008.

3.4 Conclusions

This paper sheds some light on the role of the financial system in the crisis, quantifying its impact on growth in countries in the Euro area. In order to do this, we combine data at country, sector, and firm level, and quantify the effect of financial development on growth, isolating the effect of financial integration on financial development and therefore on economic growth.

The evidence shown in the paper confirms the intense growth in financial development since 1999. This increase has occurred in an environment in which European financial markets are more integrated, especially wholesale markets. Furthermore, the international financial crisis that we have been witnessing since mid-2007 has caused financial development to rapidly decrease, and has slowed down (even decreased) European integration. The protectionist measures implemented in many countries, lack of trust in international markets, the fall in funding sources, and so on, have increased home bias, while cross-border activity across European countries has decreased. However, although the degree of integration fell in 2008, this only accounts for a small part of the decline in the degree of financial development given that the fall in capitalization has been indiscriminate, affecting equally countries from the EU-15 and from elsewhere.

Estimates in this paper demonstrate that both financial development and financial integration have been fundamental in driving the recent growth in European economies. Specifically, from 1999 to 2008 the economic impact of progress in the degree of financial development has contributed 0.09 pp. of annual GDP growth in the Eurozone, which accounts for on average 4.7% of the observed economic growth.

Given that the financial crisis which started in the summer of 2007 in the USA with the sub-prime crisis led to a general decline in the values of total capitalization in national economies, financial development dropped in 2008. This drop in financial development meant a lower contribution to GDP growth in comparison to that observed up to 2007. To be specific, the degree of financial development fell on average some 9.4% in the Eurozone from 2007 to 2008, which explains a decrease of 0.75 pp. in annual GDP growth. Taking into account that Eurozone GDP fell by 1.3% in 2008, the reduction of total capitalization accounts for 58% GDP reduction, demonstrating the importance of the financial crisis as a trigger for the crisis in the real sector.

Results indicate that EU-15 GDP increased by 0.021 pp. per year from 1999 to 2008 owing to progress in financial integration, and that financial development would have progressed at a slower pace in the absence of integration. European financial integration accounts for 65% of the growth of financial development and 1% of GDP growth. Nonetheless, with the crisis and the consequent decline in the degree of integration, its contribution to the decrease of financial development is very low (1.4%), and thus accounts for a very small percentage (only 2.2%) of the fall in GDP in 2008.

The results obtained indicate that as the financial crisis and national protectionist reactions have led to a reversal in integration (and therefore in financial development), it is necessary to return to the pace of progress in integration before the crisis, given the cost in terms of economic growth of not moving forward. Initiatives such as the G20, which seek coordinated measures at an international rather than a national level, are moving in the right direction. However, the decline of financial integration in 2008 explains only a small percentage of the drop in both financial development and GDP. This reflects the global nature of the crisis, even without funding from other European countries decreasing in relation to that from third countries.

Acknowledgements

The authors acknowledge the financial support of the Spanish Ministry of Education-FEDER though project SEJ2007–60320. Joaquin Maudos also acknowledges the financial support of the Valencian Government (PROMETEO/2009/066).

Notes

1. See more details in Fernández de Guevara and Maudos (2010).
2. More details on the data used and on the decomposition can be found in Fernández de Guevara and Maudos (2010).
3. EU-15 aggregates do not include UK, Luxembourg, Ireland and Denmark. In the three first countries, the reason is that Eurostat does not provide information for them. In the case of Denmark, the reason is that the ECB does not provide information about cross-border activity of the MFI.

References

Cetorelli N. and Gambera M. (2001). Banking market structure, financial dependence and growth: international evidence from industry data. *Journal of Finance* 56, 617–648.

Claessens S. and Laeven L. (2005). Financial dependence, banking sector competition, and economic growth. *Journal of the European Economic Association* 3(1), 179–207.

European Central Bank. (2009). *Financial Integration in Europe*, April, Frankfurt.

European Commission. (2009). *European Financial Integration Report*, Brussels.

Fernández de Guevara J. and Maudos J. (2009). Regional financial development and bank competition: effects on firms' growth. *Regional Studies* 43(2), 211–228.

Fernández de Guevara J. and Maudos J. (2010). financial crisis, financial integration and economic growth: the European case, working papers. FBBVA, forthcoming.

Goldsmith R. (1969). *Financial Structure and Development*. New Haven and London: Yale University Press.

Guiso L., Jappelli T., Padula M. and Pagano M. (2004). Financial market integration and economic growth in the UE. *Economic Policy*, October, 523–577.

King R. and Levine R. (1993a). Finance and growth: Schumperter might be right. *Quarterly Journal of Economics* 108, 717–737.

King R. and Levine R. (1993b). Finance, entrepreneurship and growth: Theory and experience. *Journal of Monetary Economics* 32, 513–542.

Levine R. (1993). Financial development and economic growth: Views and agenda. *Journal of Economic Literature* 35, 668–726.
Levine R. and Zervos S. (1998). Stock markets, banks, and economic growth. *American Economic Review* 88, 537–558.
Levine R., Loayza N. and Beck T. (2000). Financial intermediation and growth: causality and causes. *Journal of Monetary Economics* 46, 31–77.
Levine R. (2005). Finance and growth: theory and evidence. In Aghion P. and Durlauf S. (eds.), *Handbook of Economic Growth*. The Netherlands: Elsevier Science.
Loayza N. and Rancière R. (2006). Financial development, financial fragility, and growth. *Journal of Money, Credit and Banking* 38(4), 1051–1076.
Maudos J. and Fernández de Guevara J. (2006). *Bank Competition, Financial Dependence and Economic Growth*, Working Paper No. 269, Fundación de las Cajas de Ahorros.
Rajan R. and Zingales L. (1998). Financial dependence and growth. *American Economic Review* 88, 559–587.

4
Can Financial Supervision Enhance the Central Bank's Independence?

Elena Seghezza and Giovanni B. Pittaluga

4.1 Introduction

The financial crisis of 2008 demands an urgent review of financial regulation supervision. It is widely believed that sharing supervision amongst various agencies is in part the cause of the recent crisis.

Not surprisingly, the American administration's recent proposal for reform of banking supervision looks to give broader powers to the Federal Reserve System, the Fed. Attributing further supervisory duties to a central bank raises the question whether it is appropriate to concentrate monetary policy and supervisory policy in a single institution. The literature currently favours a separation of these two functions.[1] The main reason for separating monetary and supervisory responsibilities is to avoid a conflict of interest between these functions. However, albeit in a political economy perspective, conclusions regarding the assignment of monetary and regulatory functions to one institution may be different. In fact, a central bank with goal independence can be viewed as a political player in competition with other political players: in order to compete effectively and realize its objectives, it needs the support of some interest groups.

When central banks have supervisory and regulatory powers they, as political players, can and do seek support from banking interest group Commercial banks, in exchange for favourable regulatory measures, can back the central bank to protect its independence from government incursion. The interaction of central and commercial banks is realized in a *political exchange*. This hypothesis is illustrated intuitively and analytically respectively in sections 4.2 and 4.3 below.

Clear examples of this kind of exchange can be found in the supervisory activities carried out by the Fed. Evidence can be found from the Volcker and Greenspan years that supports this hypothesis. We discuss this evidence in section 4.4. Some policy indications are drawn out in the conclusions.

4.2 The central bank's independence and financial supervision functions: what kind of interconnections?

In the past, most central banks were responsible for both monetary functions and banking supervision. More recently, numerous central banks in industrialized countries have lost their supervisory function. What accounts for this ongoing process?

In the last few decades the recognition of time-inconsistency in the implementation of monetary policy (Kydland and Prescott, 1977) has given rise to a debate about the institutional tools that can be used to overcome this problem (Barro and Gordon, 1983). One of the solutions is to give an independent role to central banks. When we talk about central banks' independence from political pressure, we need to distinguish between *instrumental independence* and *goal independence*.[2] As is widely known, instrumental independence is the potential for a central bank to change monetary instruments autonomously in order to meet the goals established by government. Goal independence, on the other hand, refers to the potential for a central bank to set and follow monetary policy objectives in complete autonomy, without deferring to government.

Instrumental independence can be viewed in terms of a principal-agent contract. This hypothesis is the foundation of the literature on central bank independence, based on performance contracts (Persson and Tabellini, 1993; Walsh, 1995). In a principal-agent contract framework, assigning supervisory and regulatory duties to the central bank in addition to its monetary policy responsibilities appears unsatisfactory. Firstly it would inevitably reduce the central bank's anti-inflationary credibility, as private individuals might expect that when carrying out monetary policy the bank focuses above all on the stability of the banking system. Secondly, assigning to the central bank two different functions (monetary policy and banking system oversight) complicates government monitoring of its agent. Goal independence of central banks is seen by Rogoff (1985) as a way of resolving the time-inconsistency problem: the government's time-inconsistency behaviour can be reduced, if not eliminated, by appointing a 'conservative' central banker.

However, the conservative central banker hypothesis does not allow us to resolve once and for all the time-inconsistency problem. Government can, in fact, always revoke the central bank's independence and as long as this possibility exists, the anti-inflationary credibility of monetary policy is fundamentally weakened. Various scholars have analyzed the strength of the central bank's *de iure* independence. Most of them have considered the trade-off between, on one hand, the removal of the anti-inflationary bias achieved by delegating monetary policy to a conservative central bank and, on the other, the ensuing loss of the government's ability to stabilize output in the event of negative shocks. Lohmann (1992) has shown that two central banks may have the same degree of legal independence, but enjoy different levels of *de facto* independence, principally due to the costs incurred by government in suspending the independence of the central bank.

These costs are also examined by Jensen (1997), who, using a deterministic inter-temporal game model, shows that the higher the costs are for the government in removing independence from the central banker, the lower the inflationary bias is. For both Lohmann (1992) and Jensen (1997), the costs of a government decision to revoke central bank independence are exogenous: this perspective neglects the fact that an institution like a central bank, with goal independence, tends to resemble a political player.[3] This kind of player competes constantly in the political arena to maintain or achieve power by seeking the support of interest groups. In the social arena, by contrast, the parties conflict in order to achieve distributional gains, by offering support to political players in exchange for favourable policy measures.

Interdependence between the political and the social arena is expressed in the form of a political exchange. Political players seek support from interest groups in return for political choices in these groups' favour. Regulation and supervision of the banking system can be seen as an instrument that provides a political player like the central bank with the opportunity to earn the support of the banking lobby in the face of attempts by government to reduce its degree of independence. With this in mind, when a central bank is assigned both monetary and supervisory functions, this, rather than weakening its anti-inflationary credibility, actually strengthens it: the costs of removing its independence are higher when it has been attributed both functions, and this helps to protect it against adverse political pressure.

4.3 A formal representation of the political exchange hypothesis

In order to provide a formal representation of the ideas expressed so far, we use a Rogoff framework which allows us to examine the case of a goal-independent central bank. We assume that the government grants partial independence to a conservative central banker who places a higher emphasis on inflation stabilization than the government. The government retains the option to override the central bank's decision for positive gains: in normal times the central bank sets the inflation rate, but in extreme situations the government overrides the central bank policy and applies its preferred inflation rate. In Lohmann (1992) and similar contributions (Jensen, 1997), the cost of overriding the central bank's decision is exogenous. This assumption, while convenient, does not take into account that to override central bank independence, the government needs consensus. The present paper models this fact, assuming that the cost of overriding central bank independence depends on pressure from bank interest groups on government in order to preserve central bank independence.

We assume, using Grossman and Helpman's (1994) framework, that the central bank makes an offer to commercial banks. It offers a particular level of banking regulation in exchange for a certain level of political pressure. There are three players in the economy: the government, the central bank, and the bank interest groups. The government's preferred policy outcomes are reflected in the loss function $L^G = (y - \hat{y})^2 + \lambda\pi^2 + \delta c^2$, where the first term represents deviations of output, y, from the government's bliss point, $\hat{y}$, the second term represents deviation of the inflation rate, π, from its zero bliss point, and c is the cost that the government incurs when it reneges on its commitment to maintain central bank independence.

Monetary policy is delegated to a conservative central bank, which places a higher weight on inflation stabilization: $L^{BC} = (y - \hat{y})^2 + (\lambda + \epsilon)\pi^2 + \vartheta(R - R^*)^2$. Since the central bank has supervisory and regulatory functions, its loss function depends also on deviation of banking regulation from an optimum level R*. The latter is the level that allows for an efficient allocation of resources. We assume that the higher the level of regulation, the lower the banking sector profits,[4] and that lobbying is costly. Formally, the loss function of the banking sector may be modelled as: $L^B = \alpha R + \frac{1}{2}c^2$. The final equilibrium is represented in Figure 4.1.

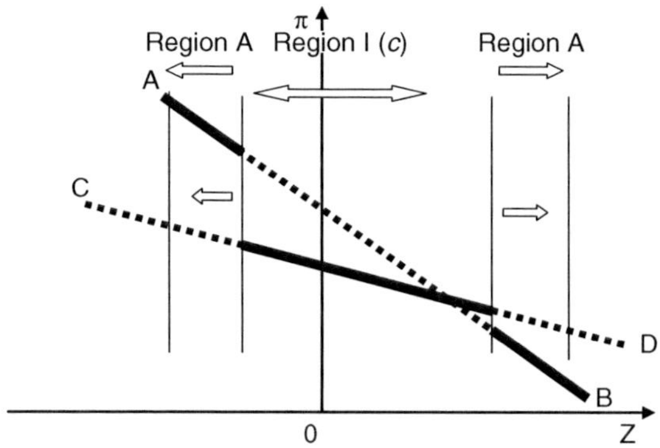

Figure 4.1 The final equilibrium graph

The abscissas show shock to the economy: if the shock is positive the economy is experiencing a boom; if the shock is negative the economy is going through a recession. The ordinates show the inflation rate. The line AB represents the optimal monetary policy for the government in response to the shock. The line CD indicates the optimal monetary policy for the central bank. Monetary policy decisions – which affect the inflation rate – are taken by the central bank if the shock occurs in region I.

Monetary policy is decided by the government if the shock happens in one of the A regions. In that case, the political cost for the government of removing independence from the central bank is less that the gains it can obtain in terms of output stabilisation. The extent of regulation when a central bank is independent depends on lobbying efforts by the banking sector. The more favourable to the banking sector the regulation offered by the central bank, the larger its degree of independence. The optimal value of regulation chosen by the central bank is lower than the optimal value of regulation in terms of financial efficiency. The central bank, therefore, chooses a level of regulation taking into account its effect on banks' ability to support it.

The model allows three main conclusions:

1. The central bank provides a banking regulation that enhances banks' capability to exert political pressure to defend its independence.
2. The higher this pressure, the higher the cost of overriding the central bank by the government. Therefore these costs are endogenous and depend on the behaviour of the political and social players.

3. When the central bank uses banking supervision and regulation to increase its independence, it may jeopardize the efficient allocation of resources.

4.4 The Federal Reserve under Volcker's and Greenspan's presidencies: a case of the political exchange hypothesis

Currently, in most industrialized countries, especially following changes made in recent decades, monetary and supervisory functions have been separated. The attribution of supervisory responsibilities to the central bank is somewhat rare in industrialized countries, with notable exceptions like that of the US Federal Reserve.

The Fed has, on one hand, goal independence and, on the other, in addition to responsibility for monetary policy, supervisory and regulatory powers over the banking system. These powers allow the Fed to turn to those constituencies – principally the banking industry – that lobby in its favour. Banks provide their support both through the reserve banks and through directly lobbying the political class.[5] The political influence of the reserve banks derives from the fact that, in each one, six of the nine board members are elected by member banks of the Federal Reserve System.

In addition, the American Banking Association can exert lobbying pressure on the political class: it calls on an army of lobbyists with previous experience on Capitol Hill, at the US Treasury, or at the Fed itself.[6]

Commercial banks give support to the Fed in several ways, firstly in the form of monetary policy management. For example, when in 1979 the US central bank drastically changed its monetary policy stance, bankers at the Federal Advisory Council encouraged the Fed's chairman to continue with, and where possible increase, the rigor of measures being undertaken.[7] A second form of support consists of opposition by banks to the government's attempts to reduce the independence of the Fed. A surreptitious way of reducing the central bank's independence is seen in attempts to loosen the Fed's ties with the commercial banks through reform of financial governance of the reserve banks. For example in 1982, when the social costs of Volcker's disinflationary policy were particularly high, government put forward proposals for the overhaul of the financial regulatory system with the aim of reducing the Fed's role in this system.

Other attempts to limit the Fed's independence by weakening its constituencies took the form of proposed changes to the governance of the reserve banks. These attempts were aimed at breaking the strong link between the reserve banks and the commercial banks. Once such attempt occurred in mid-1993 when the chairman of the Congressional Banking Commission, Gonzales, proposed that regional reserve bank chairmen were to be appointed by the US president with Senate approval, and not by the boards of the banks.[8] In the same period the vice-chairman of the Joint Economic Committee together with another Congressman, Lee Hamilton, put forward the idea of removing the reserve bank chairmen's voting rights on the FOMC. Both attempts sought to weaken the Fed's constituency. The first tried to substantially alter the public-private hybrid nature of the reserve banks, whilst the second attempted to reduce their power over monetary policy-making.

Attacks on the Fed's independence in those years were repelled thanks to the US central bank's ability to operate as a political player, and to the support commercial banks provided – in particular the pressure the latter managed to exert on the political class. What did the Fed do in return for such support? The Volcker and Greenspan years have shown that both chairmen attributed a special role to the commercial banks in the intermediation of savings, protecting their interests during a period of intense deregulation. The special role played by the banks led Volcker and Greenspan to favour supervisory and regulatory measures that benefited the banks more than other financial intermediaries (Table 4.1).

Volcker, in particular, stimulated banks' competitiveness by supporting the removal of interest rates ceilings, by favouring the fixing of reserve obligations for monetary mutual funds that offered current-account deposits, and by allowing branch opening in other states.[9] Greenspan loosened the restrictions on branch openings, benefiting the holding banks which were subject to the supervision of the Fed, which increased its power at the expense of other supervision agencies. Large banks, in particular bank holding companies, benefited also from the intense merger and acquisition process (M&A) process that marked the 1980s and 1990s, as well as the granting of authorization to carry out investment banking activities.

Under Greenspan's chairmanship, consolidation of the US banking industry was considerable: in the two decades after 1984, the number of US banks dropped sharply, from around 13,800 to 7800. The liberalization of branch openings, the authorization of commercial banks to offer investment banking activities, and the process of M and A favoured mainly large banks, Greenspan's main supporters.[10] The

Table 4.1 Examples of Volcker and Greenspan regulatory measures in favour of larger banks

Ceilings on interest-rate deposits	Interest ceilings were removed by Volcker.
Compulsory reserve on deposits of mutual funds	During Volcker's presidency a compulsory reserve on deposits of monetary mutual funds was established.
Inter-state branching	The Volcker Fed supported inter-state banking. His design was completed by Greenspan.
Mergers and acquisitions	The Fed, in the Greenspan era, supported large bank mergers.
Fannie and Freddie post-2000	Once the political climate had become less risky, the Greeenspan Fed became a vocal proponent of reform, with strong support from large banks.
Investment banking powers	The Fed led the efforts to expand banking powers, particularly in the area of underwriting corporate securities.

Source: Hawke (1988) and Calomiris (2006).

political exchange between the Fed and commercial banks, just illustrated, has been summed up by Hawke (1988: p. 21): "Fed theologians have felt that preservation of its role in supervision and regulation ... is important to the preservation of its political independence".[11]

4.5 Conclusions

The financial crisis of 2007–2008 will inevitably lead to major reforms in the banking regulation of industrialized countries. The debate regarding these reforms will inevitably include the question of concentrating monetary policy and supervisory policy functions around a central bank. In the past, various arguments have been used against attributing supervisory and regulatory functions to central banks. Without doubt the most important of these arguments is that of the conflict of interest that arises between managing monetary policy and conserving financial stability. This position has been strongly argued above all in the literature based on the time-inconsistency hypothesis. This literature has underlined the fact that attributing these dual functions to a central bank damages its anti-inflationary credibility.

There can be little argument with this position in the case of instrument-independent central banks, that is those institutions that operate as an agent for a principal (the government). However, in the case of the appointment of a conservative central banker *à la* Rogoff, the time-inconsistency problem is not definitively solved: government may in fact remove by law previously-granted central bank independence. Various authors have shown that the chance of this happening depends on the political costs incurred by such legislation. In the current literature these costs are assumed to be exogenous. In reality, a goal-independent central bank is a political player which, equipped with supervisory functions, can seek the support of commercial banks and offer them favourable regulatory measures. The commercial banks offer their support to the central bank by exercising pressure on government in return for regulations in their favour. In this way there is a political exchange between commercial banks and the central bank.

In such a framework the costs incurred by removing central bank independence become endogenous, depending on how the central bank performs its role as a political actor. This leads us to conclude that supervisory and regulatory functions, instead of damaging a central bank's anti-inflationary credibility, may actually enhance it. However, the use of a central bank's supervisory and regulatory powers to increase the support of specific interest groups may lead to an inefficient allocation of financial resources and hamper the introduction of financial innovation.[12] This inevitably raises some issues worthy of deeper consideration. Does the attribution of banking supervision to a central bank favour an inefficient allocation of financial resources? When monetary and supervision functions are concentrated in a single institution, is financial innovation hampered? Such questions represent possible future developments for this area of research.

Notes

1. For an overview of the literature see Goodhart and Schoenmaker (1995) and Haubrich (1996).
2. See Fischer (1994).
3. Calomiris (2006; p. 170) draws attention to this aspect when, writing about the US Federal Reserve, states: '*There is fairly straightforward logic to the Fed's regulatory advocacy. To understand it, one must consider the Fed as a political player in the Washington drama ...*'. And Woolley (1984; p. 1) writes: '*Plainly, the Federal Reserve is a key political institution. It defines, sets, and implements public policy in a central arena*'.
4. What really matters is that banks' profits depend on banking sector regulation.

5. Pierce (1990; p. 155) described the situation as follows: *'Armed with its control over banks and bank holding companies, and its legions of Federal Reserve Bank boards of directors, the Federal Reserve can, and does, bring forth tremendous lobbying efforts by its constituents in opposition to attempts by Congress to put the Fed on a shorter leash.'*
6. The pressure exerted by the US banking lobby can also be measured in terms of the generous contributions it makes to senators and members of congress in their election campaigns, see Greider (1987).
7. See Greider (1987; p. 115).
8. In presenting his proposal, Gonzales (1993) claimed: *'In general, the Federal Reserve Banks decision-makers are bankers or friends of bankers. Decision-makers representing the concerns of agriculture, small businessmen, labor, consumer and community groups are almost unheard of. Yet, advocates of price stability even at the price of stagnation are well represented at the FOMC'.*
9. For an analysis of Volcker's supervisory policy see Hawke (1988).
10. See Calomiris (2000).
11. Similarly, Havrilesky (1990; p. 40) writes: *'On many occasions the Federal Reserve has enlisted the support of private bankers to lobby against bills that would reduce its autonomy... in exchanges at Congressional hearings, its officials tend to support the regulatory policies favored by the most important financial services' interest groups...'.*
12. Concerns that concentrating monetary policy and supervisory policy around the Fed may produce allocative inefficiencies could convince some that separating these functions would be better. See Calomiris (2006).

References

Barro R. and Gordon D.B. (1983). A positive theory of monetary policy in a natural rate model. *Journal of Political Economy* 91, 589–610.

Calomiris C.W. (2000). *US Bank Deregulation in Historical Perspective.* Cambridge: Cambridge University Press.

Calomiris C.W. (2006). The regulatory record of the Greenspan era. *American Economic Review,* AEA Papers and Proceedings, 96, 170–173.

Fischer S. (1994). Modern central banking. In Capie F. et al. (eds.), *The Future of Central Banking.* Cambridge: Cambridge University Press.

Gonzales R. (1993). *Open Letter to President Clinton,* 22 July.

Goodhart C.A.E and Schoenmaker D. (1995). Should the functions of monetary policy and banking supervision be separated?. *Oxford Economic Papers* 47, 539–560.

Greider W. (1987). *Secrets of the Temple.* New York: Touchstone.

Grossman G.M. and Helpman E. (1994). Protection for sale. *American Economic Review* 84, 833–850.

Haubrich J.C. (1996). Combining bank supervision and monetary policy. In *Federal Reserve of Cleveland,* Economic Commentary, November.

Havrilesky T. (1990). The influence of the Federal Advisory Council on monetary policy. *Journal of Money, Credit and Banking* 22, 37–51.

Hawke J. (1988). Paul Volcker and domestic bank regulatory policy. Paper presented at the Annual Meeting of the American Economic Association.

Jensen H. (1997). The credibility of optimal monetary delegation. *American Economic Review* 87, 911–920.

Kydland F.W. and Prescott E.C. (1977). Rules rather than discretion: The inconsistency of the optimal plans. *Journal of Political Economy* 85, 473–491.

Lohmann S. (1992). The optimal commitment in monetary policy: credibility versus flexibility. *American Economic Review,* 82, 273–286.

Persson T. and Tabellini G. (1993). Designing institutions for monetary stability. *Carnegie-Rochester Conference Series on Public Policy* 39, 33–84.

Pierce J.L. (1990). The Federal Reserve as a political power. In Mayer T. (ed.), *The Political Economy of the American Monetary Policy.* Cambridge: Cambridge University Press.

Rogoff K. (1985). The optimal commitment to an intermediate monetary target. *Quarterly Journal of Economics,* 100, 1169–1190.

Walsh C.E. (1995). Optimal contracts for central bankers. *American Economic Review* 85, 150–167.

Woolley J.T. (1984). *Monetary Politics. The Federal Reserve and the Politics of Monetary Policy.* Cambridge: Cambridge University Press.

5
The Impact of a Housing Price Bubble on the Intensity of the Recent Credit Crunch: Evidence from Different Countries

José Manuel Pastor, Javier Quesada and Lorenzo Serrano

5.1 Introduction

For almost two years international financial markets have been under great pressure, originating with the sub-prime mortgage episode. This, in turn, was triggered by the downturn of the US housing cycle and spread quickly into third countries in the form of severe losses and an increasing lack of confidence. Market liquidity dried up almost instantly and banking sectors around the world suffered great financial distress. It became increasingly difficult for many financial intermediaries to refinance operations as overall loanable funds reduced. This process started a chain reaction in which bankers reduced exposure to loans. As a result, getting loans became more difficult for consumers and businesses, with lenders preferring to hold a very liquid position rather than risk facing a wave of bankruptcies and mortgage defaults. Consequently, interest rates skyrocketed and clear signs of an imminent severe credit crunch spread throughout the economy.[1]

Banks had been very active in raising mortgages which were then sold to secondary investors. Since the risk was transferred to the new holders, banks were not very cautious in limiting the risk involved in these loans. Other investors, looking for higher rates of return, relied on the role of rating companies to evaluate risk and insurance companies to diversify it. In fact, mortgage-backed assets were much riskier than investors had initially thought, as was made explicit in August 2007. Commercial and savings banks, which had previously shown very high activity in mortgage lending that forced them to obtain funds from international lenders, faced the need either to renew their short-to-medium-term financial requirements or to stop the automatic renewals of their own loans. The need to downsize their loan portfolios started a credit crunch in the banking sector. Banks were afraid of not being repaid their loans by other banks in the money market, even in the very short term. Given that they did not know the borrowing partners' risk exposure, they preferred to stay liquid and deposited their excess reserves at the central bank. Consequently, a much higher risk premium in inter-bank loans reduced the volume of transactions in the market.

The need to refinance their operations in a very hostile market led banks to reduce the refinancing of many regular loans made to customers. It was not long before safe businesses and consumers with stable banking relations started to perceive a radical change of attitude on the part of banks, which were reluctant to maintain the easy-loan policy followed until only a few months earlier. Banks rejected many of the loan requests that they used to accept before, and when accepted, borrowers were charged a much higher interest rate. Thus many households and businesses, who previously would have been able to borrow from banks, were now turned down. The credit market dried up.

With much less credit available, consumers and businesses, with expectations of an immediate recession of unknown severity, reduced their demands, stalling the economy completely. This paper analyzes whether the tightening of the credit market has been more severe in those countries that had formerly experienced a housing price bubble. We claim that in those countries with a higher presence of mortgage lending in the balance sheets of their commercial and savings banks we should expect a more severe credit tightening after the housing prices stopped rising and started falling.

Section 5.2 shows the pattern of housing prices and credit aggregates over the expansionary period 2003–2008, prior to the credit crunch. We classify the countries into bubble, non-bubble, and deflationary economies. Section 5.3 analyzes the evolution of housing prices, credit aggregates, and indicators of the real economy. Finally, section 5.4 concludes.

5.2 Pre-crunch period: international evidence on housing prices, credit market conditions, and construction investment

Figure 5.1 shows housing prices for nine different EU countries as well as the EMU aggregate since March 1996. According to the accumulated

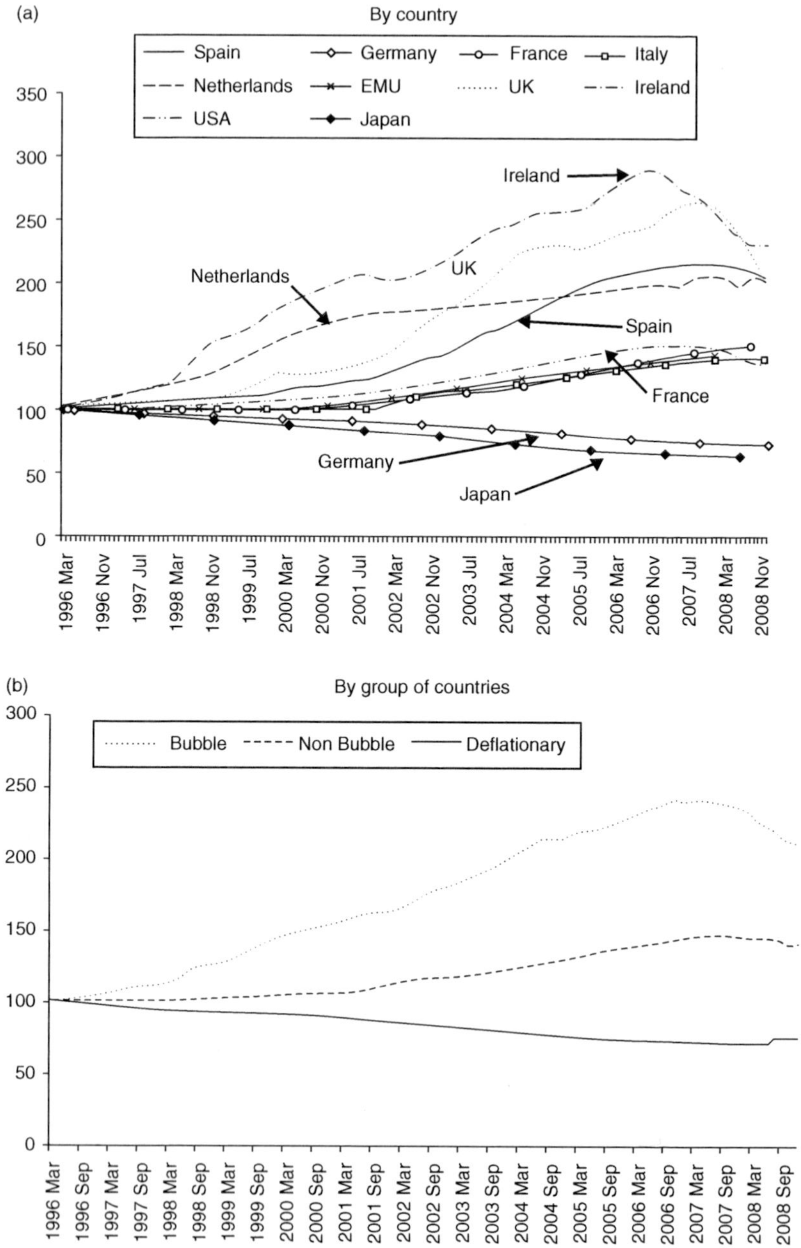

Figure 5.1 House price indices (Q1 1996 = 100)

Table 5.1 Annual rate of inflation in housing prices (computed monthly)

	Bubble countries				Non-bubble countries				Deflationary countries	
	Ireland	**Netherlands***	**UK**	**Spain**	**USA**	**EMU**	**France**	**Italy**	**Japan****	**Germany**
Inflation in housing prices (%)	12.01	10.71	9.92	7.07	3.95	3.05	2.96	2.55	–3.24	–2.00
Period	Mar 96–Jan 07	Mar 96–Sep 02	Mar 96–Aug 07	Mar 96–Mar 07	Mar 96–Dec 06	Mar 96–Dec 07	Mar 96–Sep 08	Mar 96–Dec 08	Mar 96–Jun 08	Mar 96–Dec 08

*The Netherlands will not appear as a bubble country below when we concentrate on the 2003–2008 period: see Figure 5.1. **Japan experienced a real-estate bubble in the 1985–1990 period when an index of land prices tripled in real terms. See Barsky (2009).

housing price inflation rates, we classify these countries into three different groups: bubble, non-bubble, and deflationary countries. Table 5.1 presents the annual inflation rate in housing prices by country. Spain, Ireland, the UK, and the Netherlands belong to the first group with annual sustained price hikes above 7%. Italy, France, and the USA form the second group of non-bubble economies with positive annual inflation rates under 7%. Germany and Japan belong to the group of deflationary economies.

Figure 5.1a shows that Ireland is the most inflationary country in terms of housing prices, followed by the UK and Spain. We see that the Netherlands started its inflationary period at about the same time as Ireland but its much shorter bubble had burst by 2001.

Figure 5.1b shows the behaviour of housing prices as simple averages of different countries' indices. We can see that on average the group of bubble economies saw housing prices rise by a factor of 2.5 over 11 years. Similarly, this factor was 1.5 for the group of non-bubble economies.

Housing inflation can also be very unsteady over time. Figure 5.2 shows the Financial Times Housing Price index for the UK. During the 1970s and 80s, inflation in housing prices was quite high in this country, with 3 peaks and more than 10 years of annual rates above 10%. Except for the first half of the 90s, housing price inflation was high again until the burst of the bubble in 2007.

In the case of the US, we have double-checked the housing inflation index with that of Standard and Poors-Schiller. Figure 5.3 shows for this latter one an accumulated price hike that exceeds that given by the alternative data set by a factor of six.

As for the credit market conditions, we consider two different sources for interest rates. Figure 5.4 shows typical mortgage interest rates over the period 1998–2008. There is a clear path of convergence of interest rates for all countries considered. Excluding Greece, the geographical maximum spread of interest rates between countries was 2.4 pp. in 1998 and only 1.2 pp. 10 years later.

The evolution of 10-year mortgage rates appears in Figure 5.5. All rates follow a similar path since all are EMU countries. However, the maximum difference between countries is almost 2 pp., with Denmark at the upper level and Finland, France, and Spain at the lower level.

It is well known how dependent housing purchases are on credit availability. Figure 5.6 shows the share of housing credit over total credit for households of some European countries. This share is lowest in Austria and Italy with values around 55%, and is highest in the Netherlands,

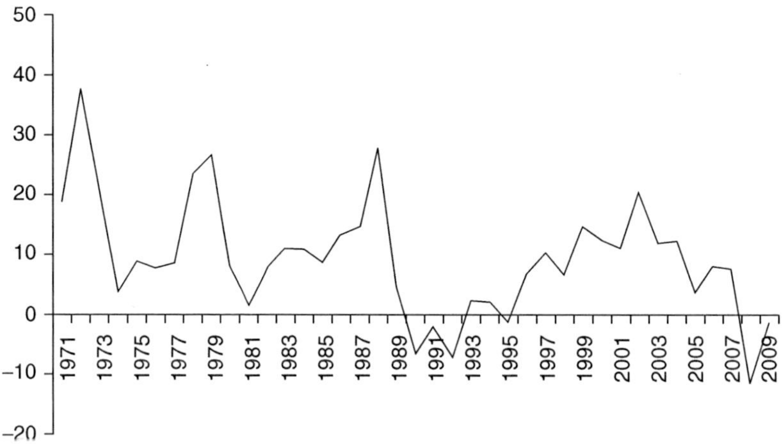

Figure 5.2 FTHPI annual rate of change

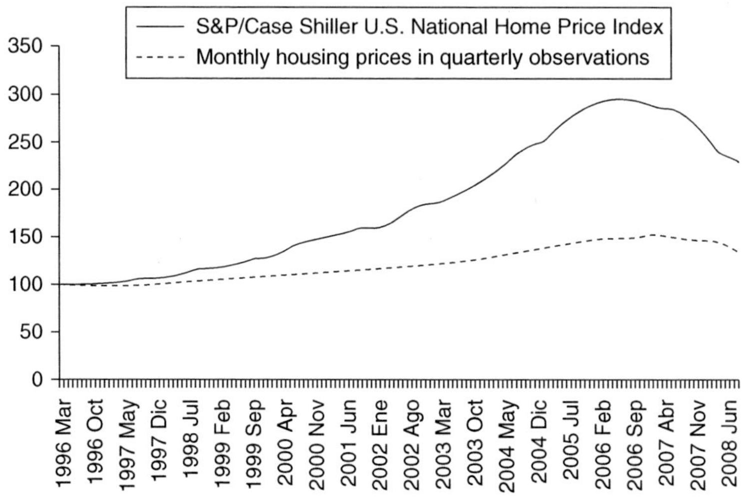

Figure 5.3 US Housing prices

Denmark, and the UK (90%, 85% and 80%, respectively). It is true that a higher share means that housing finance is a larger burden on household total indebtedness, although it might reflect only a lesser use of credit for purposes other than housing (consumption, and so on).

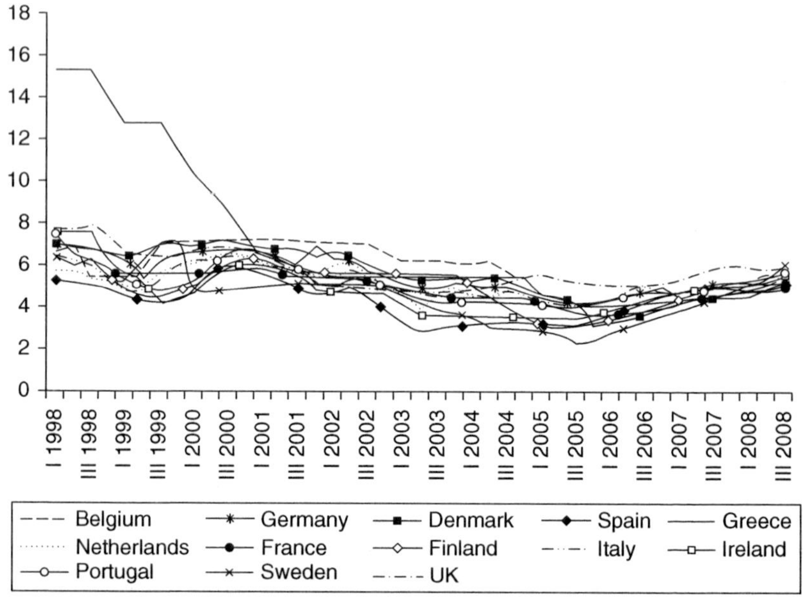

Figure 5.4 Typical mortgage interest rates (%)

Figure 5.6 also shows that the share of housing over total household credit has increased in all countries (except for Hungary), particularly strongly in Latvia, Italy, and Luxembourg.

Apparently those countries with the lowest share of housing over total credit at the beginning of the period have experienced the highest relative increase. To test for this possibility, Figure 5.7 replicates a β-convergence test. We regress the share of housing over total credit at the initial year of 2003 against its growth rate over the period. Results show that there is β-convergence since those financial systems with the lowest share of housing credit have experienced the highest rate of increase in mortgage loans. Figure 5.8 also confirms this result by means of a sigma-convergence exercise. As can be observed, the deviation coefficient of the share of housing credits among countries is lower in 2009 than in 2003. In other words, housing credit conditions in countries are now more homogeneous than they were six years ago.

Housing loan trends appear in Figure 5.9. Ireland and Spain show the highest average growth rates over the 2003–2009 period, around 16% of annual rate. The second group of countries, Finland and Austria, show

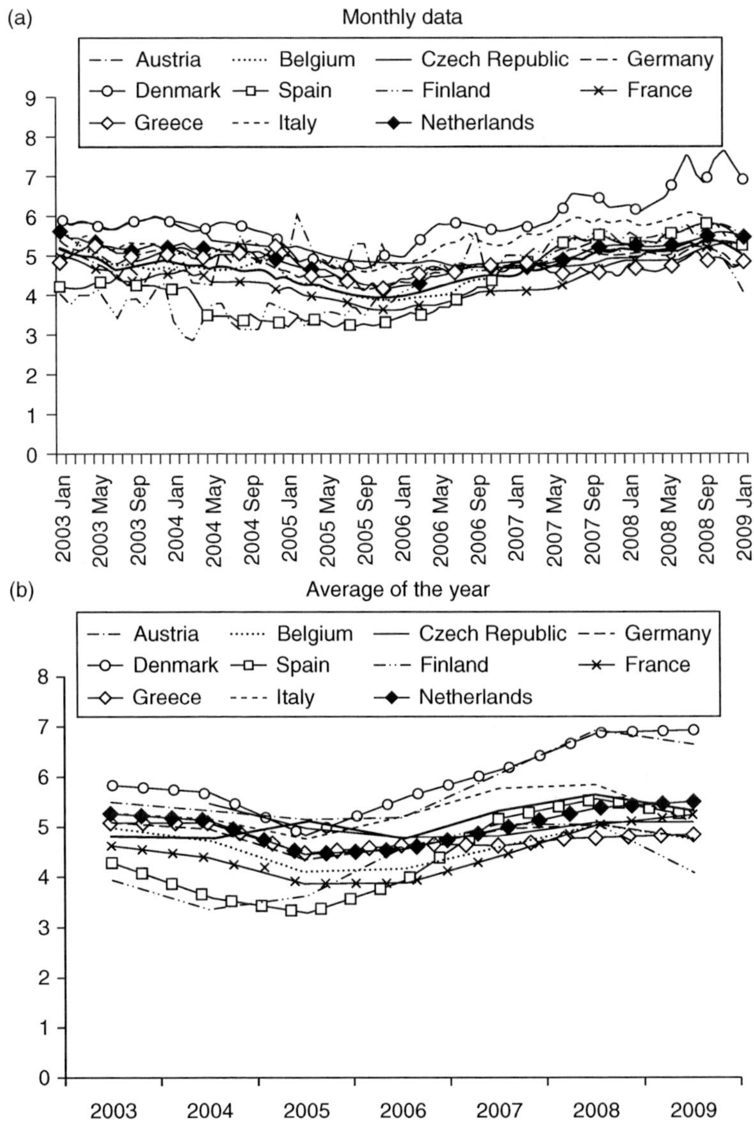

Figure 5.5 Interest rate of loans for house purchases

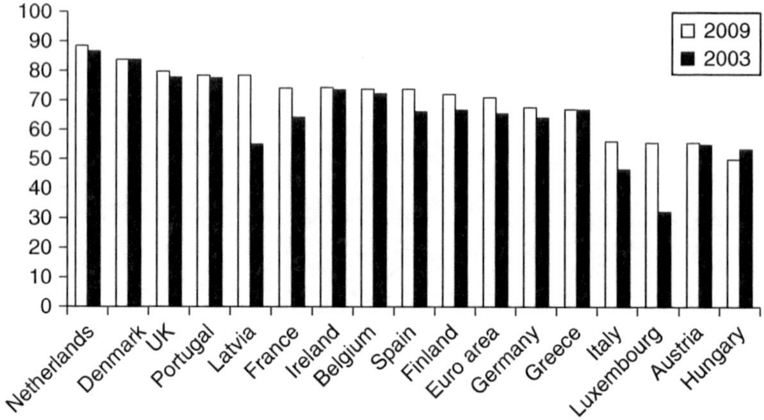

Figure 5.6 Share of housing over total credit

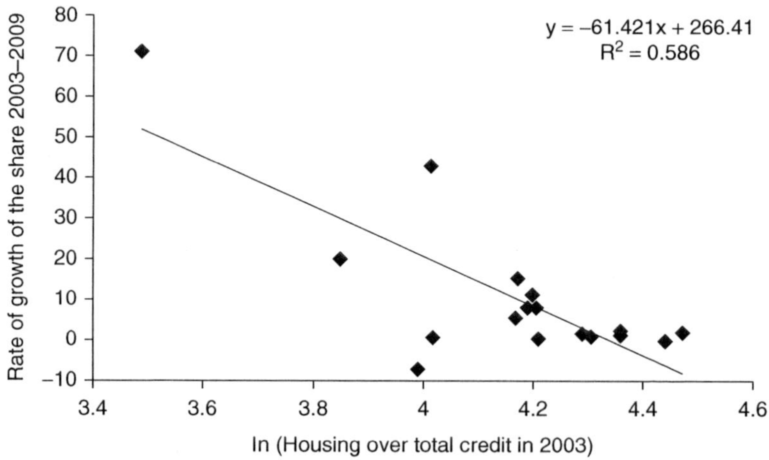

Figure 5.7 β-Convergence of the share of housing over total credit

a much lower rate of increase of 9.2%. Surprisingly the UK, one of the bubble countries, shows a much lower rate of increase until 2007 and a negative one thereafter.

Table 5.2 shows a clear correspondence between housing loan growth rates and housing price inflation.

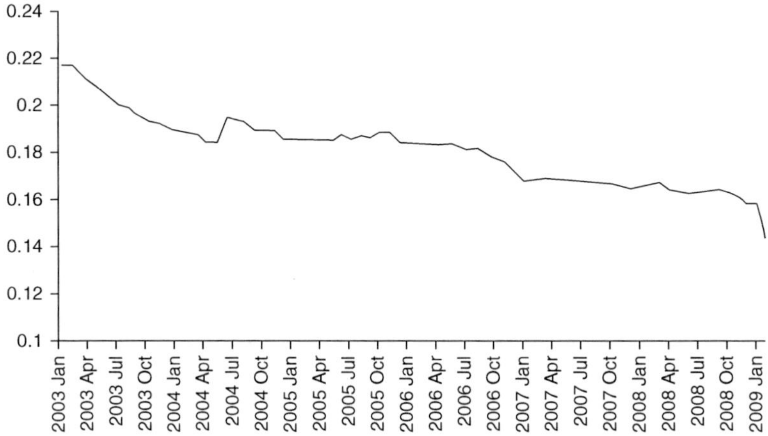

Figure 5.8 Sigma-convergence of the share of housing over total credit

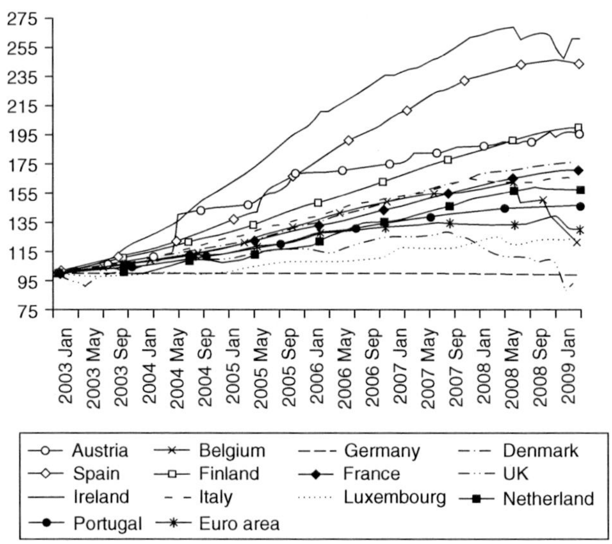

Figure 5.9 Housing loans

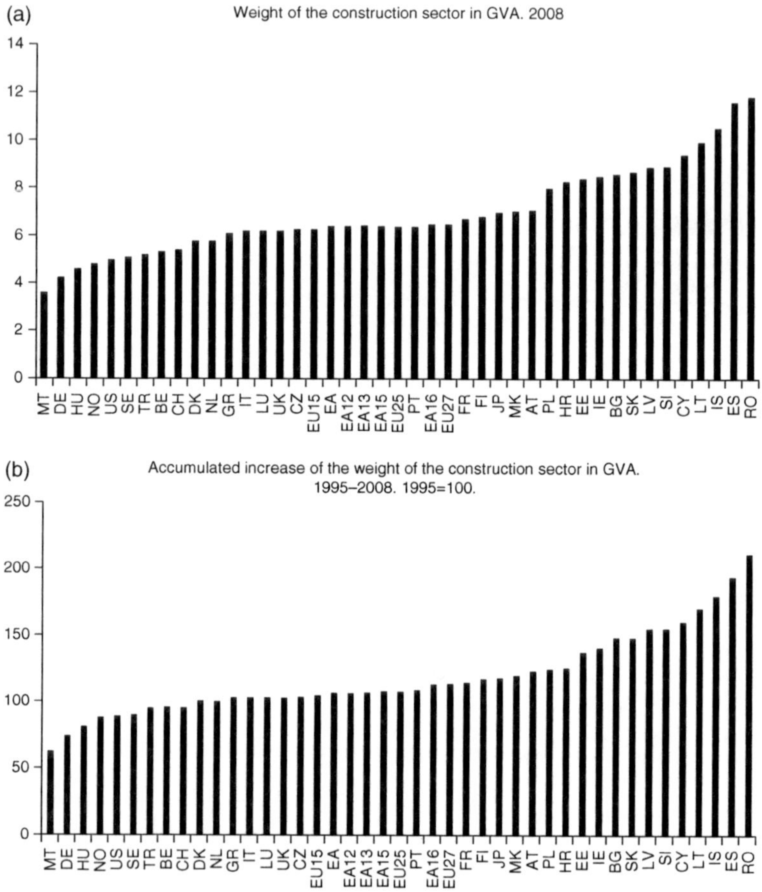

Figure 5.10 Relative weight of the construction sector in GVA

Finally, a look at the country-relative weight of the construction sector as a share of GVA explains the different quantitative implications of a credit crunch that originated in the housing sector. Figure 5.10a shows that this share is around 4% in countries like Malta and Germany and is three times higher in countries like Spain and Romania. It is interesting to note that the order of countries by the size of the construction sector is almost identical to the ordering by accumulated growth from 1995 to 2008. That is, countries with a high share of the construction sector have experienced a higher growth rate over the last 13 years.

Table 5.2 Housing loans (rates of growth in pp.)

	Bubble countries	**Non-bubble countries****	**Deflationary countries***
2003	16	14	2
2004	22	16	1
2005	24	16	1
2006	15	14	2
2007	9	12	–1
2008	–1	2	–1

*Only Germany; **including the USA.

5.3 The crunch period

We now turn to the analysis of the crunch period defined as March 2008 to March 2009. In a series of tests, we want to check whether the intensity of the deceleration in credit growth is related to the relative size of the housing credit sector in the market.

We find that those countries in which housing loans were relatively more important (representing a higher share of total loans) in March 2008 experienced – over the crunch period – the lowest growth in total loans (Figure 5.11a), in loans to non-financial companies (Figure 5.11b), in loans to purchase houses (Figure 5.11c), and finally, in consumer credit (Figure 5.11d).

However, we find no evidence as to whether the weight of the housing sector in the loan industry has influenced the increase in unemployment (Figure 5.12). Apparently, the almost unanimous worsening of the unemployment situation in all countries over the last year had no relationship to banking specialization in lending to the housing sector.

We provide evidence of the influence of the weight of the housing loan industry on the intensity of the credit crunch. We define the intensity of the credit crunch as the difference between the growth rate of loans to house purchases during the crunch period and the annual average rate of growth over the expansion period of March 2003 to March 2008. Evidence of this measure of deceleration appears in Figure 5.13. We find that loans for house purchasing decreased more than total

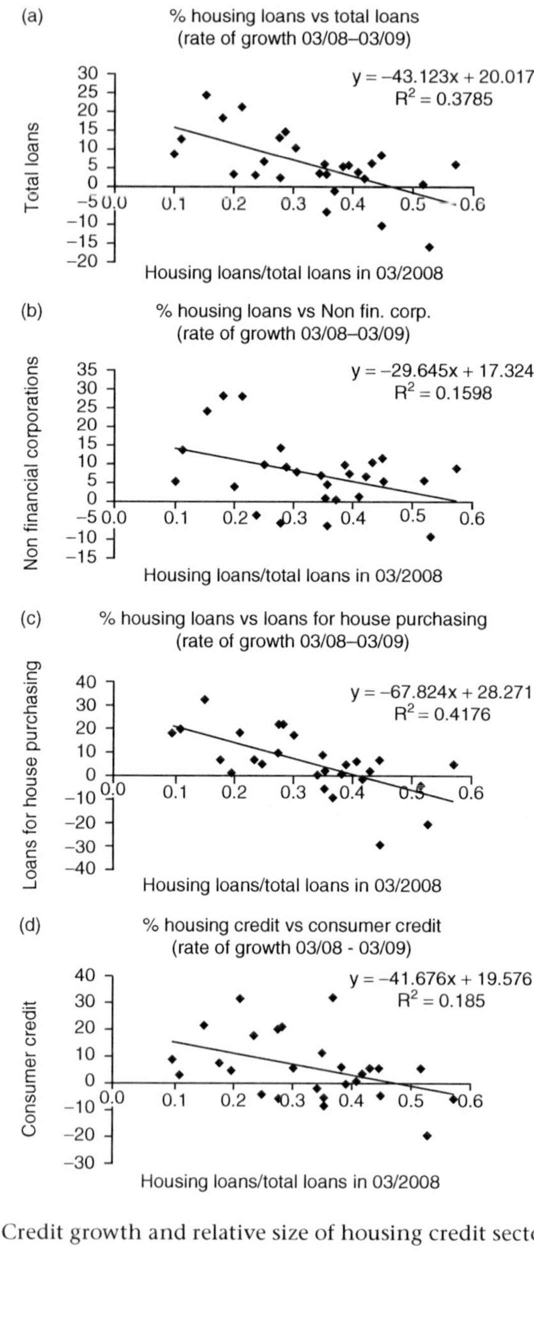

Figure 5.11 Credit growth and relative size of housing credit sector

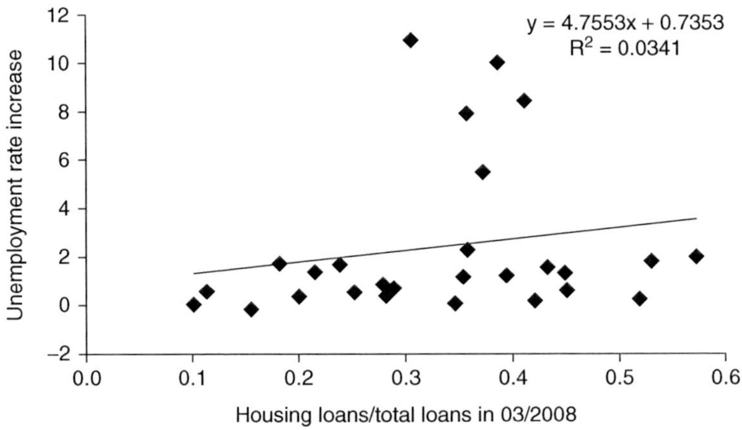

Figure 5.12 Percentage housing credit vs. unemployment rate increase

loans (panel a), loans to non-financial firms (panel b), consumer credit (panel c), or household loans (panel d).

Again, we find no relationship between the intensity of the credit crunch and variations in inflation or unemployment rates (see Figure 5.14).

Credit deceleration is plotted in Figure 5.15 on the vertical axis. We can see that it is negative for most of the countries except in the cases of credit to non-financial firms and consumer credit values.

We find no evidence for the importance of housing loans in the aggregate loan industry and the deceleration figures for total loans (Figure 5.15a), non-financial businesses (Figure 5.15b), housing loans (Figure 5.15c), or consumer credit (Figure 5.15d).

5.4 Concluding remarks

We find positive country evidence regarding the impact of the relative size of the housing sector on the intensity of the recent credit crunch period. Countries which experienced the highest housing price hikes are also countries where the credit deceleration has been more intensive. The size of housing loans relative to banks' portfolios, together with a much higher correspondent risk in the inter-bank markets, has probably been the main cause of the liquidity constraint crisis over the last year.

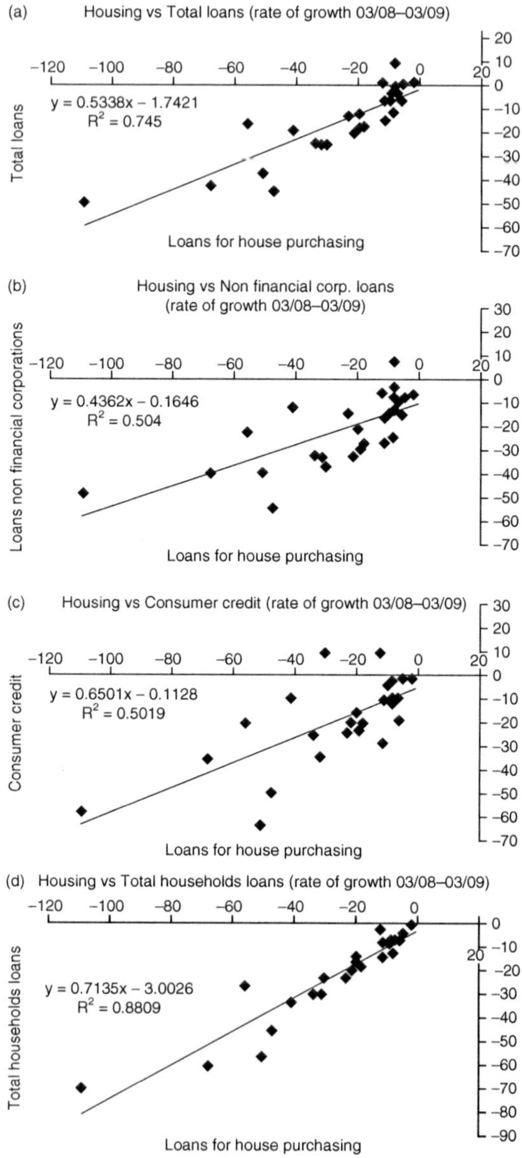

Figure 5.13 Weight of the housing loan industry and intensity of the credit crunch

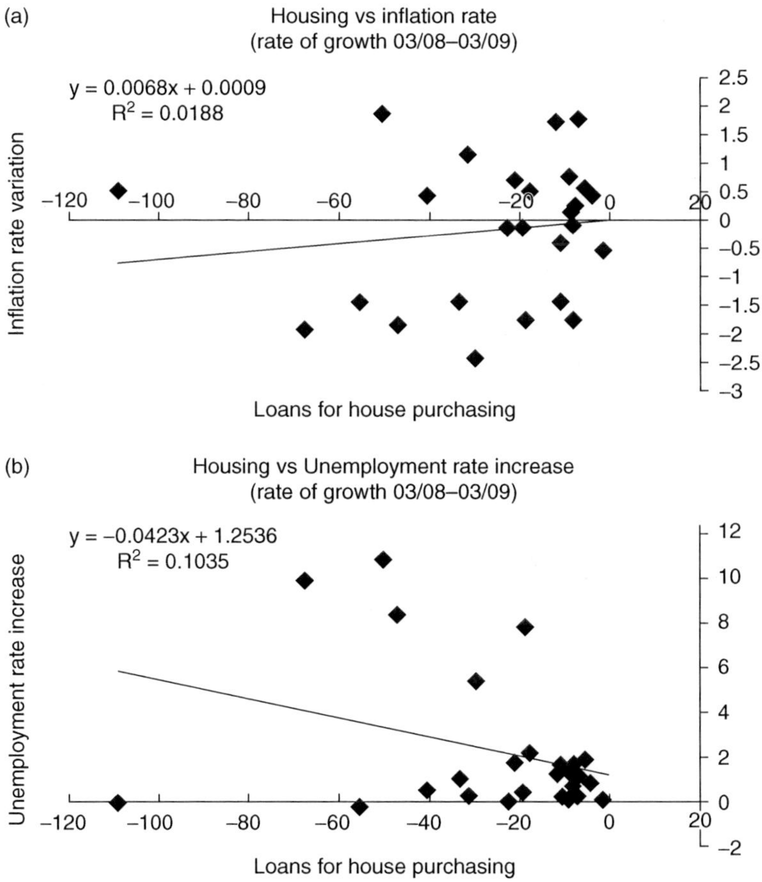

Figure 5.14 Credit crunch vs. inflation and unemployment rate

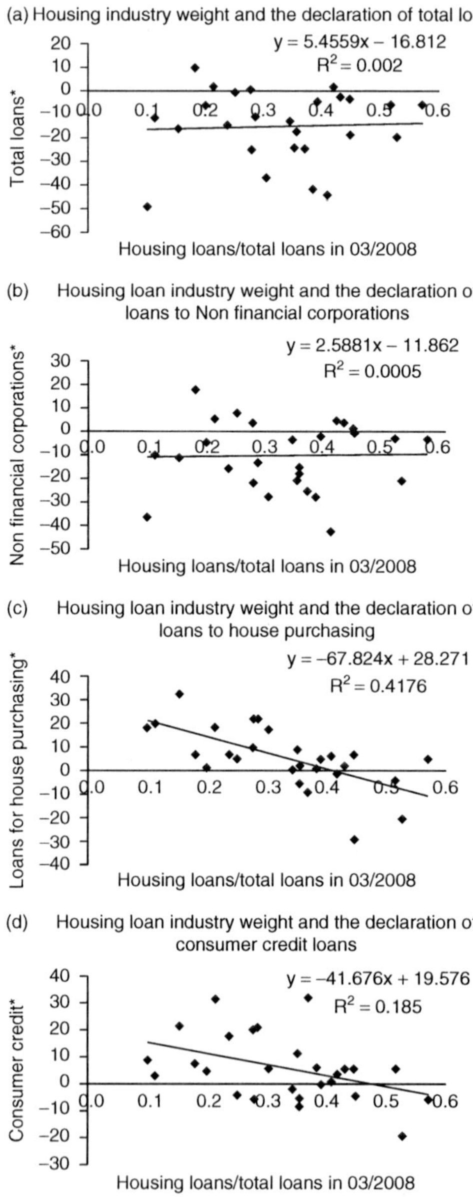

Figure 5.15 Importance of housing loans and the deceleration figures for total loans

Acknowledgement

Authors acknowledge the financial support of the Ministerio de Ciencia e Innovación (ECO2008–03813/ECON.

Notes

1. The economics profession is unclear as to what constitutes a 'credit crunch'. In simple terms, credit crunch is a situation in which lenders will not lend, borrowers cannot borrow, builders cannot build and buyers cannot buy. Essentially a credit crunch is a sudden cut in the availability of credit or loans, including mortgages, credit cards and inter-bank lending as banks worry about a lack of liquidity. If there is a significant reduction in the supply of loans, the economic outlook quickly becomes depressed. The crucial differences in definition depend on the cause of the contraction and whether credit is rationed by means other than price. Bernanke and Lown (1991) define a credit crunch as a decline in the supply of credit that is abnormally large for a given stage of the business cycle. While credit normally contracts during a recession, an unusually large contraction could be seen as a credit crunch. See Clair and Tucker (1993) and Parkinson et al. (2009).
2. In order to borrow from the central bank, an anonymous procedure was introduced in many countries to avoid the negative signalling effect on borrowing banks.
3. Kindleberger's definition of bubble is 'an upward price movement oven an extended range that then implodes', see Kindleberger (1996).
4. Interestingly, the US – blamed for starting the international financial crisis after the sub-prime episode – shows one of the lowest relative size of the construction sector as well as one of the lowest accumulated growth rates.

References

Barsky R.B. (2009). The Japanese bubble: a 'heterogeneous' approach". NBER Working Paper 15052, June.

Bernanke B.S. and Lown C.S. (1991). *The Credit Crunch*. Brookings Papers on Economic Activity, No. 2: 205–247.

Clair R.T. and Tucker P. (1993). Six causes of the credit crunch (or, why is it so hard to get a loan?). *Economic Review*, third quarter.

Kindleberger C.P. (1996). *Manias, Panics and Crashes*. Basic Books.

Parkinson M., Ball M., Blake N. and Key T. (2009). *The Credit Crunch and Regeneration: Impact and Implications*. An independent report to the Department for Communities and Local Government.

6
Inter-bank Market and Liquidity Distribution during the Great Financial Crisis: The e-MID Case

Gianfranco A. Vento and Pasquale La Ganga

6.1 Introduction

For many years, the unsecured inter-bank market has been considered the archetype of an efficient market. The participants are all professionals, and consequently they are supposed to be adequately equipped to assess the risks related to market participation. The efficiency of the inter-bank market worldwide is also confirmed by the high number of participants, the significant degree of market breadth and depth, and the narrow bid-ask spreads.

Nevertheless, during the Great Financial Crisis, many of the certainties concerning inter-bank markets suddenly disappeared, also affecting financial intermediaries which were not involved in sub-prime business. Among other factors, the fact that in the last few years many large financial groups, mainly based in the most advanced financial countries, used to adopt Originate-to-Distribute (O-t-D) business models increases the strategic significance of the global inter-bank market. Actually, the adoption of O-t-D models on a large scale requires an efficient inter-bank market where banks and Special Purpose Entities can easily, and without additional costs, raise the necessary funds to manage their liquidity mismatching.

However, since summer 2007 a major liquidity shortage has affected inter-bank markets all over the world, producing consequences that go beyond the liquidity management of financial intermediaries.

The aim of the paper is to analyze the operational solutions recently adopted by the e-MID inter-bank market for unsecured inter-bank transactions. For this purpose, the paper analyzes inter-bank transactions within the Euro area since the current financial crisis started, in both the e-MID and the over-the-counter inter-bank markets, considering if the introduction of an anonymous and collateralized segment in the e-MID market since February 2009 can help improve liquidity distribution within the Euro area.

The paper is organized as follows. Section 6.2 analyzes the most significant shocks which affected the market since summer 2007, increasing the effects on volumes and interest rates, in order to discover why the usual efficiency assumptions have been not respected. Section 6.3 is dedicated to the European inter-bank market and focuses on the e-MID case. Before the crisis, this unsecured market had shown itself to be a more efficient solution for banks, enabling them to smoothly manage their liquidity shortages. On the other hand, the e-MID has an intrinsic feature (that is, transparency), which has set a limit for market participation during the recent financial turmoil. As a result of that, in February 2009 the company that manages the e-MID launched a new segment for inter-bank transaction, called 'MIC' (Collateralized Inter-bank Market), which is collateralized and anonymous. Section 6.4 explores the possibilities for inter-bank relations,starting with the unexpected reactions of markets during the crisis. Finally, section 6.5 highlights some conclusions.

6.2 Money markets and the liquidity crisis: some empirical evidence

Over the past few months the world has been witnessing financial market turmoil of global dimensions, known as the 'sub-prime crisis', which has been discussed extensively in the specialized press and official publications. It had already caused bank failures, a temporary freeze on money markets, and sharp drops in equity markets worldwide, forcing governments and central banks to step in with drastic measures. Since the second half of 2007 the functioning of international inter-bank money markets was severely impaired: they exhibited unusual signs of stress around the world. Money-market interest rates soared within a few hours, and lending dried up. Virtually all segments of the money market were affected. After a period of normalization, in September 2008 several defaults and bailouts of systemic financial institutions reinforced general concerns about solvency and liquidity.

Two types of interest rate spreads are especially helpful in tracking events as they have unfolded: the spreads of the three-month European

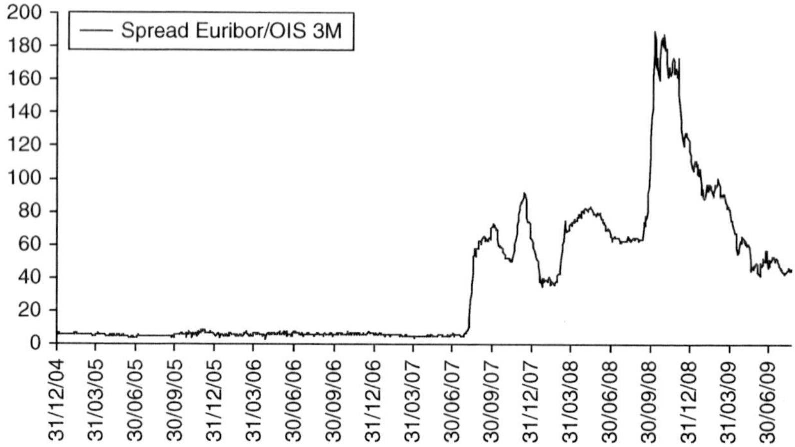

Figure 6.1 Evolution of spreads between Euribor and overnight-indexed swap (OIS) rates over 3 months

Data source: Bloomberg (http://www.bloomberg.com/markets/index.html).

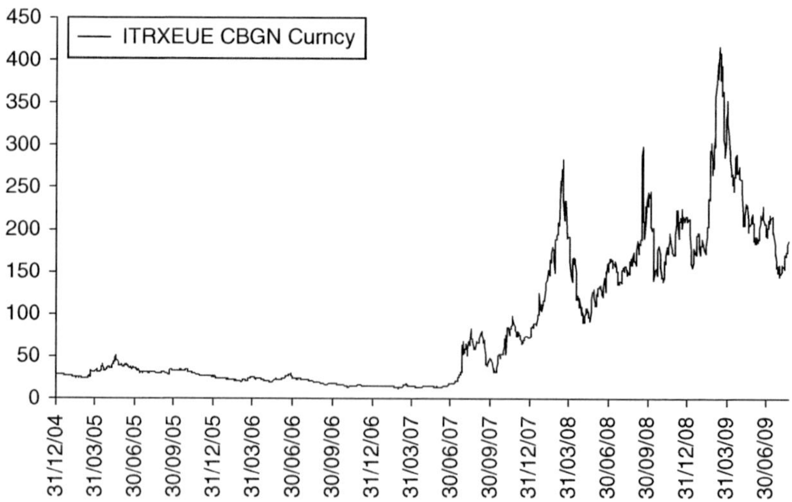

Figure 6.2 Itraxx index (generic 5 year Europe financial subordinated)

Data source: Bloomberg (http://www.bloomberg.com/markets/index.html).

inter-bank offered rate (Euribor) over the overnight-indexed swap (OIS), a standard measure of inter-bank market tensions, and spreads on credit default swaps (CDS). With the start of the financial market turbulence in August 2007 risk premia in short-term money-market rates, as represented by the spreads between Euribor and OIS rates, increased significantly in most major currencies (Figure 6.1). What is evident analyzing spreads on CDS is that concerns about counterparty risk became extraordinarily intense (Figure 6.2).

Asymmetric information about counterparty risk as an underlying friction can prolong inter-bank market tensions and affect the subsequent level achieved by inter-bank interest rates in the current financial turmoil, despite an unprecedented increase in liquidity provision by central banks. Thus, it is reasonable to assume that the level achieved by interest rates in the developed-economy inter-bank markets in the last 2 years cannot be explained only by an increase in the counterparty risk premia due to higher default probabilities of market borrowers. These rates are due to a liquidity risk premium, related to so-called 'liquidity hoarding'. In other words, banks having a surplus of funds were not able to lend to other banks, and accumulated liquidity well above their current and expected needs, due to the perception that the liquidity in the inter-bank markets might dry up suddenly.

As the financial crisis deepened in September 2008, with an additional increase in the level and the dispersion of counterparty risk, liquidity in the inter-bank market further dried up as banks preferred to hoard cash instead of lending it out, even at short maturities. During the turmoil, banks have quite probably applied stricter lending limits in the overnight inter-bank market. The remaining cash was parked with the Eurosystem, which plays the role of a risk-free counterparty without lending limits. Refinancing from the ECB implies that banks are willing to bid up tender rates, revealing a high degree of funding risk (aversion or premium) and market segmentation. Furthermore, analyzing the data on the secured segment of the inter-bank markets in the same period it is possible to find evidence that the cost of collateral had a considerable effect on short-term interest rates. Dealers in mortgage-backed securities and OTC derivatives started asking for more collateral from their counterparties. Securities accepted by risk managers were a subset of the more extended ECB collateral, due to the lower 'risk aversion' of the central bank. In repo markets, lenders sharply increased their margin calls and refused to accept as collateral anything but US treasury securities or German bunds. Since bond dealers finance themselves in the repo markets, they abruptly withdrew from the broader fixed-income markets. Liquidity in US and European fixed-income markets seemed to evaporate overnight. Trading on the inter-bank markets for maturities longer than overnight contracted sharply in a few months, and risk premiums reached very high levels due to a sharp market-wide reassessment of risk in the summer of 2007, after sub-prime mortgage-backed securities were discovered in portfolios of banks and bank-sponsored conduits; and a further increase in the level and the dispersion of counterparty risk following the Lehman's default in September 2008.

6.3 The e-MID case and the inter-bank market within the euro area

In order to analyze the reasons for the anomalous functioning of the inter-bank markets during the 2007–2009 crisis, it is useful to focus on their structural and organizational features, as well as on the type of contracts traded in these markets. A first important distinction to make is between markets in which contracts are guaranteed by liquid assets and those where negotiations are finalized without any guarantee. Inter-bank markets are distinguished between *secured* and *unsecured* markets.

Inter-bank markets worldwide are characterized by their undefined structure, and are fragmented in nature. For direct loans, which account for the vast majority of lending volume, the amount and the interest rate on each loan are agreed on a one-to-one basis between borrowing and lending institutions. Other banks do not have access to the same terms, and do not even know that the loan took place. Although quotes are sometimes displayed on screens, these are merely indicative. Trades are largely bilateral or undertaken via voice-brokers. The vast majority of transactions take place in over-the-counter markets, without specific trading regulations. Negotiations are mostly done by telephone, while quotations and other information are largely provided through information providers – Bloomberg or Reuters – which publish the quotations of inter-bank contracts for different maturities. This market organization, however, has a significant limit due to the fact that quotations are only indicative, while the actual market interest rates may vary considerably, according to the counterparties involved in the transaction.

Besides OtC inter-bank market negotiation by telephone, in Italy since the late 1980s an electronic market for liquidity has been developed. This market, which has several unique characteristics, is called 'e-MID'.

The key operative features of the e-MID can be summarized as follows:

- it is a market based on a dedicated electronic platform, in which banks can publish the liquidity amounts they want to lend or borrow, indicating different maturities and interest rates;
- the e-MID is a multi-currency inter-bank market, where financial institutions can negotiate short-term funds in euros, US dollars, GB pounds, and Polish zlotys (however, the vast majority of negotiations take place in euros);
- the market makes it possible to negotiate standardized inter-bank deposits of different maturities, which vary from overnight to 1 year;
- the e-MID offers an automatic settlement facility for contracts in euros at European level;
- market participants are committed to obeying a set of common rules created by the company that manages the market;
- the e-MID is a quote-driven market in which, once the quotations are entered into the system, contracts can be simply closed with the counterparty's acceptance;
- the Bank of Italy, according to article 79 of the Italian Finance Law (d.lgs. n. 58/98), maintains continuous supervision of the market, to determine safer operation than bilateral telephone deals;
- besides the unsecured inter-bank market, the e-MID company, since 2000, manages an OIS market, called *e-MIDER*, in which 113 European and US banks participate, with 28 central banks as observers.

The success of the e-MID market up to the crisis was evidenced by the increasing number of market participants, as well as by the volume of trade over time. In May 2009, 244 banks from 29 European countries and from the United States participated in the market; among these were 30 central banks (as observers of the market) and two ministries of finance. Before the Great Financial Crisis, the ECB estimated that 17% of inter-bank transactions within the Euro area used to transit through the e-MID platform.

Since August 2007, however, overall inter-bank trading decreased at a global level, affecting the Italian electronic market disproportionately. The average daily volumes on e-MID rose from 24.2 billion euros in 2006 to 22.4 billion in 2007, and dropped to 14 billion in 2008.[1] However, recent difficulties in the functioning of the e-MID are demonstrated by other indicators. In the last 2 years the activity of foreign operators decreased, the concentration of negotiations on the overnight segment strongly increased, and there was an increase in bid-ask spreads.[2] The trends registered in the e-MID appear much more significant than the trends analyzed in the O-t-C unsecured inter-bank market in the Euro area. A survey conducted by the European Central Bank (2009b) with a panel of 85 large banks in the Euro area highlighted that in 2008 the reduction of volume and the concentration on very short-term maturity affected the overall Euro area inter-bank market, but with a lower intensity than the e-MID (Figure 6.3).

As mentioned above, the drop in traded volumes in the inter-bank market and the increase of volatility and concentration on short-term negotiations do not depend on an increase in counterparty risk premia only. Thus, it is useful to discern the reasons why the spread between Euribor and Eurepo rates, usually close to 10 basis points, increased to

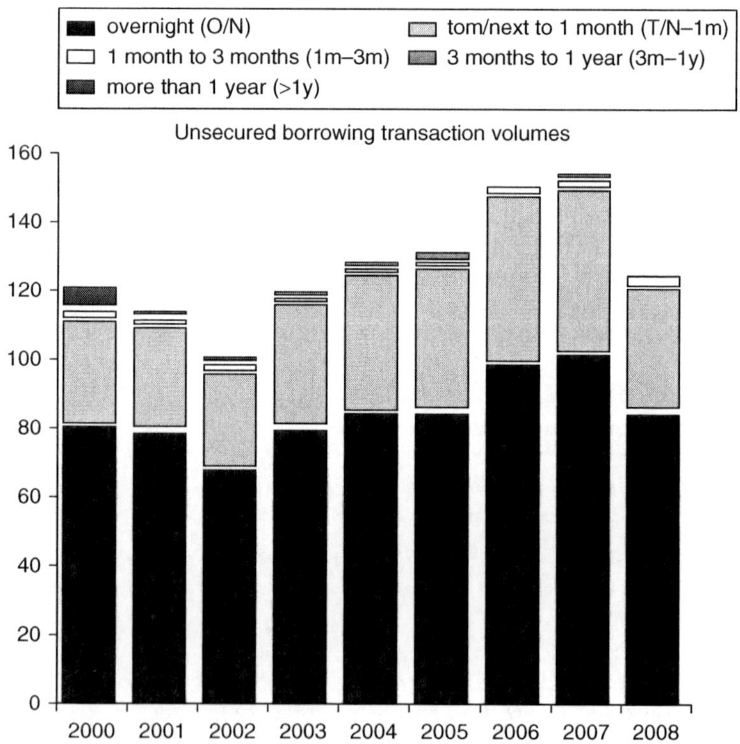

Figure 6.3 Daily turnover in unsecured inter-bank borrowing (cash-borrowing volume in 2002 = 100)

Source: European Central Bank (2009b), p. 13.

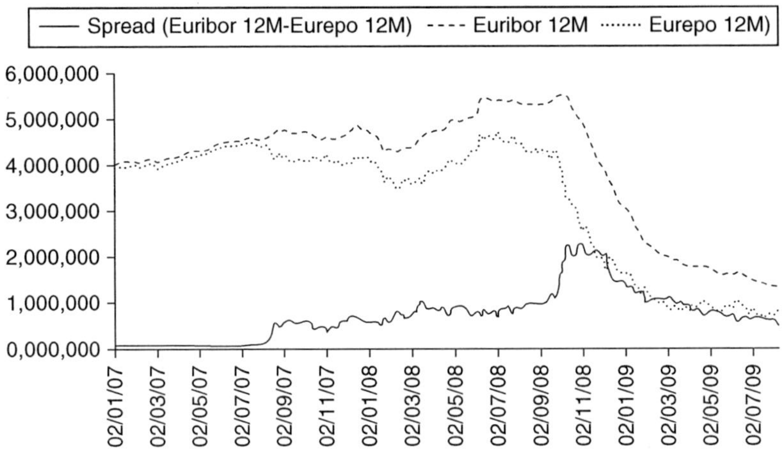

Figure 6.4 Euribor and Eurepo rates during the crisis
Source: Own interpretation of Bloomberg data.

about 70 basis points since the beginning of the crisis, and jumped above 200 basis points just after the Lehman Brothers default, in October 2008 (Figure 6.4).

A first interpretation of this data could might lead one to believe that the market participants required a higher return for unsecured inter-bank loans because, in the context of financial turmoil, the default probabilities of counterparties increased. However, such interpretation does not appear completely supported by the evolution of the risk premia on the securities issued by the banks.

Comparing the spreads between Euribor and Eurepo with the spreads on CDS for a panel of European banks, Eisenschmidt and Tapking (2009) conclude that there are other components, different from credit risk, which determine the increase in unsecured inter-bank rates. The factor that, beside credit risk, seems to have affected inter-bank interest rates during the turmoil, is so-called 'liquidity hoarding'.[3] On the other hand, banks reduced their participation in inter-bank markets, being afraid that in a context of general uncertainty and tension on the markets, raising funds in such a market could be interpreted as a dangerous signal of liquidity shortage, which could generate further funding difficulties (the so-called 'stigma effect'). Finally, despite the lack of official data, other factors – such as counterparties' size, their capital adequacy,

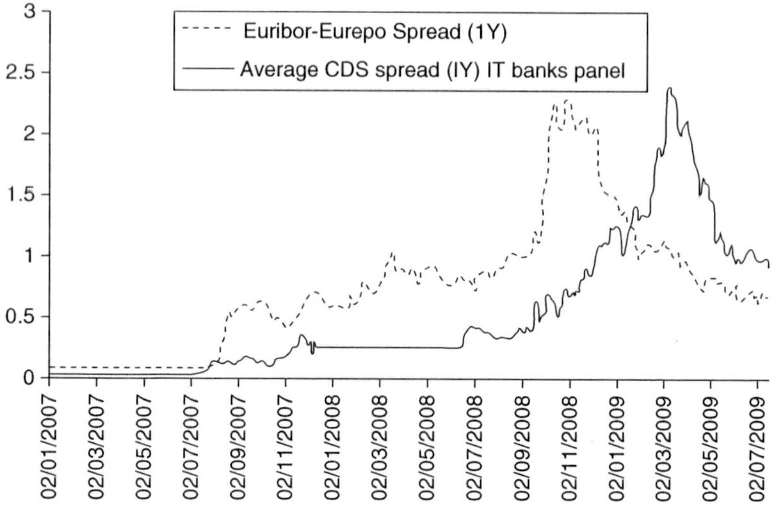

Figure 6.5 Euribor-Eurepo spread and average CDS spread with a panel of Italian banks

Source: Own interpretation of Bloomberg data.

rating, and country of origin – seemed to play a part in dealing decisions. In particular, the smallest banks within the Euro area seem to prefer to manage their financial disequilibrium with domestic counterparties, for which they have more information and are able to perform a more careful counterparty risk analysis, whereas the biggest banks – which are more capitalized and often have a better rating – mostly deal with international counterparties which have similar features.

The empirical evidence about CDS spreads analyzed by Eisenschmidt and Tapking (2009) for the Euro area seems not completely consistent with a similar analysis we undertook for the Italian market. In fact, comparing the 1-year Euribor-Eurepo spread with the average 1-year CDS spreads for a panel of six top Italian banks (of which two are also part of the Euribor panel), we find that up to the Lehman's bankruptcy the trend of the Italian sample is very similar to the European one; however, from October 2008 onwards, the latter spread is greater than the former (Figure 6.5).

This evidence for the Italian banks – which is not in line with the trends at European level that could justify liquidity-hoarding behaviour – can be interpreted as an indication that in the most acute phases of the crisis the risk perception of some banks was extremely high, well above the average for European banks. Thus, it can be affirmed that the Lehman's default and the subsequent turmoil affected different banks with varying intensity.

The above-mentioned phenomena concerning inter-bank markets, peculiar to the recent financial crisis, influenced both transactions on traditional OTC markets and e-MID deals. Nevertheless, negotiations on e-MID are characterized by a higher transparency level than bilateral telephone-based markets, because in the former all the bid and ask volumes are known by the other participants. Thus, this evidence can be considered as one of the most significant factors that caused progressive withdrawal from the e-MID during the crisis, pushing the operators towards collateralized operations or bilateral and less transparent transactions.

Since September 2008 the volumes on the inter-bank market have registered a further reduction and, at the same time, the functions of the market have been performed by the Eurosystem, which arranged special monetary policy operations in order to avoid the complete collapse of the market. In this context, the company that manages the e-MID market decided to offer services which fitted more closely the needs of market participants. In order to deal with the volume drop, since the end of November 2008 the e-MID made it possible to negotiate inter-bank deposits through the so-called 'depo auction' facility. This lets the participants request specific quotations from a number of counterparties, between one and five. Alternatively, the banks can propose directly to a counterparty an amount and a rate, and the counterparty can simply accept the proposal, formulate a new proposal, or refuse the transaction.

However, a more significant innovation has been registered since February 2009, when the Bank of Italy started – together with the company that manages the e-MID market, the Italian banking association (ABI), and the Italian association of banking treasures – a new initiative called 'MIC' to create a new inter-bank segment, guaranteed by collateral, in which is possible to trade inter-bank funds with maturity between one week and six months.

6.4 Prospects for inter-bank market and liquidity distribution

A major lesson of the recent financial crisis is that the ability of banks to withstand liquidity shocks and lend to one another depends on the functioning of the inter-bank lending market. In this section we want to investigate the impact of the financial crisis on the Italian money market in order to analyze the general impact on inter-bank lending patterns and predict the effects on inter-bank lending networks in the future.

With this aim, we use data on transactions in the Italian inter-bank money market, e-MID. As previously mentioned, this market is unique in the Euro area in being screen-based and fully electronic: information about the rates and the trades is made public. Our dataset includes most overnight trades made through e-MID between January 2005 and June 2009. During our sample period overnight loans accounted for over 75% of the total amount lent (anecdotal evidence suggests that this is a common feature of most inter-bank markets). After considerable growth in recent years when the market was fully used by major European banks (non-Italian banks account for about 43% of daily trades as of June 2008) the data confirms that the market was severely affected by the turmoil. A strong decline in the overall electronically-traded market volume (right axis) and the number of contracts (left axis) can be observed, most evidently since November 2007. In the same period, a large number of intermediaries were active with less intensity (Figure 6.6).

The information collected provides evidence of borrowers switching from a transparent electronic dealership market to a more opaque O-t-C bilateral market. The decline in e-MID's volume stands in contrast to a weak drop in Italian inter-bank trading volumes. It seems that banks prefer borrowing in a less transparent environment in order to avoid being openly seen in the market on the borrowing side.

As the empirical analysis shown in our paper suggests, it is plausible that market discipline (or adverse-selection-based process) in the e-MID operated through rationing, perhaps to a greater extent than through a price mechanism. It effected an increasing concentration on volume (Figure 6.7) as underlined by the Herfindahl index, estimated on bid and ask volume of Italian banks compared to the overall volume on e-MID.

To foster a recovery in trading on the inter-bank circuits and a greater diversification of contract maturities, the Banca d'Italia, together with e-MID SIM Spa and the ABI, has introduced a temporary guarantee scheme, the MIC. The MIC, which originally was to remain active up to the end of 2009 but has been prolonged for one more year, consists of Italian banks (no more than one for each banking group) and EU banks (by agreement with the national central bank of the country of the participating bank) which satisfy a limited set of conditions for all participants equally.

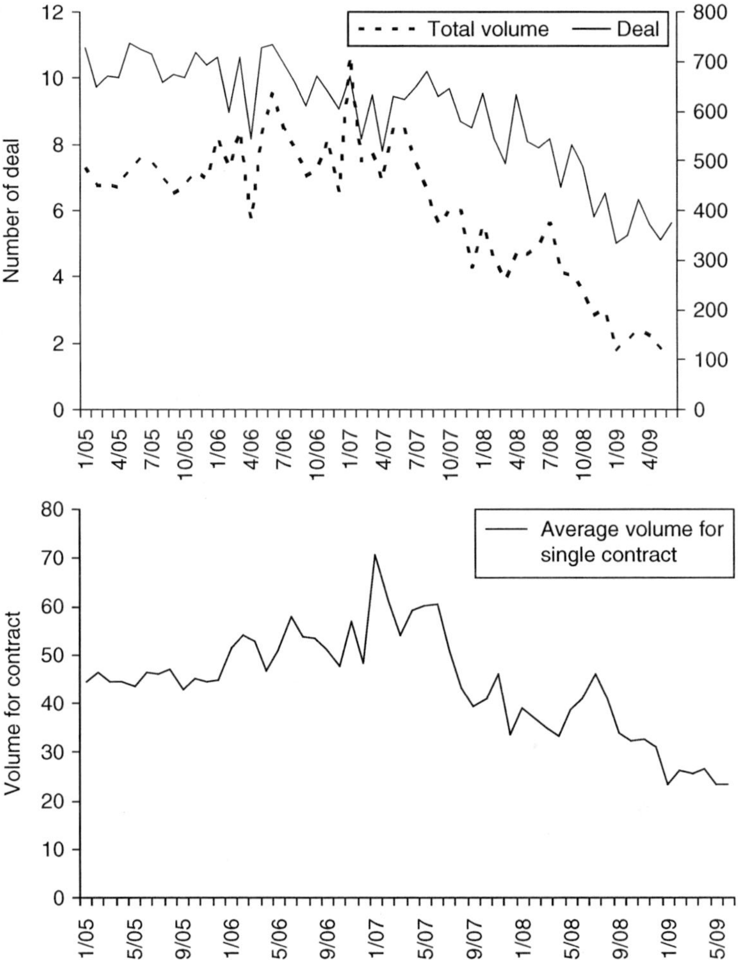

Figure 6.6 Monthly volumes, number of deals, and average volume for single contracts on the e-MID

Source: Own interpretation of e-MID data.

The trading on MIC is supported by a specific guarantee by the Bank of Italy of the obligations of market participants, the Italian central bank having an active role in the custody, administration, and evaluation of collateral, as well as ensuring the complete anonymity of counterparties. Thanks to the contribution of MIC, duration-weighted volumes on e-MID fixed-term maturities are recovering from lows (Figure 6.8).

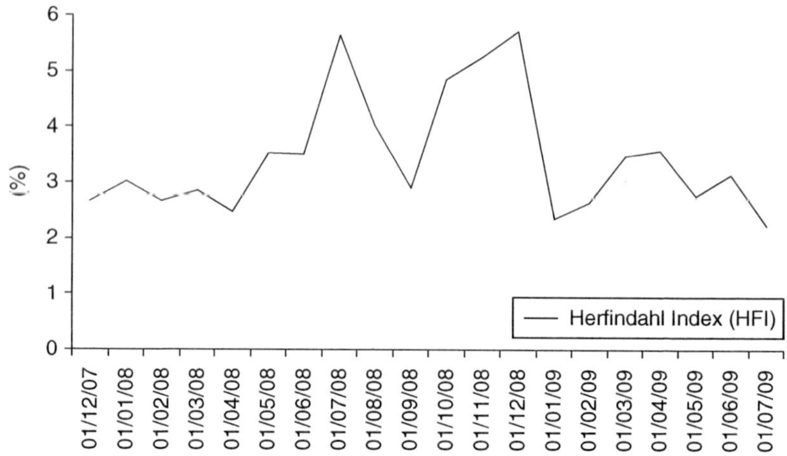

Figure 6.7 Concentration of volumes on e-MID from 31 December 2007 to 31 July 2009

Source: own interpretation of e-MID data.

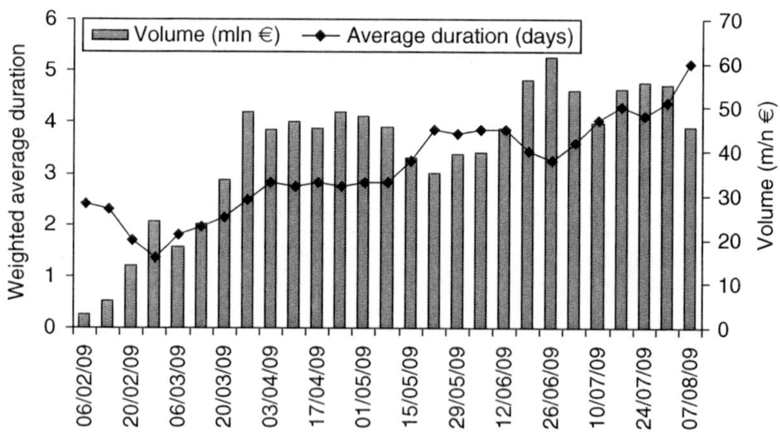

Figure 6.8 Outstanding volume (millions of euros) and average maturities (days) trend on MIC

Source: Own interpretation of e-MID data.

According to the Bank of Italy and the company that manages the e-MID, the MIC makes it possible to eliminate the credit, liquidity, and reputational risks which caused the reduction of market volumes on e-MID between the end of 2007 and 2008. In particular, financial guarantees cancel the counterparty and liquidity risks, while the fact that the inter-bank market is anonymous lets the banks which need funds avoid informing other intermediaries of their financial needs, preventing the so-called 'stigma effect'. Finally, the guarantee of the Bank of Italy confers another important advantage, lower regulatory capital need compared to traditional unsecured inter-bank loans.

As highlighted by Saccomanni (2009), in the near future the new market could be used as a template for setting up a similar scheme at a pan-European level.

6.5 Conclusions

The Great Financial Crisis, among other consequences, had peculiar and unexpected effects on the functioning of the inter-bank market. According to the analysis here, the fall in traded volumes mainly depended on a lack of confidence in banks' treasures towards other banks, perceived as being too risky for operations not collateralized or for maturities longer than overnight. At the most critical stage of the crisis, the Lehman Brothers' default, banks worldwide decided to hoard liquidity – suffering a significant opportunity cost – being afraid of a decline in market liquidity risk which could generate higher funding costs as well as increased shortage of funds. At the same, liquidity accumulation was addressed to avoid sending signals to the market, which could be interpreted as a warning sign of liquidity tension, potentially followed by a default.

This empirical evidence affirms that the current unsecured inter-bank market segmentation within the euro area – where the e-MID electronic platform coexists with over-the-counter bilateral exchanges and negotiations made through voice-brokers – functions to meet different needs of the market participants. Despite the e-MID having clear advantages in trading efficiency and in facilitating the transmission of monetary policy demands, the other segments of the OTC inter-bank market offer better dealing in undisclosed conditions, whenever market participants do not intend to reveal their liquidity needs. Since February 2009, in order to reacquire market shares lost during the crisis, such a facility has been offered by the e-MID platform.

On the other hand, the crisis demonstrated how the systematic underestimation of credit risk, typical of the financial system up to summer 2007, involved the inter-bank market too, in which risk premiums were not priced and not consistent with the concrete counterparty risk. The current differences between the unsecured inter-bank rates and the collateralized ones now seem more consistent with the counterparty risk, and so we may assume that the spreads between secured and unsecured rates will remain at levels well above those reached before the crisis.

Furthermore, as long as money managers are analyzing counterparty risk in the inter-bank market, it is reasonable to expect an improvement of the models adopted by banks in order to assess the probability of default by financial institutions. It is also likely that the money market will be able to take from the crisis the right stimulus in order to improve its the procedures to ensure a stronger analysis of liquidity risk and counterparty risk in inter-bank transactions. The Eurosystem and the supervisory authorities must have a role in incentivizing the European banking industry to adopt more adequate methodologies for the assessment of market liquidity risk, while at the same time the authorities can implement clearing and settlement systems that are more responsive to the needs of banks in the Euro area.

It is reasonable to assume that the counterparties' current assessment procedures within the inter-bank market, according to their relative size, capital adequacy, and ratings, could become a structural feature of money and inter-bank markets. In such a framework, the smallest banks seem to prefer to manage their financial disequilibrium with domestic counterparties, for which they have more information and are able to perform a more careful counterparty risk analysis, whereas the biggest banks – which are more capitalized and often have a better rating – mostly deal with international counterparties which have similar features.

The overall reduction of volumes on the inter-bank market does not appear to be a short-term phenomenon. This suggests that the current reduction in credit supply will persist, the volumes being intermediated by the banks, and it seems that, at a global level, banks are abandoning business models based on large-scale recourse to inter-bank funding to boost their credit-supply capability. In this context, supervisory authorities are tending to push the banking industry towards a closer relationship between retail funding capability and development of loan portfolios.

The Great Financial Crisis has established a structural divergence between the official monetary policy rates and the money-market rates.

This phenomenon does not seem to depend on short-term tensions, and generates serious doubts about the capability of central banks in the future to address the yield curve solely by means of traditional monetary policy instruments.

In the framework described above, the new Italian MIC, along with the traditional e-MID and the other OTC market segments, may offer money managers a viable alternative to the Eurosystem. The presence of the MIC makes possible the evolution of interest rates for different money-market maturities, and the fact that the collateral deposited by the banks involved largely exceeds the current traded volumes may signal a further development of the market in the future. Part of the picture is the central bank which supports the MIC, provided it does not have a role of market- maker. The risks are significantly less than a massive liquidity supply through the main refinancing operations, whereas the contribution to the monetary policy impulse transmission may be considerable. For all these reasons, the Eurosystem now offers the possibility of a pan-European platform for the exchange of collateralized inter-bank funds, thus facilitating a European money market in which bilateral transactions, voice-brokers, and electronic platforms coexist, enabling appropriate responses to different financial needs.

Acknowledgements

The opinions expressed in this paper do not necessarily correspond to those of the Bank of Italy. All errors remain the responsibility of the authors. This paper is the result of research jointly carried on by the authors. Sections 6.1, 6.3 and 6.5 can be attributed to Gianfranco A. Vento, while sections 6.2 and 6.4 have been written by Pasquale La Ganga.

Notes

1. See Banca d'Italia (2009).
2. The Banca d'Italia (2008 and 2009) shows how the bid-ask spread on e-MID passed from one basis point to six basis points in the last quarter of 2007. At the same time, the traded volumes on overnight maturity increased above 90% in 2007 and 2008.
3. As we underlined before (see para 3), in this framework, treasurers preferred to accumulate significant volumes of liquidity, and subsequently decided to deposit such liquidity at the national central banks, rather than lending it on inter-bank market, obtaining an interest which usually represent the lowest rate in the official corridor.

References

Banca d'Italia. (2008). *Annual Report,* May.
Banca d'Italia. (2009). *Annual Report,* May.
Eisenschmidt J and Tapking J. (2009). Liquidity risk premia in unsecured interbank money markets. *Working Paper Series,* European Central Bank, no. 1025, March.
European Central Bank. (2009b). *Euro Money Market Study,* February.

7
Quantitative Easing vs Credit Easing

Frans H. Brinkhuis

7.1 Introduction

On 18 March 2009 the Federal Reserve (Fed), the central bank of the United States, announced that it would pump an additional 1.15 trillion dollars into the financial markets. The Fed announced that "in the light of increasing economic slack, the Committee[1] expects that inflation will remain subdued and sees some risk that inflation could persist for a time below rates that best foster economic growth and price stability in the longer run".[2] To provide greater support to mortgage lending and housing markets, the committee decided to purchase up to $750 billion of agency- and mortgage-backed securities (MBS), bringing its total purchases on these securities up to $1.25 trillion. It would also increase its purchases of agency debt by $100 billion. Moreover, to help improve conditions in private credit markets, the Fed decided to purchase up to $300 billion in longer-term Treasury securities over the next six months.

Initially investors responded with surprise and enthusiasm. The Dow Jones index, which had been down about 50 points just before the announcement, jumped immediately and ended the day at almost 91 points. The 7-year Treasury yield plummeted 54 basis points to 2.08%, 10-year Treasury bonds went down 51 basis points to 2.49%, and the 30-year yield decreased by 28 basis points to 3.52%.[3] Daily changes in Treasury bond yields of this magnitude are quite rare. Changes in the 30-year yield were smaller than changes in the shorter segments, because the Fed indicated that it would "concentrate purchases in the 2- to 10-year sectors of the nominal Treasury curve".[4]

But there were also indications that the markets judged that the Fed was taking too much risk in its operations, and setting the stage for further inflation. Commentators remarked that with this extra 1 trillion dollars, the Fed's balance sheet would amount to $3,000 billion. A swollen Fed balance sheet runs the risk that the Fed may find it difficult to manage down the money supply when the economy turns, raising the possibility of inflation.[5] On the same day, 18 March, gold prices rose $26.60 an ounce, hitting $942, a sign of declining confidence in the dollar.[6] The dollar dropped sharply against the euro. The euro rate increased from $1.2972 just before the Fed's announcement to $1.3730 one day after the announcement, an increase of 5.8% in two days.

7.1.1 Problem statement

In this paper we want to investigate the consequences of the *quantitative easing* strategy for the American economy, specifically the effect on the yield curve and on possible future inflation. We want to compare the strategy of the Fed with the quantitative easing approach of the Bank of Japan (BOJ), which executed this policy from 2001 to 2006.

7.2 Quantitative easing vs. credit easing

The above-mentioned steps taken by the Fed can be characterized as part of a policy of quantitative easing. This is an extreme form of monetary policy, used to stimulate an economy when interest rates are close to zero. This means that a central bank can no longer stimulate the economy by lowering interest rates. Instead, the central bank is stimulating the economy by way of its balance sheet. In practical terms, the central bank purchases financial assets, such as Treasury bonds, from financial institutions, so that the current-account balances of banks at the central bank are augmented. These excess reserves of banks can be used for extra lending, thereby stimulating the economy. A few months before the Fed took its steps on the path of quantitative easing, the Bank of England applied this policy; the positive experiences of the Bank of England were a source of inspiration for the Fed. However, in the context of this article we will not go into the details of the London approach.

At the beginning of this millennium, quantitative easing was executed by the BOJ. The Japanese quantitative easing policy (QEP) in 2001–2006 was an unprecedented monetary policy worldwide; the only other example is the policy of the US Federal Reserve Board during the Great Depression in the 1930s.[7] At that time Japan was in the midst of a period of deflation. The BOJ made the commitment to execute this policy until the consumer price index (CPI) started to grow again. We will go deeper into the Japanese situation in section 3.

The Fed nowadays also aims to stimulate the economy, and its balance sheet has expanded from a total of around $800 billion before the credit crisis erupted in the summer of 2007 to a total of $2000 billion at present. However, Ben Bernanke stresses that the Fed's approach is conceptually distinct from the QEP of the BOJ. Bernanke's views are well known on this topic, and he has published articles on the policy of the BOJ. In the Stamp Lecture at the London School of Economics on 13 January 2009[8] the Fed chairman stated that "in a pure quantitative easing regime the focus of policy is the quantity of bank reserves, which are liabilities of the central bank; the composition of loans and securities on the asset side of the central bank's balance sheet is incidental". The Fed approach can at best be called *credit easing*. The credit easing approach "focuses on the mix of loans and securities that it holds and how this composition of assets affects credit conditions for households and business".

In the following paragraphs we will show how these two different approaches of the BOJ and the Fed have worked out in practice until now, and we will ask what lessons can be learned from the Japanese experience.

7.3 The experience of the BOJ with the QEP

From 2001 to 2006, the BOJ executed a QEP, which forms an interesting reference-point for examining the present-day policy of the Fed. Hiroshi Ugai, researcher at the Monetary Affairs Department of the BOJ, gives an overview of the extensive literature which tries to assess the empirical results of the QEP of the BOJ.[9] In the 1990s Japan experienced prolonged stagnation with a very low inflation rate. From 1998 to 2005 the growth of Japan's CPI was even negative, so that Japan experienced a period of deflation. In 1999 the BOJ executed a zero-interest-rate policy (ZIRP), but as it felt that this policy was no longer effective, it changed its course towards a QEP, which was implemented from March 2001 to March 2006.

The QEP was based mainly on the following three principles:

1. The main operating target for money-market operations will be changed from the uncollateralized overnight call rate to the outstanding current-account balances held by financial institutions at the BOJ. The BOJ will provide ample liquidity to realize a CAB target substantially in excess of the required reserves.
2. The BOJ makes the commitment that the ample liquidity provision will stay in place until the CPI registers stably at zero per cent, or an increase year on year.

3. The BOJ will increase the amount of outright purchases of long-term Japanese government bonds (JGBs) should the BOJ consider such an increase to be necessary for providing liquidity smoothly.[10]

In March 2006 the BOJ stated that the year-on-year growth in the core CPI was expected to remain positive, so that the period of inflation had come to an end. The QEP was exited and the main money-market instrument of the BOJ again became the uncollateralized overnight call rate.

7.3.1 The impact of the QEP on Japan's financial sector and economy

In this section we will examine the impact of the QEP on Japan's financial sector and its economy, and we will focus on the effect of the commitment to maintain the QEP as long as deflation continued.

The impact of the expansion of BOJ's balance sheet and the effect of the change in composition of BOJ's balance sheet on Japan's economy and financial sector showed a weaker empirical relation than the effect of the commitment.

7.3.1.1 Overview of empirical analyses into relation between QEP BOJ and yield curve 2001–2006

Baba et al.[11] compare the outcome of a macro-finance model with the empirical data of the yield curve in 2002 and 2003. The model consists of aggregate demand and supply equations and a monetary policy rule, which is an augmented Taylor rule that incorporates slow policy adjustments and zero bound constraint on interest rates, which implies that the short-term interest rate is explicitly assumed to be non-negative.

The authors estimate 3-, 5- and 10-year interest rates according to the expectations theory, which implies that the long-term interest rate consists of the weighted average of expected future interest rates. The interest rates with the zero-rate commitment conform to the actual yield curve, while the interest rates without commitment follow from the used model. See Figure 7.1.[12]

In 1999–2000 the BOJ executed a ZIRP and from 2001 a Quantitative (Monetary) Easing Policy (QMEP); both policies were characterized by a zero-rate commitment.

In Figure 7.1 it is clearly seen that the zero-rate commitment of the BOJ has led to a decrease in 3-, 5-, and 10-year interest rates. The interest rate differentials (between the rates with and without commitment) are larger in 2003 than in the years before. This can be explained by the fact that in 2003 the Japanese economy recovered which resulted

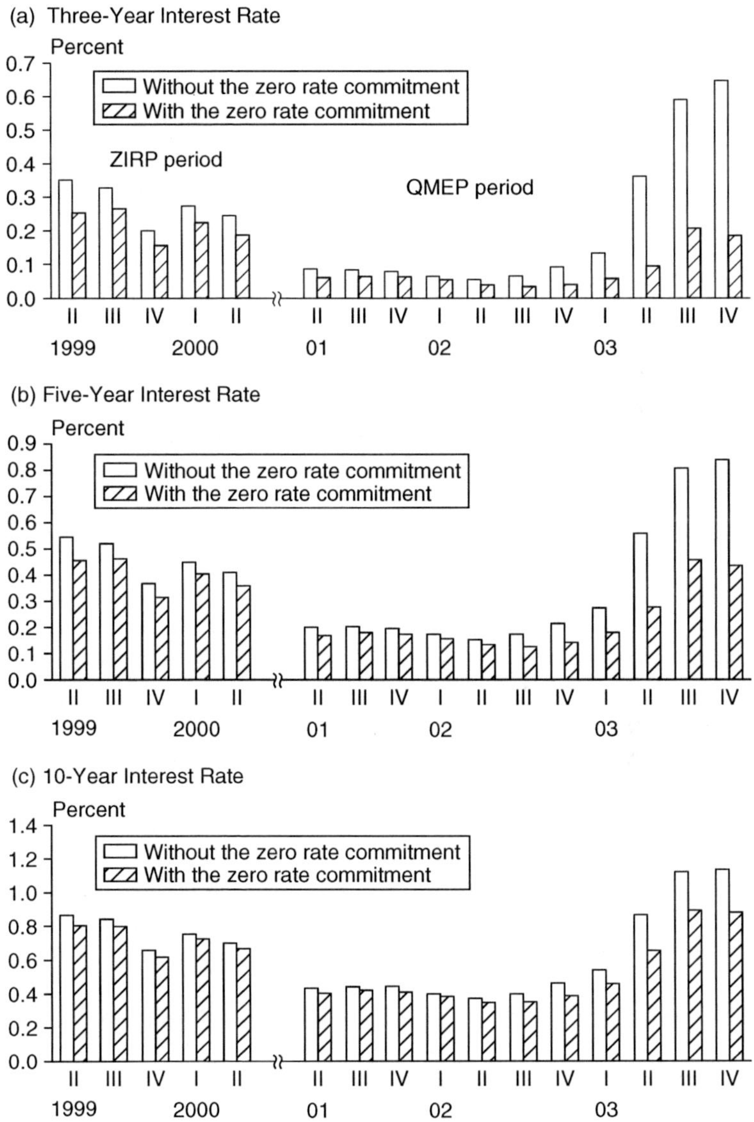

Figure 7.1 Effects of the zero-rate commitment on medium- and long-term interest rates Japan 1999–2003

in relatively high interest rates, calculated by the model used. The commitment contained the increase in interest rates to a large extent.

It is also apparent that the interest rate differentials for the 3- and 5-year interest rates are higher than those for the 10-year interest rate (around 0.45% and 0.2% respectively in 2003). An explanation could be that a zero interest-rate commitment will unlikely be maintained for a duration of 10 years, so that the commitment will lower the yield curve more on the short than on the long segments. Baba et al. also remark on the issue that the market might have expected that the future inflation rate would become higher due to the effect of lowering the yield curve. So QEP has led to lower interest rates, which stimulate economic growth so that inflation expectations increase which result in higher long-term interest rates. So quantitative easing can induce negative secondary effects.

Bernanke et al.[13] also used a macro-finance model similar to Baba et al. They show that during the period of the QEP, the actual yield curve lowered in a manner similar to the expected yield curves estimated from past economic variables under a zero bound constraint on interest rates. Two other studies, using a somewhat different methodology, found a statistically significant relation between the QEP and a lowering of the yield curve in 2002.

To sum up, all major empirical studies on BOJ's QEP found out that there is a statistically significant relation between QEP's commitment linked to the actual CPI performance and a lowering of the yield curve, especially in the short- and medium-term segments.

7.3.2 Concluding remarks on the relation between QEP and Japan's financial sector and economy

From the empirical studies, it is clear that the strongest link exists between the commitment of the BOJ to maintain zero interest rates and the yield curve: the commitment clearly led to a lowering of the yield curve. The current-account balances of Japanese banks and purchases of long-term JGBs by the BOJ had weaker empirical links to the yield curve: an inverse relationship is even detected. The importance of the commitment of the central bank implies that communication of the central bank to the public about its intentions is vital for a successful implementation of its monetary policy decisions.

7.4 The *Credit Easing* approach of the Fed

The Fed has responded aggressively to the financial crisis since its emergence in the summer of 2007. The reduction in the target federal

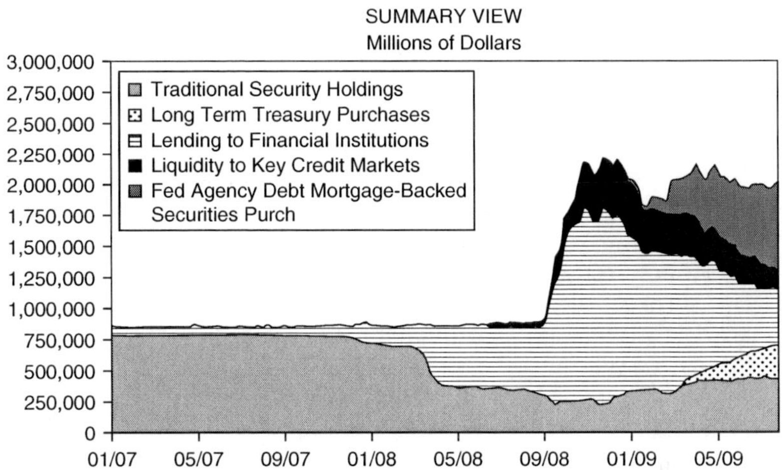

Figure 7.2 The balance sheet of the Fed 2007–2009.[14]

funds rate from 5–1/4 percent to effectively zero resulted in a rapid easing in the effects of monetary policy. In addition, the Fed has implemented a number of programs designed to support the liquidity of financial institutions and foster improved conditions in financial markets. These new programs have led to a significant change in the Fed's balance sheet.

From Figure 7.2 it is clear that the balance sheet of the Fed expanded considerably since the situation as the financial markets deteriorated in September 2008. But the balance sheet total did not attain the 3 trillion dollars which some pundits feared. That is because some balance-sheet items have decreased since 2007.

Traditional security holdings decreased from around $780 billion at the beginning of 2007 to $450 billion in January 2010. This contraction was caused by redemptions and sales which "were largely arranged to drain reserves from the banking system to prompt Fed funds to trade at the target rate".[15] In other words, the Fed wanted to tighten the money markets because the Federal funds rate was below the target rate. This lower volume of security holdings, mainly consisting of US Treasury securities, made room for other balance-sheet items that made ground from autumn 2008.

The balance-sheet item *lending to financial institutions* made a large expansion in 2008 with massive loans to institutions like Morgan Stanley, City Group, and AIG. But from the beginning of 2009 this item began to decrease at a rapid pace. Lending to financial institutions reached its peak in December 2008 with a level of $1590 billion, while it now stands at $230 billion (January 2010).[16] The reason for this rapid decline is that the majority of these loans have relatively short maturities of around 90 days. At this moment most of these loans have been repaid by banks and other financial institutions.

The items on the balance sheet which are rising are the *purchases of government securities, agency debt,* and *MBS*. In January 2010 the level of long-term Treasury securities amounted to $316 billion, slightly above the announced ceiling of $300 billion. Agency and MBS on the Fed balance sheet now amount to $1079 billion, while the announced target value is $1450 billion ($1250 trillion for MBS and $200 billion for Agency debt).[17] This could mean that the Fed's balance sheet could increase further, depending on whether decreases for some balance-sheet items could compensate for the increases in other items. The Federal Open Market Committee expects that the Fed's balance sheet "might peak late this year [2009] and decline gradually thereafter".[18]

7.5 Quantitative easing vs. credit easing

In this paragraph we try to compare the policy instruments of the BOJ and the Fed, and the economic circumstances in which both executed their easing policies.

7.5.1 The commitment

It is obvious that there is a fundamental difference in attitude between the BOJ and the Fed in their easing policies. The BOJ had a strong commitment, which implied that the QEP would be maintained as long as deflation continued. In empirical research it was shown that the commitment clearly led to a lowering of the yield curve. Purchases of long-term government securities and increases in the current-account balances of banks at the central bank had much weaker links with the yield curve, and in some instances an inverse relationship was detected.

The Fed on the other hand has no clear-cut policy target for its credit easing policy, which can be expressed in simple numbers. The FOMC has indicated several times that "inflation is expected to remain subdued for some time, so that interest rates are likely to remain low for an extended period".[19] But there is no clear link between the inflation rate and the lifting of the easing policy. Ben Bernanke recognizes this problem. In a speech at the London School of Economics he said that "the lack of a simple summary measure or policy target poses an important communications challenge. To minimize market uncertainty... the

Fed is committed to providing the public as much information as possible about the uses of its balance sheets, plans regarding future uses of its balance sheet and the criteria on which the relevant decisions are based".[20]

As Japan's commitment has worked out best in practice, we wonder what the impact is of the Fed's policy.

7.5.2 Possible inflationary consequences of purchases of Treasury securities by the Fed

In the context of the BOJ buying JGBs, empirical analyses have shown that anxieties about a loss of financial discipline led to an increase in the yield of 7-year JGBs instead of the decrease which was intended. Could the credit easing strategy of the Fed also lead to an increase of inflationary expectations? The purchases by the Fed of MBS, agency debt and long-term Treasury securities caused an increase in bank reserves. These are the reserve balances of banks with the Fed. See Figure 7.3.

We see an enormous increase since September 2008 when reserves jumped from around $45 billion to over $100 billion, increasing further afterwards, and in August 2009 attaining a level of roughly $800 billion. Data at St Louis Fed goes back to January 1959, and from then till 2008 bank reserves have always stayed below $100 billion. But a rise in bank reserves as such does not necessarily lead to inflation. Only if banks lend out money, will this lead to a growth in the money supply, which can be inflationary. Bank reserves belong to the so-called

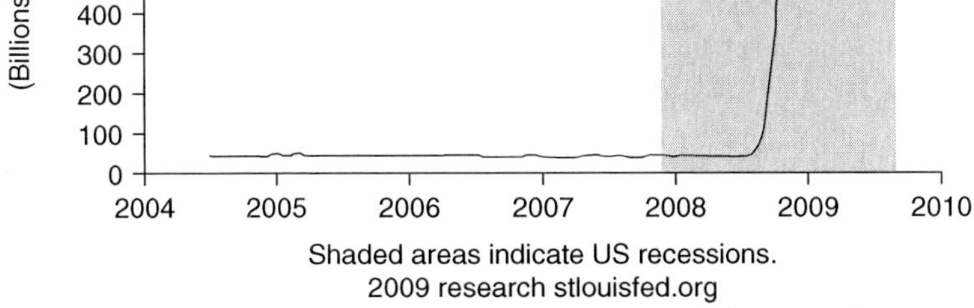

Figure 7.3 Board of Governors, total reserves, adjusted for changes in reserve requirements (TRARR)

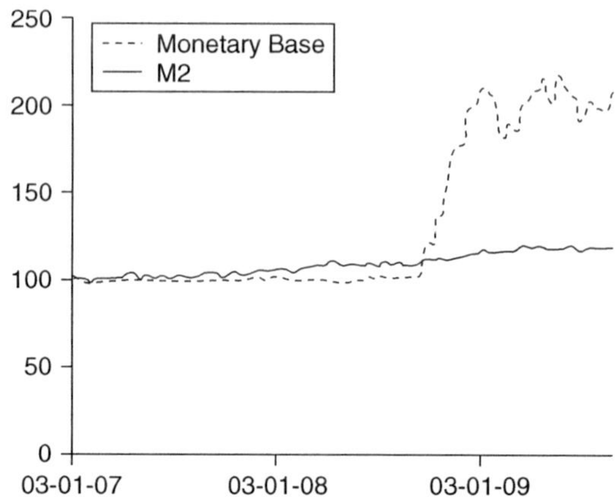

Figure 7.4 Money supply and base money, US 2007–2009

Note: Monetary Base consists of currency in circulation + reserve balances with Federal Reserve banks. M2 consists of M1 + savings deposits + small-denomination time deposits + balances in retail money market mutual funds. Both series are indexed in order to make them comparable with January 2007 = 100.

Source: research.stlouisfed.org.

monetary base (M0), consisting of currency in circulation plus reserve balances. In Figure 7.4 the money supply (M2 is the definition which is most used in the US) is depicted, in combination with M0.

Figure 7.4 shows that the monetary base (M0) has risen much less than the bank reserves. This is caused by the fact that M0 also consists of money in circulation, and that factor has remained constant for the last 2 years. More important for the inflation rate is the fact that the money supply (M2) has grown 17% from January 2007 to August 2009. This rate of growth is lower than in the preceding years because of the impact of the credit crisis on the economy. In general, the data up till now gives no evidence of an accelerating pace of inflation. In the summer of 2009 the US economy is in a recession, with a CPI oscillating around zero. In the short term the measures taken by the Fed will not have inflationary consequences. In the long run the situation may be different.

7.5.2 The exit strategy of the Fed

Although the credit easing policy of the Fed will in the short term have no inflationary consequences, the central bank must be cautious for the longer-term effects of its policy. When the economy starts to grow again, the Fed will have to let its balance-sheet shrink. Chairman Bernanke of the Fed is aware of this issue. In his Stamp Lecture on 13 January 2009, he asserts that "a significant shrinking of the balance sheet can be accomplished relatively quickly" as a substantial portion of the assets the Fed holds are short-term in nature, like loans to banks and currency swaps. But although longer-term securities can also be sold, the Fed would not anticipate disposing of more than a small portion of these assets in the near term, which will slow down the rate of shrinking.[21]

7.6 Conclusion

We wanted to investigate the consequences of the credit easing strategy for the American economy, specifically the yield curve and the effect on future inflation, thereby learning from the experiences of Japan in the beginning of this decennium.

From the empirical studies of the quantitative easing strategy of the BOJ (Bank of Japan) it is clear that the commitment of the BOJ to maintain zero interest rates till the economy is out of inflation has led to a lowering of the yield curve. The bank reserves and purchases of JGBs had no clear relationship with the yield curve.

As the Fed has no clear-cut commitment like the BOJ's, it is vital for the Fed to communicate its strategy in a clear way to the public and the financial markets. Only then can credit easing have consequences for the yield curve. The macro-economic effects of the Japanese credit easing were limited, due to erosion of the financial intermediary functions of banks burdened by non-performing loans and corporate balance-sheet adjustments. This could very well be the same for American banks. They are plagued with toxic assets, which contaminate their balance sheets and prevent them increasing their lending activities, despite a swollen level of bank reserves at the Fed. It could well be that in the short term the Fed policy will not result in extra lending by banks and will not lead to a decrease in yield curve. In the longer term, fears of inflation as a consequence of the credit easing policy can only be conquered if the Fed is able to let its balance sheets shrink at the appropriate pace.

Notes

1. This is the Federal Open Market Committee, the commission that takes and executes economic policy decisions.
2. Federal Reserve System, *Statement of the Federal Reserve*, Wednesday 18 March 2009.
3. Financial Times, 19 March 2009 *Treasury Bonds gyrate on Fed's shock move.*

4. Federal Reserve Bank of New York, *Permanent Open Market Operations Treasury: Frequently Asked Questions,* at www.newyorkfed.org/markets/pomo_faq.html
5. Financial Times, 18 March 2009, *Federal Reserve Plan Stuns Investors.*
6. New York Times website 19 March 2009, *Fed Plans to Inject Another $ 1 trillion to Aid the Economy.*
7. Christina Romer is an authority in the field of economic history on this topic. See *What Ended the Great Depression?*, Journal of Economic History, December 1992, pp. 757–784, cited in Ben S. Bernanke and Vincent R. Reinhart, *Conducting Monetary Policy at Very Low Short-Term Interest Rates,* American Economic Review, vol. 94, no. 2, May 2004.
8. Federal Reserve's website at www.federalreserve.gov/newsevents/speech/bernanke20090113a.htm
9. Hiroshi Ugai, *Effects of the Quantitative Easing Policy: a Survey of Empirical Analyses,* Bank of Japan Working Paper Series, no. 06-E-10, July 2006.
10. Ugai (2006), p. 2.
11. http://www.imes.boj.or.jp/english/publication/mes/2005/me23–1–2.pdf
12. Baba, Nishioka, Oda, Shirakawa, Ueda and Ugai, *Japan's deflation, problems in the financial sector and monetary policy,* Monetary and Economic Studies, BOJ 2005.
13. As cited in Ugai (2006), p. 14.
14. *Source:* Federal Reserve Bank of Cleveland, Research department at:http://www.clevelandfed.org/research/data/credit_easing/index.cfm
15. Federal Reserve Bank of New York: *Domestic Open Market Operations During 2008,* January 2009.
16. Federal Reserve Bank of Cleveland, Research department at http://www.clevelandfed.org/research/data/credit_easing/index.cfm
17. Statement of the Federal Reserve, March 18, 2009, 3:57 PM.
18. Minutes of the Federal Open Market Committee, June 23–24, 2009.
19. See among others: Ben S. Bernanke, *The Federal Reserve's Balance Sheet,* at the Credit Markets Symposium, Charlotte, North Caroline, April 3, 2009.
20. Speech of Chairman Ben S. Bernanke at the Stamp Lecture, London School of Economics, January 13, 2009 at: www.federalreserve.gov/newsevents/speech/bernanke20090113a.htm
21. Speech of Chairman Ben S. Bernanke at the Stamp Lecture, London School of Economics, 13 January 2009 at: www.federalreserve.gov/newsevents/speech/bernanke20090113a.htm

8
Financial Reforms, Competition, and Risk in Banking Markets

Barbara Casu, Alessandra Ferrari and Tianshu Zhao

8.1 Introduction

The analysis of the relationship between financial reforms, competition, and bank risk-taking incentives is of particular interest in the wake of the recent financial turmoil, as banks and regulators are currently facing unprecedented challenges. As new regulations and infrastructures are created and the old ones discarded or reformed, it is necessary to foster understanding of the implications of the crisis on the banking sector.

Most of the legislation following the 1930s financial crisis was based on the assumption that competition makes banks more risk-prone, and competition should therefore be restrained to preserve stability. During the 1990s this view was questioned and fundamental programmes of liberalization were carried out by many governments. Deregulation was, however, often accompanied by prudential re-regulation to ensure that bankers took only 'prudent' risks. There is a vast literature examining the relationship between financial reforms and competition, and between competition and risk exposure. Both theoretical and empirical findings are mixed, however, and recent research questions the causal negative link between competition and stability (Boyd and De Nicolò, 2005).

The economic rationale for financial deregulation is commonly based on the assumed positive effect it will have on competition, and consequently on efficiency and productivity. However, there is also often a concern that increased competition may discourage banks from engaging in effective monitoring and screening in the provision of loans, hence exacerbating the fragility of the banking system. The literature on competition and bank performance is relatively well developed, whereas much less is known about the links between competition and financial stability (Wilson et al., 2009; DeBandt et al., 2010), the main issue being to what extent a competitive banking sector is compatible with the ultimate goal of financial stability.

To correct the potential increase in risk-taking incentives, regulators tend to accompany deregulation with prudential re-regulation which, unlike economic regulation, is 'market-friendly': it targets risk-taking in the presence of intense competition, rather than limiting competition. Research on the effects of financial reforms on banks' competitive conduct, risk- taking, and production performance has very important policy implications for improving the supervision and regulation of banking in order to embrace market forces and sustain economic stability and growth. This chapter contributes to the current debate with an extended review of the theoretical and empirical literature on the effects of financial reforms on competition and the relationship between competition and banks' risk-taking behaviour.

8.2 Financial deregulation, competition, and risk-taking incentives

A large number of developed and developing countries have deregulated their banking systems over the past two decades, removing restrictions on entry, business activities, and price and number of financial intermediation. The primary objective of such reforms was to improve the productivity, efficiency, and profitability of the banking systems, thereby increasing international competitiveness and promoting economic growth. This positive effect of reforms on financial sector performance is, however, not always validated by empirical studies. Indeed, the outcome of deregulation policies seems to reflect several country-specific demand-and-supply characteristics, so that an increase in competitive pressure may sometimes exacerbate the inherent fragility of banking systems. For this reason, as we said before, deregulation has often been accompanied by prudential re-regulation.

The idea that a too-competitive banking sector will be prone to excess risk has had a substantial impact on contemporary financial policies, but only recently has this issue been addressed directly, and the theoretical literature is not yet as well-developed as it should be (Carletti, 2007). Many theoretical models do not distinguish between observable market structure (such as concentration ratios and the number of market participants) and competition, but rather assume a one-to-one mapping between the two (Carletti and Hartmann, 2003; Beck, 2008), in conflict with the growing notion that competition is a type of conduct

(Berger et al., 2004; Claessens and Laeven, 2004). Moreover, most theoretical models assume that price, risk, and return characteristics of assets are exogenous to banks (Boyd and De Nicolò, 2005), in contrast with the stability literature whose focus is on the endogenous risk-taking behaviour of agents (Carletti, 2007). Finally, the existing theoretical frameworks typically treat banks as homogeneous. Since competitive selection among heterogeneous firms is the key to efficiency and productivity improvements, this creates inconsistency among the interrelated theoretical streams.

8.2.1 The theoretical framework

The theoretical literature is divided on the assumptions made about the behaviour of banks in an increasingly competitive environment, emphasizing either the adverse selection or the moral-hazard aspects (Koskela and Stenbacka, 2000; Canoy et al., 2001; Carletti, 2007).

Taking banks' behaviour as exogenous, the first strand of theoretical literature concentrates on the adverse selection problem that banks face with respect to borrowers. An increase in the number of banks increases informational imperfections because borrowers are more likely to obtain loans elsewhere. As a consequence, increased competition may have an adverse impact on banks' solvency.

The alternative approach considers risk-taking behaviour as endogenous, and identifies its link with competition in the change in the relative costs and benefits of informational specialization. Informational activities are costly and cannot be sold at exit, so the crucial point is how competition affects the private rents banks derive from them: if they diminish, then banks' incentive to engage in them will decrease, the exploitation of the safety-net arrangement becomes more attractive, and the moral-hazard problem is exacerbated (Besanko and Thakor, 1993). Along these lines, some recent studies have suggested that this perverse link between competition and risk-taking is not robust (Allen and Gale, 2004; Boyd and De Nicolò, 2005). In particular, this theoretical literature argues the uniqueness of bank loans vis-à-vis arms'-length debt in terms of information production. Hence, the higher additional value that borrowers could receive from loans granted by banks with a higher reputation for informational specialization. Consequently, borrowers' preferences act as a market-based endogenous incentive mechanism to induce banks to engage in informational specialization, in order to gain and maintain a reputation. With the involvement of the demand side, the increase in banks' efforts towards informational specialization appears to reconcile with the increasingly competitive environment (Besanko and Thakor, 1993; Boot, 2001). This will be particularly true if banks are competing for good lending opportunities (Allen et al., 2006), or if their main competitive pressure comes from inter-bank competition rather than capital markets (Boot and Thakor, 2000). Prudential re-regulation could also correct for excessive risk-taking incentives, but only if it coordinates effectively with the market-based discipline (Demsetz et al., 1996; Galloway et al., 1997; Flannery, 2001): banks are self-interested decision-makers, and they will react to prudential re-regulation in a way that best serves their own interests, not the regulators' interests.

8.2.2 The empirical evidence

The vast body of empirical work on competition and banks' risk exposure has produced very mixed findings. We categorize this literature into four types: (a) studies in the SCP tradition that infer competition from observable market structure indicators; (b) studies that infer the increase in competition from the relaxation of regulatory restrictions; (c) studies that follow the new empirical industrial organization (NEIO) approach; and (d) studies developed under the charter-value hypothesis (CVH).

The first type of study measures competition by observable market structure indicators, so that a lower concentration ratio and/or Herfindahl-Hirschman Index (HHI), and a higher number of market participants, are treated as a sign of increased competition. Rhoades and Rutz (1982) is one of the earlier studies of this type; it finds a positive correlation between the three-bank deposit concentration ratio and risk indicators in the US banking market in 1969–1978, therefore implying that banks in more competitive markets are in a more risky position. Based on figures from 69 countries over the 1980–1997 period Beck et al. (2006) also find that banking crises are less likely in more concentrated markets. This finding is robust to a number of different specifications and controlling for an array of other factors potentially associated with crises. The opposite in found by De Nicolò et al. (2004) and Boyd et al. (2007), suggesting that competition improves financial stability.

The second type of study infers competition indirectly from the implementation of deregulation policies or from the extent of regulatory restrictions. The underlying assumption is that competition increases in a deregulated environment, and the finding of a positive relationship between risk indicators and the easing of restrictions is interpreted as an adverse impact of competition on risk-taking. Using aggregate data of US banks between 1975 and 1992, Jayaratne and Strahan (1998) find that branching relaxation sharply reduces banks' risk, therefore concluding that competition lowers risk-taking. Dick (2006), on the other hand, finds a positive link between the removal of geographic restrictions and risk indicators over the period 1993–1999 in US banking, and concludes that competition worsens risk-taking. Finally, the cross-country studies by Beck et al. (2003) and Barth et al. (2001, 2004) find that banking crises are less likely in less regulated markets, consistently with the view that competition enhances stability. In addition, there is evidence of the importance of the institutional environment for the occurrence of banking crisis. Demirguc-Kunt and Detragiache (1999) show that banking and financial crises are more likely to occur in a liberalized financial system with a weaker institutional environment. Institutional settings are crucial to the success of a prudential approach at ensuring banking stability.

The third type of study follows the NEIO approach to measure competition. Yeyati and Micco (2007) estimate the H-statistic for eight Latin American countries over the period 1993–2002 and find that it appears to be negatively correlated with risk-taking, indicating that competition leads banks to behave more prudently.

To summarize, these three types of study produce controversial results. Moreover, they focus on testing for the existence of a relationship between competition and risk-taking, but do not analyse the means by which this relationship takes place, despite the policy relevance of the issue. Without digging into banks' risk-taking incentives, empiricists spin answers in every possible direction. Relaxing restrictions on banking activities might decrease banks' risk-taking by providing more opportunities, or it could increase it by increasing scope for diversification (Gonzalez, 2005). A higher number of market participants may lead to riskier bank portfolios and higher failure probabilities because it worsens banks' screening abilities (Shaffer, 1998). Yet, it could also induce banks to increase the intensity of soliciting borrowers. It also has to be noted that the various measures of competition used are not immune to criticism. The contestability literature suggests that the degree of competition should be analyzed through firms' conduct and threats of entry rather than the observable market structure, which is mainly reflective of industry-specific production characteristics. For instance, the presence of asymmetric information in corporate relationships, and of switching costs and networks, would have an impact on the industry structure and lead to an ambiguous relation between the number of banks and the competitive outcome (Carletti, 2007). Also, economies of scale may question the relationship between concentration and competition (Canoy et al., 2001). Finally, whilst the widely-used H-statistic falls into the conduct-analysis category, it does not map directly into a static or dynamic oligopoly-equilibrium concept. As a result, although it provides an informative sign, its specific value carries an unclear interpretation for the strength of market power (Shaffer, 2004; Carbò Valverde et al., 2007). All in all, one seems to have reason to query whether the results presented in these three types of studies can robustly support their conclusions.

The fourth type of study is developed under the CVH. By definition, charter value is the present value of the current and future profit that a firm can earn as an ongoing concern. The value of charters in banking arises from two main sources: market regulation, which by limiting competition can provide market power, and bank-related sources, which are associated with bank-specific reputation, economies of scale, and superior information in financial markets (Demsetz et al., 1996). According to CVH, banks have higher charter value in a less competitive environment, which provides a higher opportunity cost of bankruptcy and deters risk-taking incentives. An increase in competition then leads to a decline in charter value, and is associated with increased risk-taking. Therefore, the CVH portrays a chain reaction from competition to charter value and from charter value to risk-taking. While the empirical work on competition and charter value does not find a definite link between the two, the majority of the empirical studies on the relationship between charter value and risk suggests a negative link, supporting the idea that higher charter value reduces risk-taking incentives (Keeley and Furlong, 1990; Demsetz et al., 1996; Galloway et al., 1997; Anderson and Fraser, 2000; Salas and Saurina, 2003; Konishi and Yasuda, 2004; Gonzalez, 2005). However this effect should not be overemphasized; charter value can be effective in limiting leverage risk, credit risk, and liquidity risk, but it fails to alleviate asset risk. Moreover, its effectiveness depends on how it is generated in the first place, on the diligence of the regulator, and on the changes in economic conditions. For example, a larger charter value may lead to a higher risk if it results from a forbearance regulatory policy (Nagarajan and Sealey, 1995), if the regulator is less effective in sorting out the risk position of banks (Park, 1997) and when economic conditions are in a downturn (Saunders and Wilson, 2001).

Overall the results of these studies indicate that whether more competition induces more risk-taking via a reduction in the charter value is essentially an empirical issue. An additional possible weakness of these studies is the reliability of their chosen proxies for competition, which are usually the extent of regulatory restrictions and market structure indicators. Finally, although CVH studies endogenize banks' risk-taking incentives and attempt to link competition and risk-taking in a moral-hazard framework, their focus is on the charter value as a whole. The market-related and bank-related components of the overall charter value are not distinguished. The variation of charter value across banks due to bank-specific informational capacity is not recognized. The effect of competition on banks' informational rents, which the theoretical literature identifies as the key determinant of risk incentives, is left unexplored.

A recent study by Zhao et al. (2009) on India develops a structural model of competition in the lending market to examine the impact of financial reforms on competition and the change that this induces in banks' risk-taking incentives. Following the NEIO literature, the authors model banks as price-setting profit maximizers and measure the dynamics of competition on the estimation of a conjectural variation parameter. They base the analysis of banks' risk-taking incentives on the changes in responsiveness to demand according to lenders' monitoring and screening capacity. Their results show that competition in the lending market increased along with the reform process and concurrently with the introduction of tighter prudential norms, therefore implying that these may not necessarily hinder competition (consistently also with Zhao et al., 2010). Their results also show that borrowers favour lenders with lower monitoring and screening capacity when the market becomes more competitive. This supports the view that competition increases banks' risk-taking incentives. These results are particularly important in light of the proposed reforms to strengthen the stability of the banking sector in the wake of the 2007–2009 financial crisis, since they highlight that the introduction of tighter prudential norms may not automatically correct banks' excessive risk-taking.

8.3 Conclusion

The objective of financial reforms is to foster a well-functioning financial system via an optimal balance between efficiency and stability. Financial deregulation and concomitant prudential re-regulation policies have recently been a dominant feature of regulatory policies of both developed and developing countries. The purpose of this chapter has been to review the theoretical arguments and the empirical evidence of the impact of financial reforms on the banking sector. Overall, the impact of financial reforms on banks' competition, risk-taking incentives, and production performance has not been studied as extensively as one might expect. Despite a growing number of studies, the literature is still rather limited and inconclusive in many aspects.

The most important point that has not been fully recognized in the literature is the change in the role of banks as the regulation regime switches from economic regulation to prudential regulation. Whilst under the former banks are passive investors who simply take what the market offers them, with the operational freedom of the latter banks behave as market-oriented economic agents and interact with market forces. Consequently, the evaluation of the impact of regulatory reforms has to be studied through an analysis of the behaviour of banks in a changing environment. However, the literature seems to have considerable flaws in endogenizing banks' behaviour in the empirical analysis. In particular whilst the increase in competition depends on how market participants react to regulatory reforms, with few exceptions the literature lacks a measure of the evolution of competition. Indeed the *a priori* expectations of regulators about the effects of policy changes on competition are not always fulfilled. Similarly the effects on banks' risk-taking depend on the change in banks' informational rents in an increasingly competitive environment. Although banks are special players in the market for information, they must be motivated by the correct incentives to do their job properly. Taking into account the borrower-lender relationship and banks' information production, some recent theoretical contributions have suggested that the widely accepted perverse link between competition and risk-taking is not robust (Allen and Gale, 2004; Boyd and De Nicolò, 2005). The empirical literature, however, has typically focused on the mere existence of a relationship between competition and risk, without explaining what it originates from and how it develops. CVH studies do attempt to link competition and risk-taking in a moral-hazard framework, but their attention is on the charter value as a whole. The market-related and bank-related components of the overall charter value are not distinguished. The effect of competition on banks' informational rents, key in determining the impact of competition on risk-taking incentives, is left unexplored. In addition, whereas the effect of financial reforms on competition and that of competition on risk are inextricably intertwined, the existing literature treats them as separate issues. The objective of financial reforms is to achieve a proper balance between efficiency and stability with appropriate market forces. A complete evaluation of the impact of financial reforms cannot therefore be limited to an analysis of production performance and competition if it is to offer a sound base for proper policy reforms.

References

Allen F. and Gale D. (2004). Competition and stability. *Journal of Money, Credit and Banking* 36(3), 453–480.

Allen F. Carletti E. and Marquez R. (2006). *Credit Market Competition and Capital Regulation*, Working Paper, University of Pennsylvania.

Anderson, R.C. and Fraser, D.R. (2000) Corporate control, bank risk-taking and the health of the banking industry. *Journal of Banking and Finance* 24, 1383–1398.

Barth JR., Caprio G. and Levine R. (2001). Banking systems around the globe: do regulations and ownership affect performance and stability?. In Mishkin FS (ed.), *Prudential Supervision: What Works and What Doesn't*. Chicago: University of Chicago Press.

Barth J.R., Caprio G. and Levine R. (2004). Bank regulation and supervision: what works best?. *Journal of Financial Intermediation* 13, 205–248.

Beck T. (2008). Bank competition and financial stability: friends or foes?. Policy Research Working Paper Series 4656, The World Bank.

Beck T., Demirguc-Kunt A. and Levine R. (2003). *Bank Concentration and Crises*. University of Minnesota, Carlson School of Management.

Beck T., Demirguc-Kunt A. and Levine R. (2006). Bank concentration, competition and crises: first results. *Journal of Banking and Finance* 30, 1581–1603.

Berger A.N., Demirguc-Kunt A., Levine R. and Hubrich JG. (2004). Bank concentration and competition: an evolution in the making. *Journal of Money, Credit and Banking* 36, 433–453.

Besanko D. and Thakor A.V. (1993). Relationship banking, deposit insurance and bank portfolio. In Mayer C. and Vives X. (eds), *Capital Markets and Financial Intermediation*. Cambridge, UK: Cambridge University Press, 292–318.

Boot A.W. (2001). Regulation and banks' incentives to control risk. *Sveriges Riksbank Economic Review*, Sveriges Riksbank, 2, 4–24.

Boot A.W. and Thakor A.V. (2000). Can relationship banking survive competition? *Journal of Finance* 55, 679–713.

Boyd J.H. and De Nicoló G. (2005). The theory of bank risk-taking and competition revisited. *Journal of Finance* 60, 1329–1343.

Boyd J.H., De Nicoló G. and Jalal A. (2007). Bank risk-taking and competition revisited: new theory and new evidence. IMF Working Paper No. 06/297.

Canoy M., van Dijk M., Lemmen J., de Mooij R. and Weigand J. (2001). *Competition and Stability in Banking*. CPB Netherlands Bureau for Economic Policy Analysis.

Carbò Valverde S. and Rodriguez Fernandez F. (2007). The determinants of bank margins in European banking. *Journal of Banking and Finance* 31, 2043–2063.

Carletti E. (2007). Competition and regulation in banking. In Boot AWA and Thakor AV. (eds), *Handbook of Corporate Finance: Financial Intermediation and Banking*. London: North Holland.

Carletti E. and Hartmann P. (2003). Competition and stability: What's special about banking?. In Mizen P. (ed.), *Monetary History, Exchange Rates and Financial Markets: Essays in Honour of Charles Goodhart*. Edward Elgar.

Claessens S. and Laeven L. (2004). What drives banking competition? some international evidence. *Journal of Money, Credit and Banking* 36, 563–584.

DeBandt O., Hartmann P. and Peydro JL. (2010). Systemic risk in banking: an update. In Berger A., Molyneux P. and Wilson JOS (eds.), *The Oxford Handbook of Banking*. Oxford: Oxford University Press.

De Nicolò D., Bartholomew P., Zaman J. and Zephirin M. (2004). Bank consolidation, internationalization and conglomeration: trends and implications for financial risk. *Financial Markets, Institutions and Instruments* 13, 173–217.

Demirguc-Kunt A. and Detragiache E. (1999). *Financial Liberalization and Financial Fragility*, Working Paper No.1917, World Bank.

Demsetz R.S., Saidenberg M.R., Strahan P.E. (1996). Banks with something to lose: the disciplinary role of franchise value. *FRBNY Economic Policy Review* 2, 1–14.

Dick A.A. (2006). Nationwide branching and its impact on market structure, quality and bank performance. *Journal of Business* 79, 567–592.

Flannery M.J. (2001). The faces of market discipline. *Journal of Financial Services Research* 20, 107–119.

Galloway T.M., Lee W.B., Roden D.M. (1997). Banks' changing incentives and opportunities for risk-taking. *Journal of Banking and Finance* 21, 509–527.

Gonzalez F. (2005). Bank regulation and risk-taking incentives: an international comparison of bank risk. *Journal of Banking and Finance* 29, 1153–1184.

Jayaratne J. and Strahan P.E. (1998). Entry restrictions, industry evolution, and dynamic efficiency: evidence from commercial banking. *Journal of Law and Economics* 41, 239–273.

Keeley M.C. and Furlong F.T. (1990). A re-examination of mean variance analysis of bank capital regulations. *Journal of Banking and Finance* 14, 69–84.

Konishi M. and Yasuda Y. (2004). Factors affecting bank risk-taking: evidence from Japan. *Journal of Banking and Finance* 28, 215–232.

Koskela E. and Stenbacka R. (2000). Is there a tradeoff between bank competition and financial fragility?. *Journal of Banking and Finance* 24, 1853–1874.

Nagarajan S. and Sealey C. (1995). Forbearance, deposit insurance pricing and incentive compatible bank regulation. *Journal of Banking and Finance* 19, 1109–1130.

Park S. (1997). Risk-taking behaviour of banks under regulation. *Journal of Banking and Finance* 21, 491–507.

Rhoades S. and Rutz R. (1982). Market power and firm risk. *Journal of Monetary Economics* 9, 73–85.

Salas V. and Saurina J. (2003). Deregulation, market power and risk behaviour in Spanish banks. *European Economic Review* 47, 1061–1075.

Saunders A. and Wilson B. (2001). An analysis of bank charter value and its risk-constraining incentives. *Journal of Financial Services Research*, 2, 185–195.

Shaffer S. (1998). The winner's curse in banking. *Journal of Financial Intermediation* 7, 359–392.

Shaffer S. (2004). Patterns of competition in banking. *Journal of Economics and Business* 56, 287–313.

Wilson JOS., Casu B., Girardone C. and Molyneux P. (2009). *Emerging Themes in Banking: Recent Literature and Directions for Future Research*, CASS Working Paper Series, Centre for Banking Research, WP-CBR-07-2009.

Yeyati E.L. and Micco A. (2007). Concentration and foreign penetration in Latin American banking sectors: Impact on competition and risk. *Journal of Banking and Finance* 31, 1633–1647.

Zhao T., Casu B. and Ferrari A. (2009). Competitive behaviour and risk-taking incentives in the lending market: An application to Indian banking, CASS Working Paper Series, Centre for Banking Research, WP-CBR-02-2009.

Zhao T., Casu B. and Ferrari A. (2010). Total factor productivity growth, ownership structure and competitive behaviour: the role of deregulation and prudential re-regulation. *Journal of Banking and Finance* 34, 246–254.

Part II

The Lending Business: Markets and Instruments

9
The Driving Forces of Credit Brokers' Diffusion in Italy: An Empirical Analysis

Federica Poli and Teodora Erika Uberti

In the last decade, there has been a tremendous growth in the number of credit brokers (CB) in Italy. Some estimates maintain that about a quarter of residential mortgage loans are intermediated by CB (Europe Economics, 2009); their market shares of some leasing and consumer credit products are also significant. Despite the importance of credit brokerage services, little empirical research has been devoted to investigating its origins. In this paper we undertake an analysis of CB diffusion in Italian provinces (NUTS3 level) based on spatial panel data model that aims to estimate the relevance of spatial effects. Two models are developed in order to identify the determinants of this phenomenon. The results emphasize that CB diffusion is to some extent influenced by the socioeconomic and banking features of the area, but estimates reveal also the emergence of a 'herding effect' whose occurrence is probably due to the fact that access to the brokerage profession is not hindered by heavy regulatory requirements.

9.1 Introduction

Credit brokers (CB), sometimes known as third-party originators, are intermediaries performing a matching function between lenders and borrowers in credit markets (Alexander et al., 2002). Typically CB provide financial counselling to borrowers (households, firms, and so on) and carry out some phases of the origination process (collection and fulfilment of loan applications, preliminary credit risk evaluations). The presence of brokers may improve households' and firms' access to financing as well as competition in local credit markets. Reducing the uncertainty of completing a transaction, such intermediaries may increase the volume of trades and operate more efficiently than lenders and borrowers by themselves (Yavas, 1994).

Additionally, CB may be regarded as a distribution substitute whenever augmentation of bank branches is not feasible and/or convenient to satisfy a growing demand for loans. More generally, the increasing importance of CB may be sustained by the convenience they offer to lenders who are looking for new distribution vehicles: channels that are more flexible and suitable for brand and product differentiation strategies aimed at reaching new customer segments or markets, and improving 'customer proximity'.[1] Despite these benefits, in recent years increasing concerns about unfair CB conduct has been expressed by consumerist associations, supervisory authorities,[2] and lenders' associations, thus causing regulators to reconsider the existing legal framework.[3] Allegations of misconduct have been mostly associated with agency problems, due to the incentives provided by common broker-remunerations schemes.[4] Also, potential areas of conflict of interest are recognized in the case of overlapping roles, in particular real-estate agents acting as mortgage brokers.

In Italy the number of CB has impressively grown: from around 500 in 2000 to more than 100,000 in 2008.[5] Recent research by SFG (2009) into Italian house-buyers shows that 42.6% of respondents contacted CB for financial assistance. Another survey conducted by a CB association indicates that CB provide both households and firms located in their neighbourhood with numerous lending products, intermediating an annual average amount of loans per CB equal to 4.4 million Euros. Despite the absence of comprehensive official data on market shares held by CB, unofficial estimates maintain that about a quarter of Italian residential mortgage loans originated in recent years are attributable to CB (Europe Economics, 2009). CB also play an important role in the origination of some leasing and consumer credit products (Bank of Italy, 2008).

Despite the importance of this phenomenon, no empirical analyses have been carried out to help us to understand it. At an international level, determinants of CB diffusion are mostly only indirectly assessed, since the main aim of most of these studies is to investigate the behaviour of these agents in mortgage markets, and more recently in subprime markets (see LaCour-Little and Chun, 1999; Woodward, 2003; El Anshasy et al., 2006; LaCour-Little, 2009).

In this paper we undertake an empirical analysis based on spatial panel data models, following Elhorst (2009), in order to estimate the relevance of spatial effects in explaining CB diffusion. The remainder of the paper is organized as follows. Section 9.2 provides evidence of the presence of CB in NUTS3 Italian provinces from 2001 to 2007.

Section 9.3 presents the main empirical findings. Finally, some concluding remarks are provided in section 9.4.

9.2 Data and empirical analysis

Spatial distribution of CB in Italian provinces is changing over time, but seems not to be driven by random patterns, and this is confirmed by spatial indicators. Figures 9.1 and 9.2 present a graphical representation of the CB per capita distribution in 2000 and 2007 according to the location (quartile) of each province.

In 2000, CB per capita are not very numerous and no particular pattern emerges: the Moran's I computed for 2000 is positive, but very low (0.0216 significant at 5%).[6] (Table 9.1).

However, over time the diffusion of CB exhibits two patterns: the first is a shift of growth in the southern provinces, displaying a remarkable north–south differentiation; the second comprises agglomeration forces that cluster together provinces where the phenomenon is mostly concentrated. Table 9.1 shows Moran's I values that confirm clustering effects: 2007 values are positive and much higher (0.3316 significant at 1%).[7] Analysis of the distribution of bank branches per capita reveals that the geography is more unbalanced in the south than in the north,

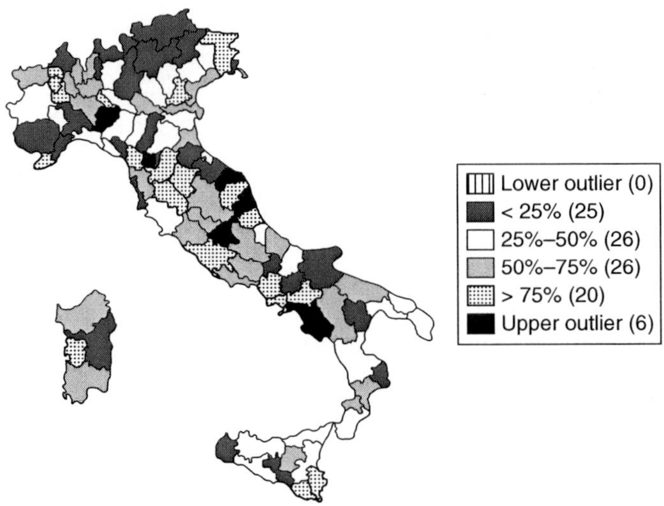

Figure 9.1 Number of CB per capita, 2000

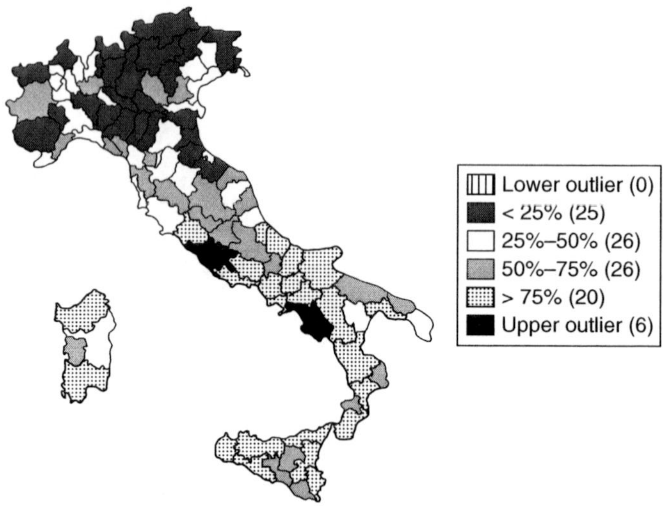

Figure 9.2 Number of CB per capita, 2007

Table 9.1 Moran's I statistics

Year	Number of new CB per capita
2000	0.0216**
2001	0.1015***
2002	0.1658***
2003	0.2166***
2004	0.2703***
2005	0.2534***
2006	0.2692***
2007	0.3316***

**significant at 5 %; ***significant at 1 %.

and this result could confirm that CB constitute an alternative distribution channel in under-banked markets.

Since according to current Italian law there are no strong requirements for registration as CB,[8] the profession might represent an appealing job opportunity, either for younger people (as the decreasing trend in the national average age shows) and for women (although almost two-thirds of CB are males). With these very simple descriptive statistics we aim to detect empirically the diffusion of CB, considering both socioeconomic and banking determinants as the literature suggests (El Anshasy et al., 2006; LaCour-Little, 2009), and also taking into account progressive spatial autocorrelation. Due to the different nature of CB in year 2000, we exclude this year from the empirical analysis.

The size of value-added per capita (*VApc*) of province *i* at time *t* represents a proxy for local *ex-ante* credit conditions or, in other words, the potential for credit. Although we do expect a positive sign of the coefficient, we should consider that CB tend to operate in low-income areas, hence we could envisage a negative sign of the variable's coefficient. In order to capture the potential need of firms for financial advice provided by CB we include the entrepreneurship vivacity index (*EV*), calculated as the ratio of the number of new-born and ceased firms to total firms in province *i* at the beginning of time *t*, whose expected sign is positive. Given the importance of CB in residential real-estate lending, we use the real-estate index (*REI*) measured as the ratio between the value of new real-estate transactions and the total value of real-estate stock existing in province *i* at time *t*. The sign of the coefficient is expected to be positive.

The unemployment ratio (*U*) of province *i* at time *t* is adopted as a proxy for local credit conditions, and its coefficient is expected to have a negative sign. However, since we suppose that the incentive to become CB may be higher in local markets with more severe unemployment conditions, a positive sign of the coefficient is likely to occur. Existing US literature on the quality of mortgage loans sold through CB shows that these latter tend to act primarily with ethnic minorities, who have reduced access to traditional credit channels. On this basis we use the immigration ratio (*Ir*) calculated as a percentage of immigrants to province *i* at time *t*, we expect a positive sign of the coefficient due to the difficulties for immigrants of accessing credit in formal markets.With regard to the socioeconomic characteristics of local Italian markets we include the education ratio (*Er*) calculated as new graduates within the resident population of province *i* at time *t*. Following the stereotype that brokers mainly operate in poorly-educated communities, we should expect a negative sign of the coefficient; on the other hand, seeing the profession of CB as an easy job opportunity for highly-educated individuals suggests that a positive sign of the coefficient would be feasible.

The structure and quality of the local credit market may affect the presence of brokers in a market. The prevalence of CB may be influenced negatively by the bank-branch density ratio, and positively by the kilometrical coverage of bank branches (*CBB*). Hence, we have computed two indicators: branch density (*Bd*), calculated as the number of bank branches per 100,000 inhabitants in province *i* at time *t*, and the kilometrical *CBB* in province *i* at time *t*.[9] Relative to these two variables we assume that, in under-banked markets, there will be room for brokers' growth. Finally we consider the credit risk proxy (*CR*) as the ratio between the value in euros of non-performing loans and the total value of loans in province *i* at time *t*, in order to test whether the presence of CB might be positively linked with the riskiness of local customers.

9.3 Empirical results

The empirical analysis has been performed for CB per capita (*CB*) calculated as the natural logarithm of newly-registered CB per 100,000 inhabitants in each Italian province from 2001 to 2007 as follows:

$$\begin{aligned}\ln CB_{it} = {} & \alpha_0 + \alpha_1 VApc_{it} + \alpha_2 Ir_{it} + \alpha_3 Er_{it} + \alpha_4 EV_{it} + \alpha_5 Bd_{it} + \\ & \alpha_6 CR_{it} + \alpha_7 REI_{it} + \alpha_8 CBB_{it} + \alpha_9 WLB_{it} + \theta_i + \epsilon_{it} \qquad (1)\end{aligned}$$

$$\begin{aligned}\ln CB_{it} = {} & \beta_0 + \beta_1 U_{it} + \beta_2 Ir_{it} + \beta_3 Er_{it} + \beta_4 EV_{it} + \beta_5 Bd_{it} + \\ & \beta_6 CR_{it} + \beta_7 REI_{it} + \beta_8 CBB_{it} + \beta_9 WLB_{it} + \theta_i + \upsilon_{it} \qquad (2)\end{aligned}$$

where variables are defined in section 9.2. WCB_{it-} is the spatially lagged dependent variable calculated on the inverse of the kilometrical distance among centroids of provinces, and θ_i is the random effect coefficient. We estimate two log-linear models (equations 1 and 2) in order to interpret the coefficients of the estimates as relative changes, and in both models results are stable (Table 9.2). Following the procedure in Elhorst (2009), in all the cases the Hausman test suggests the spatial random effects model with a spatially lagged dependent variable.

First of all the two variables used as proxies for local economic conditions (*VApc* and *U*) are not significant, hence they do not seem to play any role in determining this phenomenon. The presence of an immigrant population is negative and significant implying that, differently from the hypothesis, immigrant people may have credit access through different channels. The coefficient of the education ratio seems to reflect the fact that for highly-educated people enrolment among CB may represent a job opportunity, presumably because of the undemanding professional requirements. *EV* is not significant, implying

Table 9.2 Log-linear models with spatially lagged dependent variable and spatial random effects (dependent variable: $LnCB_{it}$)

Independent Variables	Model 1	Model 2
Constant	0.701**	0.831***
VApc	0.000	
U		–0.0001
Ir	–0.032**	–0.027**
Er	0.775***	0.782***
EV	–0.011	–0.011
Bd	–0.013***	–0.012***
CR	0.013**	0.012*
REI	0.091**	0.093**
CBB	–0.105***	–0.111***
WCB	0.910***	0.908***
θ	0.474***	0.473***
N	618	618
ni	103	103
T	6	6
Log-likelihood	–200.501	–200.793
LR test	132.213***	135.596***
Hausman Test	-52.456***	27.399**

*significant at 10 %; **significant at 5 %; ***significant at 1 %, in brackets *t*-values.

that entrepreneurship vivacity does not influence this phenomenon, while *REI* is significantly different from zero and positive, as expected, indicating that the dynamics experienced by residential real-estate markets positively affect CB presence. The *CR* coefficient seems to provide evidence that CB preferably operate in riskier areas, perhaps those neglected by bank branches. In this regard, the coefficient of *Bd* shows that under-banked markets do offer greater potential for credit brokerage activity both to capture potential demand for loans and, on the supply side, to make market penetration more efficient.

Contrary to our hypothesis, the *CBB* coefficient is negative and significant. While apparently contradicting the previous results, it simply reflects the fact that the presence of CB is more pronounced in populated provinces with a smaller kilometrical area which are not sufficiently banked.[10] Finally, the diffusion of CB in Italy seems to be highly influenced by contagious effects, in particular that of CB in nearby provinces (as defined by spatially lagged dependent variable, *WCB*), probably due to the 'herding effect' in registrations, highly favoured by the minimal requirements of current regulation.

9.4 Conclusions

The empirical results emphasize that the driving forces behind the diffusion of CB in Italy have a distinctive nature. The socioeconomic and banking characteristics of Italian provinces help to explain the proliferation of CB although we do observe the likely occurrence of the 'herding effect' on registrations, facilitated by spatial proximity. The fact remains that mild requirements, in particular the minimal demand for professional skills, make registration easy, and the threat of future legislative change has been a powerful incentive to CB diffusion in recent years: amendments to the current regulation (more stringent professional requirements) and a more effective supervision of CB appear necessary in order to minimize misconduct practices and other agency problems. The recently enacted law no. 88/2009 pursues the above targets by designing a new regulatory framework within which credit brokerage will be undertaken in Italy.

Notes

1. See Jacobides (2003) for his interpretation of the emergence of intermediate markets in mortgage banking as the result of a process of organizational unbundling.
2. For example in Italy since 2000 until nowadays there has been an increasing number of convictions reported to the Italian Anti Trust Authority for violations concerning consumers protection laws. In addition the Anti-Racket and Usury Commissioner (2008) claimed soaring violations of laws on usury/anti-money laundering related to the diffusion of CB.
3. For US see the Report of the Mortgage Bankers Association (2008).
4. Typically, CB remuneration is related to the loan origination phase and not to the effective loan stream of payments (El Anshasy et al., 2006). Additionally, there is a pervasive poor disclosure about compensations received from lenders by CB (Guttentag, 2000).
5. Italian CB are listed in an *ad hoc* national register held by the Bank of Italy and may undertake credit brokerage on behalf of individuals as well as other principals, i.e. firms. According to law n. 108/1996, brokerage services have

to be performed independently. CB may act as debt collectors on behalf of lenders.

6. We computed the spatial lag values using the proximity matrix, as the inverse of the distance among centroids of each province. To detect the robustness of these results we computed Moran's I using the rook contiguity matrix, and results are stable.
7. In 2007 the Moran's I value confirms the upward trend, showing a phenomenon that is continuously affected by spillovers effects.
8. Registration in the national register for individuals is actually subject to the possession of the following requirements: domicile in Italy, high school degree or previous registration in some specified registers and absence of conviction for several types of crimes.
9. We use the following formula: $2 \cdot \sqrt{Km_i^2 / BB_{it} \cdot 3{,}14}$, where Km_i^2 indicates the squared kilometres of province *i* and BB_{it} indicates the number of bank branches in province *i* at time *t* (Gandolfi, 2002).
10. Intuitively, also size and development of credit markets may affect the entry of new CB. However, we do not find any significant relation between CB and i.e. credit market size.

References

Alexander W.P., Grimshaw S.D., McQueen G.R. and Slade B.A. (2002). Some loans are more equal than others: Third-party originations and defaults in the sub-prime mortgage industry. *Real Estate Economics* 4, 667–697.

Anti-racket and Usury Commissioner. (2008). *Relazione annuale.* 31 January, Rome.

Bank of Italy. (2008). *Appendix to the Annual Report,* Rome.

El Anshasy A., Elliehausen G. and Shimazaki Y. (2006). *The Pricing of Sub-prime Mortgages by Mortgage Brokers and Lenders.* Georgetown University, Credit Research Center, Working Paper 70.

Elhorst J.P. (2009). *Spatial Panel Data Models.* In Fischer M.M. and Getis A. (eds), *Handbook of Applied Spatial Analysis.* Springer.

Europe Economics. (2009). Study on credit intermediaries in the internal market. DG Internal Market and Services, MARKT/2007/14/H, 14 January.

Gandolfi G. (2002). *La concorrenza bancaria nel settore bancario italiano.* Rome: Bancaria Editrice.

Guttentag J. (2000). *Another View of Predatory Lending,* Wharton Financial Institution Center, Working Paper 01-23-B.

Jacobides M.G. (2003). *How do Markets Emerge? Organizational Unbundling and Vertical Dis-integration in Mortgage Banking.* London Business School, Centre for the Network Economy, Working Paper 8.5.

LaCour-Little M. (2009). The pricing of mortgages by brokers. An agency problem?. *Journal of Real Estate Research,* 2, 265–266.

LaCour-Little M. and Chun G.H. (1999). Third-party originations and mortgage prepayment risk. an agency problem?. *Journal of Real Estate Research,* 17, 55–70.

Mortgage Bankers Association. (2008). *Mortgage Bankers and Mortgage Brokers: Distinct Businesses Warranting Distinct Regulation,* May.

SFG. (2009). *Evoluzione del mercato immobiliare e finanziario.* Survey presented at the Unione del Commercio in Milan, 29 January.

Woodward S.E. (2003). *Consumer Confusion in the Mortgage Markets.* Sand Hill Econometrics, Working Paper 14.

Yavas A. (1994). Middlemen in bilateral search markets. *Journal of Labour Economics* 12, 406–429.

10
Financial Constraints to Italian SME Growth: A Proposed Solution through VC and PE Financing

Vincenzo Capizzi, Renato Giovannini and Valerio Pesic

10.1 Introduction

The last few decades have seen increased emphasis on the dynamism of small and medium enterprises (SMEs) to accelerate economies. This has been accompanied by a greater focus on creating financial markets that efficiently meet the needs of these businesses. These trends are of particular interest in Italy, whose economy has traditionally depended on the wealth produced by its industrial districts.

Several studies have shown that SMEs account for an exceptional degree of product innovation and R and D, which helps to explain these companies' rapid sales growth rates. This is particularly true for high-tech and industrial enterprises (Audretsch et al., 1999), Verheul et al. (2002) show that among 18 OECD countries, higher levels of entrepreneurship accompany faster growth and lower unemployment in the overall economy. Studies focused on the development of particular regions confirm this finding, indicating that young and small firms devoted to innovative businesses are the leading drivers of economic growth in their respective areas.[1]

The availability and cost of finance is a key factor determining the ability of businesses to grow. Carpenter and Petersen (2002a) show that in a panel of more than 1600 small US firms, the growth of most of them is constrained by internal finance, together with a small leverage effect. In contrast, growth rates of the small fraction of firms that heavily use new share issues outstrip what internal finance can support. In particular, the phase that separates the identification of the innovative project from the marketing of the product appears to be crucial. In part because they do not have the financial and other resources to survive long periods of poor performance, small organizations have high failure rates; accordingly, potential investors are prone to see that losing their money is a likely outcome. Consequently, a small business with little track record that is looking for external capital may face constricted funding sources, because of the difficulty of evaluating its historical performance.

For entrepreneurs trying to start a company (especially where intangible assets are at the core of the business), venture capitalists (VCs)[2] are often the only available sources of financing. VCs act as professional investors with deep knowledge of the market based on their previous managerial experience. Their involvement usually implies sharp changes to both corporate governance models and relations with stakeholders, factors that are often seen as essential for better future performance (Hellmann and Puri, 2002), Similar changes also accompany the involvement of private equity firms (PEs),[3] which serve larger established companies that need to improve their results or resolve issues of ownership succession.

Empirical evidence from the US highlights some common factors of the VC and PE industries: financing is directed mainly to smaller firms operating in high-tech sectors and which had significantly outperformed similar firms. Performance leads were found in many areas, including research and development (R and D) intensity, sales growth, and investment.

The European investment market differs significantly from North America's. For example, the American capital market is much larger and more developed, and it includes a different composition of investments (for example, a greater proportion of start-up and high-tech firms) as well as financing sources. (Pension funds constitute a larger share of the US market, while banks are the main source of company financing in Europe.) Given such differences, it might be assumed that determinants and effects of VC and PE in European countries differ from those in the US.

10.2 The role of SMEs in economic literature

10.2.1 About SMEs

During the post-war period, there has been widespread agreement among academics and practitioners that SMEs share several shortcomings when compared to larger firms. Empirical evidence consistently indicated that SMEs were less efficient, paid their employees less, and were less innovative; consequently, they hindered economic growth.

Generally, small size was perceived as a preparatory step before consolidation into efficient large firms (Audretsch et al., 2002), Since the 1980s this position has been reconsidered, however, due to the increased numbers and impact of SMEs in the most developed industrial economies.

Recent economic literature cites several reasons for this changed situation. A loosening of the traditionally close relationship between size and efficiency has transformed production processes; this change has especially benefited those companies which have been able to recognize technological gaps and create flexible organizations. Workers have generally liked this new flexibility and have adapted to it in ways that improve productivity. On the demand side, specialized markets expanded according to changes in customers' tastes; this required specialized production and more highly targeted allocations of resources. With these changed circumstances, in particular the recognition of the importance of a knowledge-based economy, new theories have reappraised SMEs as fundamental contributors to new patterns of economic growth. One key advantage for SMEs is that the tiny revenue margins that flow from continuous incremental improvements to products, materials, and processes can often be sufficient for small businesses to be profitable; this is less often the case for large firms.

While SMEs were being reappraised as entities capable of helping to drive the general economy, a large body of literature focused on the financial constraints that may hinder the birth and development of such new businesses. Lack of internal financial resources especially intensifies operating risks for nascent firms. Young SMEs also face increased financial risks due to market imperfections, such as information asymmetry, and transaction and agency costs. More generally, such enterprises face a financial system that is inadequate to meet their needs. First, smaller and younger firms usually lack managerial skills and the ability to convey structured information to investors (Caselli, 2004), Second, the operations and finances of SMEs are often highly opaque; this is because the identity of owners and managers often coincide. Consequently backers, while running their evaluations, often privilege real guarantees to the future returns indicated by the firm, because of the difficulty of evaluating it. Finally, the risk of revealing proprietary secrets often makes innovative entrepreneurs reluctant to disclose details of their businesses (Ueda, 2004).

10.2.2 VCs as a solution

In line with the above, several authors have suggested that VCs and PEs are the financial intermediaries best suited for situations where information is significantly asymmetric. Indeed, these forms of financing have been very successful in the US, having fuelled the growth of many high-technology firms. The well-known fortunes of such ventures as Yahoo!, eBay, Microsoft, and Apple convinced many policymakers and entrepreneurship scholars to regard start-ups and VCs as driving forces for economic growth, job creation, and structural change. Regarding the Italian case, data gathered by the Private Equity Monitor (PEM©) on PE funding transactions occurring in 2005 and 2006 confirm the close relationship between SMEs and PE.

There are many factors that favour the involvement of VCs and PEs in funding SMEs. First, they hold stakes in all firms they back, and keep greater control rights where they believe that the entrepreneur must be induced to greater effort to ensure a project's success. Their role as stakeholder is enforced by an optimal mix of debt securities and equity securities that ensures the possibility that the backer may become a creditor or a partner according to what it perceives is needed to keep the entrepreneur fully engaged. Kaplan and Strömberg (2004) refer to this feature as a separation between control and cash-flow rights. Specifically, control rights allow the VC to participate in the entrepreneur's key decisions. Additionally, VCs and PEs often grant capital infusions in stages, periodically re-evaluating the firm's prospects before each tranche. The shorter the durations of financing rounds, the more frequently the backer monitors the entrepreneur's progress and the greater the need to gather information (Gompers, 1995), Finally, VCs and PEs serve to provide a certification effect. As we have already argued, the quality of small companies often cannot be observed directly. Thus, evaluators must appraise the company's value based on observable attributes that are thought to vary along with its underlying but unknown qualities.

10.3 Determinants and effects of VCs and PEs on SME financing

10.3.1 Introduction

The theoretical literature regarding the financing of small firms generally agrees that information opaqueness makes it more difficult for these businesses to obtain external finance. Asymmetric information problems between firms and financiers strongly affect their relationships and shape the contracts between them, especially terms about whether backing takes the form of debt or equity, and whether collateral is given for any debt, for covenants, and for the maturity of any loan.

The form of backing can create agency problems. For example, debt increases moral hazard problems. Following Jensen and Meckling (1976), firms can replace low-risk investments with high-risk projects, which increase the risk of bankruptcy but offer no offsetting gain to debt-holders in the event of success. At the same time, as Carpenter and Petersen (2002b) suggest, a small firm's marginal costs of financial debt could increase quickly because it has fewer tangible assets with which to secure loans. Thus, bank financing may not be viable. Unlike debt, equity finance does not increase the probability of bankruptcy. Moreover, agency problems are ameliorated because both entrepreneurs and equity investors share in upside returns. Aghion and Bolton (1992) and Aghion et al. (2004) propose a model based on control rights, which concludes that when size of projects becomes sufficiently large or when assets are increasingly intangible, firms will give more control rights to outside investors by issuing new equity.

Inherent characteristics of innovative companies, including unclear growth potential and large investments in intangibles assets (which is common for high-tech companies), tend to create obstacles to raising additional capital. There is increasing empirical evidence confirming the theoretical prediction that innovative firms rely more on internal finance than on leverage. It also seems clear that, at least in some countries, outside equity is a valuable source for funding innovative firms. Small firms can have more trouble in financing innovative activity. When they need to borrow, they are likely to do so on relatively poor terms (higher interest rates, shorter maturity) due to their asymmetric information problems; accordingly, outside equity seems to be their most suitable source for external financing. Borrowing can be difficult even for larger innovative firms. Based on a panel of publicly traded US high-tech companies, Carpenter and Petersen (2002a) conclude that, although large innovative companies have at their disposal more collateral to pledge against bank debt, difficulty in obtaining outside financing nonetheless constrains their growth.

Myers (1977) argues that a firm whose value largely depends upon investment in future growth options would likely make less use of debt because of a glaring agency problem: the owner/manager can undertake investment strategies that are particularly detrimental to bondholders. Rajan and Zingales (1995) give empirical support to this prediction. Testing the relationship between market-to-book ratios[4] and leverage, they find it to be negative. Similarly, Barclay and Smith (1995) find that debt maturity declines with firms' market-to-book ratio. The nature of firms' assets can also affect expected agency costs, which opens the door for VCs to step in. Williamson (1988) argues that leverage should be positively related to the liquidation value of assets. In fact, tangible assets are on average easier to sell and receive a higher fraction of repayment than do intangibles assets such as patents or copyrights. Thus, a higher liquidation value implies that default is less costly. Subsequent tests, as in Rajan and Zingales (1995), confirmed that the relationship between liquidation value (measured as the ratio of tangible assets to total assets) and leverage is indeed positive.

The framework presented gives factual hints about the role played by an external financer. Where such conditions are in place, there is scope for VCs and PEs to add more value than other intermediaries. Screening and monitoring activities, though imperfect,[5] and membership of the company's board can potentially overcome most of the problems outlined. This may not apply to banks; because regulations limit banks' ability to hold shares directly, they cannot fund projects through equity. Regarding the Italian market for SMEs funding, Panetta, Schivardi, and Shum (2004) find that a bank's merger seems to affect its specialization in terms of credit policy: the portion of credit allocated to small business decreases in the long run. This is due to size change and more complex organizational structure.

10.3.2 The economic impact of VCs and PEs on SME financing

Literature on economic impacts of VCs and PEs have focused on two issues: outcomes for the general economy, and the performance of a small business after acquiring new capital.

Regarding impacts on the general economy, numerous studies show that there is a strong positive correlation between VC and innovation. Hellmann and Puri (2000) argue that VC-backed firms appear to implement new patents more quickly. Kortum and Lerner (2000) conclude that a dollar invested by VC is three times more effective in promoting patent creation than a dollar invested from a corporation. Still, the direction of causality between VC and the degree of innovation remains an open question. Some empirical studies have found that more VC financing fosters innovation (the "VC first" hypothesis, for example Kortum and Lerner, 1998), while others have found that the external financier enters only after the discovery of a new technology and meets the need to market such innovations (the "Innovation first" hypothesis), Hirukawa and Ueda (2003) find that VC financing is more frequent in industries that have had an increase in total factor productivity, which the authors interpret as a proxy for innovation; after funding, productivity decreases.

Regarding the second focus area, several recent studies have empirically examined the relationship between receiving VC finance and firm performance. Sapienza (1992) finds that the performance of backed firms positively relates to the services that VCs provide. Two correlations particularly stand out: The more innovation a venture pursues, the more frequent are contacts between the lead investor and the CEO. And the more open communication is, and the less conflict of perspective exists between the VC and the CEO, the greater is the value of VC involvement.

Lerner (1999) evaluates the long-run success of firms participating in the US government's Small Business Innovation Research (SBIR) program, a major public-assistance initiative for high-tech firms. Those receiving SBIR assistance achieved significantly higher employment and sales growth rates than similar firms that did not receive SBIR assistance. These differences were most pronounced in ZIP codes with high VC activity. Jain and Kini (1995) add that services from VCs can include marketing advice and upgrades of the commercial network, which foster increased sales. Based on 187 Belgian VC-backed firms, the work of Manigart and Van Hyfte (1999) contrasts partially with the above results. These firms do not achieve significantly higher employment growth compared to non-VC backed firms of the same industries, of similar size, and similar age. Higher growth rates in total assets and cash flow, however, are obvious.

Summarizing, many studies have argued and shown that the presence of professional investors can strengthen a company's performance, due to many actions that these investors can take.

10.3.3 The certification effect

It is widely acknowledged that financial intermediaries can positively contribute as agents able to produce information about firms' qualities. The seminal work of Akerlof (1970) highlights the plausible failures of a market with imperfect information. The model predicts that, without both defined guarantees and distinguishable quality, the market may fail. Only the average quality of the goods will be considered. This causes a 'lemon market', in which goods of superior quality are driven out. Using the same framework, Chan (1983) shows that when all investors have positive search costs (that is, they are uninformed investors) entrepreneurs will find it in their interests to offer less desirable projects. This leads to the degeneration of projects undertaken. Thus, only 'lemons' are offered, and investors will not enter the market. Conversely, when some investors have zero search costs, the allocation of resources is improved in terms of entrepreneurs' efforts to spur projects with higher investor returns.

Both of the above studies note a lack of guarantees as a feature of imperfect markets. Investigating further, Booth and Smith (1986) find important evidence of the certification effect. The underlying theory derives from the expanding literature on the use of reputational signalling to guarantee product quality. The most notable work is by Klein and Leffler (1981), They demonstrate the conditions under which a non-salvageable capital expenditure can serve as an effective bond to guarantee the quality of a firm's products. In fact, the non-salvageable investment is perceived by customers as a commitment to product quality, which will be rewarded as long as the firm does not cheat. Booth and Smith extend the reputational capital paradigm to explain the role of the investment banker in certifying the pricing of equity and risky debt issues. In a market where insiders have an information advantage that might facilitate a wealth transfer from outsiders, issuing firms may have the option of 'leasing' the brand name of an investment banker to certify that the issue price reflects available inside information. In situations where insiders lack the ability to communicate their beliefs credibly or outsiders lack the ability to buy information, a potential market failure of the type identified by Akerlof (1970) results: other things being equal, the proportion of over-valued firms seeking new outside equity will be greater than the proportion in the general population, leading outsiders to raise their expectation that a firm is probably over-valued. This causes a decline in market value of firms.

10.4 Conclusions

In this paper, we consider the characteristics of the relationship between SMEs and VC and PE investors in Italy. The analysis has shown that VCs are more likely to step in for firms that are younger, smaller, and more endowed with intangible assets than the average. Additionally, it hints at their positive role when asymmetric information problems are of utmost importance and there is broad scope for adding value.

We confirm the hypothesis of VCs and PEs as certifying parties. Departing from the traditional background of IPO underpricing, which has been widely investigated, we focused attention on a new framework based on a cluster of balance sheet indexes. Thus, the original contribution of this study is, in our view, the confirmation of the presence of the certification effect under new circumstances and applying to SMEs, which are seldom considered.

We sustain the thesis that VC backs innovative businesses rather than supporting new entrepreneurial ideas from scratch. From a practical viewpoint, it highlights the limits of private initiative only (embodied here by VCs and PEs) in encouraging innovative companies, and leaves to policy-makers the task of bridging the gap. Not surprisingly, this is also the position expressed in several official documents issued by the European Commission.

In line with the above, we suggest as a future line of research the further investigation of the characteristics of the Italian financial system with an eye to factors that inhibit VC from achieving its full potential. (The experience of Anglo-Saxon countries indicates that this could be attained under proper regulation.) This research could include an assessment of the performance of state-owned regional agencies and the role of universities as incubators. Although we did not include these two sorts of organizations in our survey, we perceive their contributions as fundamental supports to start-up businesses.

Notes

1. Callejón and Segarra (1999) point out a positive relationship between the number of start-up companies and the growth of Spanish regions and industries. For the United Kingdom, see Hart and Hanvey (1995).
2. *VC* may refer to either *venture capital* or *venture capitalist.*
3. *PE* may refer to either *private equity* or *private equity firm.*
4. Myers suggests that a firm's market-to-book ratio may be related to the fraction of firm value that is based on future growth opportunities.
5. *Cf.*, Gorman and Sahlman (1989) and Manigart et al. (2002),

References

Aghion P. and Bolton P. (1992). An incomplete contracts approach to financial contracting. *Review of Economic Studies* 59, 473–494.

Aghion P., Bond S., Klemm A. and Marinescu I. (2004). Technology and financial structure: Are innovative firms different?. *Journal of the European Economic Association* 4, 277–288.

Akerlof G. (1970). The market for 'lemons': quality and the market mechanism. *Quarterly Journal of Economics* 84, 488–500.

Audretsch D.B., Santarelli E. and Vivarelli M. (1999). Start-up size and industrial dynamics: some evidence from Italian manufacturing. *International Journal of Industrial Organization* 17, 965–983.

Audretsch D.B., Thurik A.R., Verheul I. and Wennekers S. (2002). Understanding entrepreneurship across countries and over time, in *Entrepreneurship: Determinants and Policy in a European-U.S. Comparison*; D.B. Audretsch, A.R. Thurik, I. Verheul and A.R.M. Wennekers (eds), (Kluwer Academic Publishers, Boston/Dordrecht), 1–10.

Barclay M.J. and Smith Jr C.W. (1995). The maturity structure of corporate debt. *Journal of Finance* 50, 609–631.

Blackwell D., Wayne M., Spivey M. (1990). Shelf registration and the reduced due diligence argument: implications of the underwriter certification and the implicit insurance hypothesis. *Journal of Financial and Quantitative Analysis* 25, 245–259.

Booth J.R. and Smith R.L. (1986). Capital raising, underwriting and the certification hypothesis. *Journal of Financial Economics* 15, 261 281.

Callejón M. and Segarra A. (1999). Business dynamics and efficiency in industries and regions: the case of Spain. *Small Business Economics* 13, 253–271.

Carpenter R. and Petersen B. (2002a). Is the growth of small firms constrained by internal finance?. *The Review of Economics and Statistics* 84(2), 298–309.

Carpenter R. and Petersen B. (2002b). Capital market imperfections, high-tech investments and new equity financing. *The Economic Journal* 112(1), 54–72.

Caselli S. (2004). Corporate banking strategies: Products, markets and channels. In De Laurentis G (ed.), *Strategy and Organization of Corporate Banking*. Berlin/ New York: Springer Verlag.

Chan Y. (1983). On the positive role of financial intermediation in allocation of venture capital in a market with imperfect information. *The Journal of Finance* 38(5), 1543–1568.

Gompers P.A. (1995). Optimal staging, monitoring, and the staging of venture capital. *The Journal of Finance* 1(5), 1461–1489.

Gorman M. and Sahlman W.A. (1989). What do venture capitalists do?. *Journal of Business Venturing* 4(4), 231–248.

Hart M. and Hanvey E. (1995). Job generation and new and small firms: some evidence from the late 1980s. *Small Business Economics* 7(2), 97–109.

Hellmann T. and Puri M. (2000). The interaction between product market and financing strategy: The role of venture capital. *The Review of Financial Studies* 13(4): 959–984.

Hellmann T. and Puri M. (2002). Venture capital and the professionalization of start-ups: empirical evidence. *Journal of Finance* 57(2), 169–197.

Hirukawa M. and Ueda M. (2003). *Venture Capital and Productivity*. University of Wisconsin, Mimeo.

Jain B.A. and Kini O. (1995). Venture capitalist participation and the post-issue operating performance of IPO firms. *Managerial and Decision Economics* 6, 593–606.

Jensen M.C. and Meckling W.H. (1976). Theory of the firm: managerial behaviour. agency costs and ownership structure. *Journal of Financial Economics* 3(4), 305–360.

Kaplan S.N. and Strömberg P. (2004). Characteristics, Contracts, and Actions: Evidence from Venture Capitalist Analyses. *Journal of Finance* 59(5), 2177–2210.

Klein B. and Leffler K. (1981). The role of market forces in assuring contractual performance. *Journal of Political Economy* 89, 615–641.

Kortum S. and Lerner J. (1998). Does venture capital spur innovation?. NBER working paper no. 6846.

Kortum S. and Lerner J. (2000). Assessing the contribution of venture capital to innovation. *RAND Journal of Economics* 31(4), 674–692.

Lerner J. (1999). The government as venture capitalist. *Journal of Business* 72, 285–318.

Manigart S., Baeyens K. and Van Hyfte W.V. (2002). The survival of venture capital backed companies. *Venture Capital* 4(2), 103–124.

Manigart S. and Van Hyfte W.V. (1999). Post-investment evolution of Belgian venture capital backed companies: An empirical study. Paper presented at the Babson Entrepreneurship Conference.

Myers S. (1977). Determinants of corporate borrowing. *Journal of Financial Economics* 5, 147–157.

Panetta F., Schivardi F. and Shum M. (2004). Do mergers improve information? Evidence from the loan market. Bank of Italy discussion paper no 521.

Rajan R.G. and Zingales L. (1995). What do we know about capital structure? Some evidence from international data. *Journal of Finance* 50, 1421–1460.

Sapienza H.J. (1992). When do venture capitalists add value?. *Journal of Business Venturing* 7, 9–27.

Ueda M. (2004). Banks versus venture capital: project evaluation, screening and expropriation. *Journal of Finance* 59(2), 601–621.

Verheul, I., Wennekers A.R.M., Audretsch D.B. and Thurik A.R. (2002). An eclectic theory of entrepreneurship: policies institutions and culture, in *Entrepreneurship: Determinants and Policy in a European-US Comparison*, D.B. Audretsch, A.R. Thurik, I. Verheul and A.R.M. Wennekers (eds) (Kluwer Academic Publishers, Boston/Dordrecht), 11–81.

Williamson O. (1988). Corporate finance and corporate governance. *Journal of Finance* 43, 567–591.

11

Transparency of Price Conditions in Consumer Credit: The Usage of the APR

Massimo Caratelli

11.1 Introduction

Several studies have addressed the issue of consumer credit. Its influence on banks' profits, factors that inspired borrowing decisions, and over-borrowing have been investigated. More recently, studies have dealt with the theme of transparency of price conditions. There are two main reasons why more attention is being paid to this topic: first, the weakening of the oligopolistic structure of the credit market, which has induced credit providers to avail themselves of new competitive levers; secondly, the renewed guidelines on supervision, which are now more focused on promoting individual comparative skills and preventing information overload.

The present work examines processes of obtaining consumer credit, with the intention of adding to studies on transparency. The role of annual percentage rate (APR) in installment plan selection was investigated. The choice of APR was motivated by its wide diffusion due to mandatory disclosure acts. There have been doubts about consumer understanding of APR (Lee and Hogarth, 1999).

The paper proceeds as follow: section 11.2 considers the existing literature. Section 11.3 considers the economic convenience of lending, and section 11.4 presents an empirical analysis. In section 11.5 results are discussed. Finally, section 11.6 summarizes findings and proposes improvements of the study.

11.2 Applications to the credit market

Investigations addressing transparency of loan conditions have essentially followed two main lines of research: examining the structure of the credit market, and exploring the processes of taking consumer credit. The first stream deals with the relationship between asymmetries and competition. These studies focus on supervisory actions intended to prevent firms adopting practices which penalize consumers.

The second stream focuses on factors that affect borrowing decisions and the comparison of loan alternatives (Masini, 1979; Cox and Jappelli, 1993). With regard to the comparison between alternatives, much has been written about the purchasing of durable goods. For details, see Beatty and Smith (1987). Unfortunately, the field of financial services has not been explored to any great extent. Consumer credit has received even less attention. The most elaborate investigations have dealt with mortgages. The analyses suggest that loan choice represents the final act of a complex process, usually consisting of five phases. The first phase corresponds to the perception of the need to borrow: possibly to meet a new expense, or a real-estate investment not covered by current endowments. In the second phase, consumers search for information about credit alternatives. In particular, lenders and installment plans are identified. In the next two phases the data collected is compared and the alternatives rated (Caratelli, 2008).

The literature is unanimous in the assertion that consumers (more or less consciously) use a repertoire of decision strategies in order to formulate judgements and compare the options available. Various authors have addressed this issue, including Bettman et al. (1998) and March (1994), who have made important contributions in this area. Nevertheless, the repertoires followed by borrowers to select an installment plan have been left unexplored. Decision strategies can be divided into two main categories: compensatory and non-compensatory. The compensatory strategies are so-called because, through their use, consumers favourably judge options that have a particularly valued attribute, compensating for lower assessments assigned to other characteristics. By contrast, non-compensatory strategies do not provide such a trade-off between the levels of attractiveness of different attributes.

The scant evidence on installment plan selection suggests a bias by householders towards non-compensatory strategies, which are more simple to apply (Devlin, 2002). This preference is explained by consumers' difficulties in comparing the characteristics of different loan proposals. Usually the proposals from two, or at most three, intermediaries are examined. Those who are more proactive in their research include younger buyers and graduates (FSA, 2001). The borrowing costs are the feature most often indicated by credit applicants as definitive when selecting an option. In particular, the APR is the factor most cited by borrowers. The choice of APR should be motivated by its wide diffusion due to the mandatory disclosure acts. Under many legislative regimes, lenders are required to quote the APR. This legislation was first introduced by the United States Congress in 1968 to provide consumers with a standardized measure of loan prices. It was intended to make comparisons easier. APR was adopted by the United Kingdom in 1974, and by Italy in 1992. While the formula used is very similar, the APR value can vary from country to country due to different charges included in the computation. For more details, see Finlay (2009).

11.3 Assessment of economic convenience of loans

The term 'financial proposal' refers to a series of receipts and expenses, described as an 'investment' if negative cash-flows exceeds earnings, or 'financing' if positive cash-flows exceed expenses. A proposal is said to be 'simple' if the time series presents only one expense followed by earnings. A personal loan is a simple financial proposal. Proposals are normally subject to assessment in terms of economic convenience, sustainability, and financial flexibility. By economic convenience, one refers to a condition of balance between resources which are absorbed by the project and resources which are generated by the project. 'Sustainability' means compatibility between expenses and receipts, as determined by the decision-maker. 'Flexibility' refers to the risk that the project may not make a profit to to return the funds invested. The present analysis concentrates on the economic convenience of the personal loan. The notions of sustainability and financial flexibility – mentioned above – will be explored more deeply in future studies of this topic.

Studies of corporate finance have applied economic convenience to financial proposals (in the context of firms). Over the course of recent years, such studies have produced indicators for measuring the intensity of the relationship between 'absorbed' and 'generated' resources. The net present value (NPV) and the internal rate of return (IRR) are the measures that have gained most consensus; both are derived from discounted cash-flow techniques. The NPV is the sum of the present cash-flows of a project. The IRR is the (unique) discount rate that sets the NPV at zero.

Household finance has taken in these corporate finance indicators, applying them to consumer choices, most commonly to refinancing decisions, evaluations of lease contracts, and comparisons between fixed and adjustable-rate mortgages. The NPV allows the consumer to evaluate financing choices: if a negative value indicates an excess of absorbed resources, the loan under consideration must be rejected. Such a calculation enables discrimination between credit alternatives, giving preference to those that present greater NPV. The limit of NPV is set by the return on capital it offers, and this determines its value. The return on capital is the reward attained by households having a profile similar to the decision-maker; the return corresponds to the rate at which the borrower is able to generate a repayment cash-flow by working and investing. The average APR applied by credit providers should approximate to the borrower's repayment cash-flow. A far-sighted lender (it has to be in their interest, not the client's) charges an APR that is not greater than the capacity of the applicant to produce a cash-flow to meet the additional cost; this enables the borrower to avoid difficulties with repayment. Approximating return on capital with the average APR avoids errors of financial misjudgement by the borrower when choosing between credit proposals. The APR neutralizes the influence of commercial policies, but the NPVI also has informational worth: its positive value denotes that resources are invested at a rate less than the return on capital and greater than the funding cost. The literature uses the term 'opportunity cost of capital' to indicate this discount rate, and it corresponds to the 'standard' cost of borrowing that one gives up when opting for a credit alternative.

In this study we equate the discount rate with the average annual percentage charges calculated by the authorities who set the interest charge. This reflects a good balance between the lender's exact calculation of the cost of lending, and the desire of the borrower to disregarding calculations too complex for practical use, which demand financial information typically unavailable to them. The Bank of Italy calculates average interest rates, which it calls 'TEGM' (Tasso Medio Effettivo Globale). These rates correspond to an average of all the interest charges in the financial market, including a range of similar financial products and types of provider. The TEGM rate is weighted according to information about the number of transactions carried out by lenders. Consequently, TEGM is the optimum rate charged to a loan applicant. By law, this information must be provided to all households by means of leaflets.

The second indicator proposed by corporate finance is the IRR. It is integral to the lending process, and therefore objectively defined. If the opportunity cost is expressed as a compound annual rate, the IRR equals the loan APR. Not all loan proposals include an IRR, though Norstrøm's theorem (1972) asserts that it must be part of all simple finance agreements. Interesting links exist between NPV, APR, and the opportunity cost of capital, as the formulas below demonstrate.

$$\text{Amount borrowed} = \sum_{k=1}^{N} Mo \times (1 + APR)^{-k}$$

$$\text{NPV} = \text{Amount borrowed} - \sum_{k=1}^{N} Mo \times (1 + Op)^{-k}$$

Mo = Monthly installment

Op = Opportunity cost

The links show that selecting the loan with the highest NPV depends on opting for the lowest APR, which is less than the opportunity cost of capital. The links also reveal that an extension of the repayment period may be more important, for ease of repayment, than a competitive interest rate. A lower APR may identify the loan proposal with the highest NPV. There should be a balance between the amount borrowed and the repayment period. The second precept is based on the positive effects of extending the repayment term on the NPV curve. Competitive financing requires an interest rate which is less than the market rate (as determined by the opportunity cost of capital). The benefits are clear when the yield curve is flat. Though not infallible, this assumption is correct enough to be relevant to the present analysis. Indeed, it gives borrowers some forecasting skill when making credit choices.

11.4 Empirical analysis

With the aim of clarifying installment plan selections, a sample of 299 consumers were recruited by word of mouth in late 2009: 148 were students of a faculty of economics (graduate and undergraduate); 151 were individuals with various profiles, consisting of office workers (some employed by credit providers), self-employed professionals, and pensioners. Descriptive statistics are presented in Tables 11.1 and 11.2.

After a brief introduction to the aims of the study, the consumers were informed about interview procedure. Then they were provided with five series of loan alternatives. For each series, respondents were asked to express their preferences regarding the credit options proposed. Alternatives were represented as rows of a matrix and described through a set of features (the columns of the matrix). Features included amount financed, lifetime of repayment agreement, and four dimensions of borrowing costs: interest rate, APR, monthly installment amount, and total repayment.

After having assigned a preference, respondents were asked to justify their choice by writing down their comments. They also had to

Table 11.1 Composition of the sample

Status	A	B	C	Total
Students	47	52	49	148
Graduate	20	24	22	66
Undergraduate	27	28	27	82
Non-students	50	50	51	151
Office workers	32	30	21	83
Self-employed professionals	12	10	6	28
Managers	0	2	2	4
University lecturers	1	6	13	20
Pensioners	1	0	2	3
Other	4	2	7	13
Total	97	102	100	299

Table 11.2 Profile of participants

	Identity (%)			
Characteristic	**Students (148 respondents)**		**Non-students (151 respondents)**	
Age	Less than 25	87.16	Between 25 and 30	39.73
Gender	Male	56.16	Male	52.35
Marital status	Single	99.32	Single	48.65
Region	Latium	86.39	Latium	67.33
Educational attainment	Low	0.68	Low	0.00
	Medium	54.73	Medium	30.46
	High	44.59	High	69.54
Financial maturity	Quotient	0.1824	Quotient	0.2904
Debit card	Availability	67.57	Availability	96.69
Credit card	Availability	25.00	Availability	68.87

describe the difficulties they had experienced in making their selection. To grade the effort needed, participants were given an Osgood Scale question range from 1 (easy task) to 5 (arduous task). They were asked to report their demographic data, education attainment, and financial experience. Respondents were classified as 'low', 'medium', or 'high' according to their highest level of educational attainment, with 'low' representing no formal qualifications, and 'high' attainment of a first degree or higher. Financial maturity was determined according to the measurement introduced by Devlin (2002). The list of financial services was composed of eight instruments: current account, savings account, financing, administration of securities, investments, financial management, accident cover, and insurance company savings scheme.

To facilitate consistency of choice, some information about shared attributes was common to all questionnaires, but data about interest rates, APR, total costs (TCs), and average annual percentage charges was supplied randomly. Participants were classified into three groups according to information supplied to them. Interest rate and APR information was given to groups B and C, whereas TCs and average charges were given only to group B. Group A was provided with the most limited information.

11.5 Results

Results are discussed according to the sequence in which the five questions appeared in questionnaires. The students' responses are investigated first, then their preferences are contrasted with those of the rest of the sample. The intention was to identify differences in behaviours adopted by older individuals with greater levels of education and financial maturity (see Table 11.2).

Question one

Non-bank intermediary	Amount borrowed	Term	Monthly installment	Total cost	CIR	APR	NPV
α	10,000	12	901.40	10,816.85	14.75	15.79	–264.34
β	10,000	12	888.61	10,663.30	12.03	12.71	–119.78

Students did not experience any particular difficulties in expressing their preferences. The two alternatives offered equal amounts and durations. Students were put at ease during the delicate initial phase of the interview. They consistently indicated a mean difficulty level of 2 for the task, on a graduated scale of 1 (ease of effort) to 5 (arduous effort).

The students seemed willing to adopt the first comparison criterion mentioned above: indeed, 121 individuals (nearly 82%) of the 148 students who composed the sample indicated credit option β as their choice. Comments noted by participants on forms supplied information about students' familiarity with the first criterion. Citing the installment amount as the only reason for the selection calls into question the correct understanding of the concept. The frequency of some keywords in comments was investigated. The keywords – included in the appendix – were terms cited frequently in the questionnaires, and their occurrence was analyzed (cf. Carretta et al., 2009). A total of 101 students (68%) knew the APR value. They used 194 terms to explain their choice. A total of 48 students (46%) attributed their decision to interest rate and APR; of them, 31 cited the installment amount or TC of the loan to explain their preference. Finally, there were indications of the use of APR to support selection. However, this choice was not made confidently, as shown by the combination of APR with other measures of borrowing costs.

Selection might have been affected by data about the average annual percentage charges applied by credit providers. The Bank of Italy indicated two rates for non-bank intermediaries in the period of the investigation: 10.20 % for loans above 6000 euros, and 14 % for smaller amounts. In light of such information, the two credit alternatives should have been discarded. Of the 49 students who had access to the average data, only 7 (14 %) selected alternatives that were not economically convenient. This low number suggests a low awareness of market interest rates, or the inability to extract the opportunity cost from the average charges.

Question two

Non-bank intermediary	Amount borrowed	Term	Monthly installment	Total cost	CIR	APR	NPV
α	5000	12	445.95	5351.45	12.73	13.50	+11.53
α	5000	36	167.82	6041.56	12.73	13.50	+17.87
α	5000	60	113.08	6784.58	12.73	13.50	+19.12
β	5000	12	444.30	5331.62	12.02	12.71	+29.81
β	5000	36	166.32	5987.63	12.11	12.80	+42.95
β	5000	60	112.62	6757.33	12.55	13.30	+26.77
γ	5000	12	450.70	5408.44	14.75	15.79	−41.02
γ	5000	36	172.12	6217.81	14.75	15.79	−63.62
γ	5000	60	118.30	7097.79	14.75	15.79	−68.04

The second question examined familiarity with comparison criteria adopted in making complex decisions. Participants had to contrast a significant number of repayment plans. The students' effort showed a mean difficulty score of 2.7. A total of 116 students (78%) appropriately compared the lifetime of the repayment agreements and rejected the alternatives offered by non-bank intermediaries α and γ. This behaviour is consistent with the adoption of the first comparison criterion. The assessment then considered the 'survivors' loans: 73 students (63%) selected the option with the short duration; 27 chose credit repayments over 36 months; whereas 16 respondents opted for the long-term repayment period. This distribution of frequencies demands further investigation, which may be provided by analyzing questions three and four.

Question three

Non-bank intermediary	Amount borrowed	Term	Monthly installment	Total cost	CIR	APR	NPV
δ	3500	6	600.82	3604.95	10.21	10.70	+29.30
δ	3500	18	210.54	3788.65	10.21	10.70	+43.05
δ	3500	42	99.46	4177.14	10.21	10.70	+46.97

Some difficulty in evaluation of alternatives with the same APR was evident. Indeed, the mean level of difficulty assigned by students to the task was 2.2. If the second comparison criterion had been applied, participants would have opted for the long-term loan. Instead, just 26 students (18%) selected credit repayments over 42 months. A total of 48 respondents (32%) preferred the short-term alternative of repayments over 6 months; while 47 chose the intermediate solution. A total of 17 students (11%) identified the three options as equally attractive. This last finding indicates the weight some consumers attribute to APR values in their choices.

The analysis of keywords showed that the second comparison criterion was disregarded. Students who opted for the long-term loan were motivated in their choice by an interest in affordable installments. Only a single explicit reference to average rates was reported. No reference was made to the relative competitiveness of loans.

Trade-offs between interest rates and loan durations were included in this question: the first two alternatives presented almost equivalent APR but different lifetimes, whereas the third solution showed higher

Question four

Non-bank intermediary	Amount borrowed	Term	Monthly installment	Total cost	CIR	APR	NPV
ε	3500	6	603.33	3,619.95	11.66	12.30	+15.01
ε	3500	18	213.32	3,839.70	11.93	12.60	+18.15
ε	3500	42	103.71	4,355.67	12.73	13.50	+7.05

APR and loan duration. A total of 111 students (75%) selected either 6 or 18 months. Students were apparently guided by the desire to extinguish the debt quickly, the low interest rate, and the intermediate amount of the installments. Written comments confirmed this analysis.

As for the third question, no interest was demonstrated in the competitiveness of loans, or in extending the repayment period. Indications of an overlap between economic convenience and financial sustainability are, by now, unequivocal. However, the question posed to participants was quite clear: "Which of these loans do you consider to be the cheapest?"

Question five

Non-bank intermediary	Amount borrowed	Term	Monthly installment	Total cost	CIR	APR	NPV
κ	3500	12	309.21	3710.58	10.93	11.49	+40.74
κ	3500	36	109.39	3938.12	7.82	8.11	+149.25

Question five represented an attempt to clarify the role in credit decision-making of two key aspects of borrowing costs. Respondents had to choose from a pair of options with conflicting total repayments and APR. The second comparison criterion advises consumers to prefer the 36-month loan, based on the lower APR and the prolonged repayment period. The combination of low interest rate and long duration appropriately influenced participants: 79 students (53%) opted for the solution with 36 repayments. The TC did not mislead respondents; rather, it seemed to have guided them in their comparison, supporting the impression that differences in APR affected the economic convenience of the loan. Keywords cited were consistent with the complementary function of TC information. The students used 195 words to explain their choices: of these, 130 (67%) identified interest rates, lifetimes, and TC of loans, often cited together.

By contrast, choices assigned by non-student participants were more polarized: 6 out of 10 chose the loan with the lowest APR, whereas 2 rejected alternatives due to conditions judged excessively onerous. These numbers are in part different from those revealed by the rest of the sample: 3 out of 10 students were only guided by interest rates; 3 opted for loans with short duration and low installments; almost no one rejected alternatives. For more details on distribution of preferences, see the graphs provided in the Appendix. Evidently, maturity manifests itself in terms of a more robust awareness of APR, and a clear focus on market conditions. A mean difficulty level of 1.7 attributed to the tasks by non-students supported this conclusion, contrasting with the value of 2.3 attributed by the remaining participants to their efforts.

Keywords confirmed the hypothesis of a greater confidence with APR of non-student consumers. They used 1315 words to explain their selections. Of the non-students, 480 (37%) identified interest rates, compared with 24% of students. The latter group, on the other hand, referred more often to the installment amount, indicating the attention they paid to financial sustainability – understandably, considering the students' low level of economic independence. Installment amounts were cited by students 313 times (24%) in their comments. By contrast, the percentage was 12 in the non-students' questionnaires. With regard to comparison strategies, the wide extent of the first criterion is evident, for both students and non-students, and by contrast the generally limited extent of the second criterion. It seems that the possibility of benefiting from the competitiveness of a loan by extending its repayment period was commonly disregarded. This lack of knowledge may guide consumers to search for the lowest APR without comparing lifetimes of repayment agreements. The result may be a failure to choose installment plans with high NPVs.

11.6 Conclusion

The role of APR in installment plan selection was investigated. A sample of 299 consumers were given five series of credit alternatives. Participants presented different profiles. The descriptions of the loans included amount borrowed, duration, monthly installment, APR, total of payments, and opportunity cost of capital. Consumers were asked to select a credit option for each series, specifying the reasons for their choice. The ability to select the loan with the highest NPV was ascertained. It depends on the awareness of (i) opting for the lowest APR, which is also less than the opportunity cost of capital; and (ii) requesting an extension of the repayment period to improve the convenience of the identified competitive rate.

The analysis attested consumer failure to single out loans with high NPV. The reason may be a significant lack of information about the usage of APR: participants often selected the lowest rate but neglected to consider the opportunity cost of capital and the possible extension of the repayment period. Furthermore, they sometimes chose a loan with contrasting duration and monthly borrowing costs. The analysis of keywords supported this finding. APR usage may therefore be inappropriate since this figure is seen as a substitute for the monthly installment payment. An overlap between economic convenience and financial sustainability could explain this phenomenon. To improve disclosure, additional (or different) borrowing cost measures should be included in credit advertisements.

Finally, an assessment of costs of lack of knowledge was undertaken. The sample was able to take advantage of the cheapest charges contained in the questionnaires. However, if consumers had have been more watchful and better qualified, they could have earned much more.

A more detailed interpretation of consumer behaviours would require: a more complete and representative sample of participants; analysis of the processes of extracting the opportunity cost from the average data; and an analysis of aversion to borrowing and to financial sustainability. These topics could be examined in future studies.

References

Beatty S.E. and Smith S.M. (1987). External Search Effort: An Investigation Across Several Product Categories. *Journal of Consumer Research* 14(1), 83–95.

Bettman J.R., Luce M.F. and Payne J.W. (1998). Constructive consumer choice processes. *Journal of Consumer Research* 25(3), 187–217.

Caratelli M. (2008). Transparency between banks and their customers. In Carretta A. and Mattarocci G. (eds), *New Drivers of Performance in a Changing World*. Basingstoke, UK: Palgrave Macmillan.

Carretta A., Schwizer P. and Farina V. (2010). The 'day after' basel 2: Do regulators comply with banking culture?. *Journal of Financial Regulation and Compliance* (forthcoming).

Cox D. and Jappelli T. (1993). The effect of borrowing constraints on consumer liabilities. *Journal of Money, Credit and Banking* 25(2), 197–213.

Devlin J.F. (2002). An analysis of choice criteria in the home loans market. *International Journal of Bank Marketing* 20(5), 212–226.

Finlay S. (2009). *Consumer Credit Fundamentals*. Basingstoke, UK: Palgrave Macmillan.

FSA (2001). Choosing a Mortgage. Report of a Research Review and Qualitative Research on the Mortgage-buying Process. London, UK.

Lee J. and Hogarth J.M. (1999). The price of money: consumers' understanding of APRs and contract interest rates. *Journal of Public Policy and Marketing* 18(1), 66–76.

March J.G. (1994). *A Primer on Decision-making. How Decisions Happen*. New York, NY: The Free Press.

Masini M. (1979). *Le politiche di raccolta delle banche di deposito.* Milan: Giuffrè Editrice.

Norstrøm C.J. (1972). Sufficient conditions for unique non-negative international rate of return. *Journal of Financial and Quantitative Analysis* 7(3), 1835–1839.

Part III

Capital Markets and Risk Management

12
Asset Management and Industry Portfolio Indices: Momentum and Reversal Returns

Mario Toscano and Giuseppe Torluccio

12.1 Introduction

Identifying a robust methodology that enables periodic screening of the financial market is of one of the most covered areas of research in recent decades. Since the earliest works that defined financial markets as efficient markets (the efficient market hypothesis, or EMH Fama, 1970), efforts have been made to prove that such notions are merely utopian. Specifically, rather than destroying the foundations of the EMH, numerous studies have attempted to capture and anticipate future fluctuations of stock prices to model a portfolio that would allow investors to increase their profits and returns.

Most empirical studies have focused mainly on stocks, and only recently have a small number been dedicated to stock indices, proving the concrete existence of profitability anomalies. Some of the research has verified the existence of historically abnormal returns, also known as *momentum* and *reversal* in industry portfolio returns, both before and after the Financial Services and Markets Act 2000 was approved.

Specifically, building a portfolio of stocks is a strategy called *momentum,* if it consists of a sub-portfolio of shares that in a specific period (the 'building period') result in better performance (a 'winner'). It has been statistically verified several times that, regardless of the marketplace where the quoted company or the market represented by indicators operates, stocks or indicators that in the previous 3, 6 or 12 months performed better than other shares (the winner) usually continue to perform better in the subsequent 12 months compared to worse performers ('losers'). By contrast, a *reversal* strategy is a sub-portfolio built of stocks that have demonstrated bad performance (a 'loser') during the building period. However, it has been statistically verified that even in this case loser stocks (in the previous 3, 6 or 12 months) over the long-term (no less than 6–12 months) perform better than stocks previous defined as *winners*.

12.2 Literature review

Jegadeesh and Titman (1993, 2002) are universally known as the authors of the *momentum pattern*. Their empirical study of NYSE quoted stocks over the period July 1962 to December 1989 shows that strategies that foresee the purchase of *winners* through self-funding by selling *losers* produce significant returns in the subsequent 3–12 months. According to the authors, these results relate to the delayed reaction of stock prices and the under-revaluation of positive information (under-reaction) of determined stocks (winners). Hong et al. (1990) show that, particularly in the case of stocks with past losing performance, the phenomenon can be attributed more tangibly to the under-reaction hypothesis.

The findings of De Bondt and Thaler (1985) are contradictory: studying the performance of *losers,* they reached the conclusion that '*the earnings of winning and losing firms show reversal patterns that are consistent with over-reaction*'. Finally, in an analysis of the profitability of the S&P 500 stocks from 1970 to 2004, Figelman (2007) supports the idea that the *reversal pattern* is a phenomenon that is not only confirmed in the long-term period, but also present in the short-term (quarterly), whereas *momentum* emerges only in medium-term periods. The studies carried out by Chan et al. (1996) are in many ways similar to the study of De Bondt and Thaler (1987). From an analysis of the profitability of stocks quoted on the NYSE, AMEX and NASDAQ from July 1963 to December 1994, Asness (1997) confirms that the momentum strategy generally performs well when the investor invests in growth stocks; on the other hand, when stock choice is value-oriented it is generally losers that perform well. The same findings were previously identified by Lakonishok et al. (1994) who grouped stocks into value and growth type. Chopra et al. (1992), Aarts and Lehnert (2005) identify the existence of a significant economic over-reaction effect, even when the portfolios are based on several ratios and/or betas of specific stocks.

Mengoli (2004), in his analysis of stocks quoted on the Italian stock market covering the period between 1955 and 1995, confirms the existence of both *momentum* and *reversal patterns*. However, he reaches contradictory conclusions in correlating the effects with various risk measures. Given that the betas of winner and loser portfolios are equivalent, it would be impossible to examine any effects when considering that with the construction of a beta zero portfolio (sell loser and buy winner, or *vice versa*, with the same beta) we would expect zero performance. Griffin et al. (2004) studied the indicators of 40 countries and found that macro factors cannot explain the earnings of momentum portfolios, and that the performances of various markets are weakly correlated. In a further verification, Griffin et al. (2004) performed on the same sample, the authors correlate the performance of winner and loser portfolios with past returns. They concluded that the momentum strategy is distinguished from market trends and economic cycles. In the same arena Cooper et al. (2003) question whether momentum and reversal patterns should be seen as the results of bull and bear market trends. When testing includes assets that are different from stocks, results are not significantly different from previous studies such as Chan et al. (2005),[1] who investigate the weekly profit-making opportunity of the momentum pattern on various national indicators, and Bianchi et al. (2004), who observed the existence of the momentum pattern while analyzing the forex market performances of G7 currencies from 1980 to 2004. Finally, the existence of momentum and reversal patterns has been proven in more than one case and on various assets.

In this study, we question whether these studies were useful to investors to ensure increase profits over a number of years. Grinblatt et al. (1995), Griffin et al. (2002a) and Hwang and Rubesam (2007) have provided answers to this question.

The former, who studied mutual fund strategies, concluded that 77% of invested funds are from 'momentum investors', or those who buy stocks previously rated as winners. However, they do not sell losers on a regular basis. At the same time, funds that applied the subsequent strategies resulted in better performance when compared to others.

In the analysis of the NASDAQ 100 stock market, GHT indirectly confirm the above, concluding that winners are bought by institutional investors and are sold by retail in 65.2% of cases against 41.3% of the worst performing stocks. Finally, regardless of the fact that more than 15 years have passed since the first studies, in the analysis of stocks quoted on NYSE, AMEX and NASDAQ from June 1926 to December 2005, HR question whether the momentum pattern results in a profit increase. In this regard, the authors notice two break periods: by the end of 2000, they claim, following the second period, the momentum effect disappeared. This shows that, after being put into practice by investors, the anomalies under examination ceased to produce extra profits. Nevertheless, the question remains as to why this anomaly has lasted for so long following its detection. Perhaps, according to the authors, the answer is in the stock exchange boom in the 90s, in particular the technological and intermediaries boom that persisted during those years and is unlikely to repeat itself in the future.

12.3 Hypothesis tested, sample and methodology

The novelty of this research, which should lead us towards behavioural finance, is in the study of the profitability of industry indicators or in proving the existence of their anomalies. Specifically, this research is aimed at testing the existence of momentum and reversal patterns in the profitability of industry indicators or whether an investor who, based on historical industry performance, would buy previous winners by means of self-funding through selling losers or by building a portfolio at zero cost, managed in a medium-term period to achieve positive performance (momentum patterns) from a statistical perspective.

At the same time, we evaluate the reversal hypothesis, in other words try to establish whether an investor who, based on the assets' historical performance, would buy losers or, in a better scenario, invest the latter by self-funding by selling winners (zero-cost portfolio), would achieve positive performance (reversal patterns) from a statistical perspective. In testing the existence of both momentum and reversal patterns, we undertake an analysis of whether the former are restricted in the short and medium-term and the latter in the long-term. Thus, we shall try to indirectly evaluate Figelman's (2007) findings on the presence of a reversal pattern in the short-term.

Further, as shown by Werner et al. (1987), Chan et al. (1996), we elaborate on whether momentum and reversal patterns in different markets are related to a stationary beta in various market trends (bull and bear), or whether they may have been caused by immediate and unexpected portfolio beta changes.

The last analysis examines Hwang and Rubesam's (2007) thesis. In this case, the focus of the analysis is exclusively on zero-cost portfolios, considering the mean and median returns. The reduced number of observed cases in the 2000–2007 period could affect the final outcome. In order to test the robustness of the results we employ 'bootstrapping' sampling technique, with and without replacement (Bühlmann, 2002), with the latter to be further subjected to the permutation test.

The first and the last daily returns are on 31 December 1991 and 30 April 2007, respectively.

12.4 Momentum and reversal patterns: models and empirical testing

12.4.1 Models

In order to determine the winner and loser stocks, the following process was implemented:

1. For each '*i*' industry (where $i = 1, 2, \ldots, 18$) the cumulative return (R) during the building period ($t - n$; t where $n = 1, 3, 6, 12$ months) is determined.

   According to the aforementioned studies and after establishing the past performances of various industries, the series of returns are distributed into quartiles: that comprising the best-performance industries (winners) is identified as Π1, whereas that with the worst performance (losers) is identified as Π4. Intermediate quartiles are identified as Π2 and Π3. A fifth portfolio, Π5, or the zero-cost portfolio, is a result of the difference between Π1 and Π4. In other words, to test the existence of momentum patterns, we assume the purchase of Π1 through the sale of Π4 and *vice versa* for the reversal pattern. Under these circumstances, for the figure to be invested in the winner (loser) industries to be equivalent to that obtained by the sale of losers (winners), the sum of weights to be attributed to each portfolio, Π1 and Π4, should be equal to 1.
2. For each industry and, subsequently, for each Π the average return applicable for the retention period (t; $t + y$ with $y = 1, 3, 6,12, 18, 24, 30, 36$) is calculated.
3. The above steps are applicable to any available observations, so that for each n and y, a historical series of returns is taken as a sample, one for each Π. The distribution or average, median and statistical meaning of the t-test are determined for each industry individually.
4. In order to prove which of the two weight factors is more efficient, for each n and y, we calculate a new vector as the difference between differently weighted average returns. For each separate vector we determine the average of differences and statistical meaning of the t-test to prove whether the pre-selected weight factor significantly affects the returns of various portfolios (alternative hypothesis) or whether the use of one or other method is irrelevant to performance determination (null hypothesis).

12.4.2 Empirical analysis

The research results also confirm other industry indicators, tested by other researchers on other assets. In reality, the analysis of the five portfolios could lead to the conclusion that for industries also the momentum pattern can be extended to the short- and medium-term and *vice versa*, while the reversal pattern covers the long term. These outcomes do not confirm the existence of a short-term reversal for the industry indicators, as applying to Figelman's (2007) quoted stocks over S&P 500. More specifically, regardless of the building and retention period, the average returns of Π1, Π2, Π3 and Π4 are always positive. However, with the prolongation of building and retention periods, average returns of Π1 are subject to decline, whereas those of Π4 tend to grow. Focusing on the zero-cost portfolio (Π5 = Π1 – Π4), the existence of the momentum and reversal patterns, respectively restricted to a short and long-term period, is rather more evident. Nevertheless, as shown in Figure 12.1 below, the intensity of such phenomena depends on the building and/or retention period.

For short building periods (1–3 months), regardless of the retention period, the momentum pattern is always prevalent on the reversal pattern. In fact, significant average returns can be obtained, particularly in retention periods of 3–6 months. In this case, Π1, which substantially over performs Π4 after 6 months, the intensity increases, reaching a peak that corresponds to t + 12 (2.98% higher than the loser). When the building period exceeds 6 months, the momentum loses intensity in very short retention periods. Reversal patterns are inclined to prevail

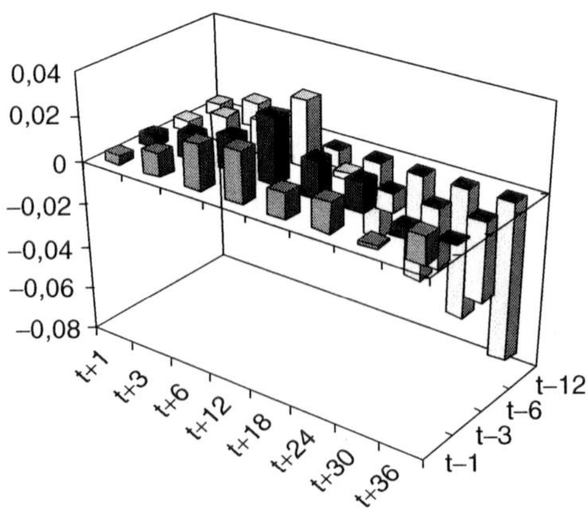

Figure 12.1 Monthly average cumulative returns for the Π5 portfolio, in different building and retention periods, for the sample covering January 1993 to April 2007. The weight (λ) that is attributed to the returns is correlated with the price of '*i*' of the industry in '*t*' or at the beginning of each retention period.

during the medium-term period (12 months) over different building periods. In this context, the reversal pattern is truly inclined to provide important statistical results after 18 months (7.25% more compared to winners), by increasing the intensity and the duration of the retention period, reaching a maximum of 36 months. Finally, we argue that both the momentum and the reversal pattern depend on the building and retention period, which is short-term in the first case and long-term in the second.

We performed the median returns test in order to verify that these results are not driven by outliers. Even in this case we can affirm that the momentum and reversal patterns are related to short-to-medium and long-term retention periods. However, at the median returns, the reversal pattern loses intensity, whereas it increases in momentum.

Finally, if we were to build an investment portfolio that maximally increases returns, which we recall varies according to the investment horizon, the following approaches should be adopted from a strategic perspective:

Momentum	**Reversal**
Portfolios created in short-term building periods	Portfolios created in long-term building periods
Portfolios built on the basis of median returns	Portfolios built on the basis of median returns
Portfolio-building with a view of short-to-medium term view	Portfolio-building with a long-term view
Industry weighted without distinction, based on prices and/or past returns	Industry weighted only based on prices

12.5 Betas of winner and loser portfolios and upward and downward market trends[2]: results

Analyses of the various up and down market beta trends are performed only on Π1, Π4 and Π5. However, before performing this analysis to identify their significance and for information purposes, the beta of each portfolio is determined in relation to various building and retention periods. Betas are calculated by reducing the cumulative extra-median returns (net risk free rates) of the portfolios in different retention periods against the cumulative market extra-return for the same period of time.

The analysis of betas in different market trends (up/down) shows that in the market up-trend (+), the beta of Π1 is generally inclined to be higher than that of Π4. However, given that the former is reduced with the extension of the retention period and the latter decreases at the beginning and then increases, the difference between the two betas is inclined to disappear. On the basis of this results and mainly in the short-term retention period, it would be relevant to assume that a bull market Π1 should outperform a Π4, which would actually confirm the momentum pattern, by outperforming the market itself when $\beta > 1$. During market reverse down trends (–), the Π4 beta is inclined to be generally higher than that of Π1. Considering that with the extension of the retention period the Π4 beta increases at the beginning to subsequently reduce, the difference between the two betas is consequently inclined to reduce to zero, and, in the most extreme case, to be exchanged for long-term retention periods. These results confirm that these two patterns exist. In fact, when the building and retention periods are short-term and Π4 beta is higher than Π1, the former experiences greater losses than the latter in a down market (momentum pattern). On the other hand, for long-term building and retention periods or when the Π4 beta is lower than that of Π1, the former loses less than the latter in a down market (reversal pattern). Summarizing the above, given that the momentum and reversal patterns are phenomena related to the short-to-medium term and long-term respectively, and given that we have just seen that the beta of Π1 and Π4 have varying dynamics based on the building and/or retention periods, as well as due to the up/down market trends, it is thus not to be excluded that the above phenomena take place due to market trends and portfolio betas.

12.6 Structural breaks: results

In order to test whether there is a breakpoint for industry indicators by the end of 2000, as identified by Hwang and Rubesam (2007), the study tested the existence of momentum and reversal patterns on a subsample of what was previously available.[3] The returns of both samples are different when there is a breakpoint in nodes, the marks of average returns and/or of portfolio Π5. The 1993 sample was re-collected more than once when analysing the average returns for long-term building and retention periods or when the reversal pattern is applicable and when excluding a few sample exceptions from 2000. On the other hand, for short-term building and retention periods or when momentum patterns emerged from 1993, they almost always over perform compared with 2000. However, there are three exceptions where the average of the two samples is the same. These three exceptions obviously support the theory according to which a breakpoint was marked in 2000. The conclusion is that breakpoints exist only and exclusively for momentum patterns (the return turning from positive to negative with the sample change).

The analysis includes data of the unique sample starting from 2000, but the size of the sample is rather reduced and thus potentially abnormal returns may affect the calculation of the median and, therefore, in determining the breakpoints. In order to avoid these problems the test was implemented by using the median and not the mean returns. Conversely, in this case, from the analysis of the median returns we obtain five breakpoints and not three. Thus, when the test focuses on the medians, the breakpoints exist both in momentum (returns change from positive to negative with the sample change), as well as in reversal patterns (from negative to positive with the sample change).

In order to validate the test performed up to this point, we tried to prove that breakpoints are not simply random or a result of the time structure of returns. We therefore proceeded with a double test based on bootstrapping techniques. In the first test, the first sample and sub-sample were collected with replacement, 500 times each. The mean of the differences by bootstrapping is similar to that observed originally, adding validity to the breakpoints identified by the means. In the second test (the permutation test), both samples are re-collected without replacement, 500 times each. The mean of the differences by bootstrapping is confirmed as valid only in the reversal breakpoints (from negative to positive).

In summary, when the breakpoints are determined based on the median return the sample shows three breakpoints and all require the application of the momentum pattern. On the other hand, when defined on the basis of the mean return, five breakpoints are present, three of which pertain to the momentum pattern and two to the reversal pattern. When bootstrapping is applied on the last nodes, the results differ depending on whether sample collection is with or without replacement. In the former case, all breakpoints are considered statistically meaningful, while in the latter case, the p-value test shows that only breakpoints subject to reversal patterns are significant.

12.7 Conclusions

A number of studies have found the existence of momentum and reversal patterns several times and in various markets. With few exceptions, most of these studies looked at the first pattern in the short-to-medium term and the second in the long-term. Even the results of this study on the performance of DJ Euro Stoxx industries confirm the absolute prevalence of the short-term momentum pattern and long-term reversal pattern. Quite similar results are achieved when the industries are weighted, for both price and profitability in the building and retention period. However, in this case, results are quite different (better) in the reversal pattern.

In essence, there is no change when the test is performed on median returns (instead of the mean) but the momentum gains intensity compared to losers. If wanting to make a strategic investment by following the indications of a momentum pattern, it would be advisable to build the winner portfolio on the basis of median returns. Otherwise, for a reversal pattern, losers are preferable on the basis of mean returns. The results, in correlating the momentum and reversal patterns with the up and down market trends, were rather surprising. In fact, the test results indicate that the zero-cost portfolio beta is positive in the up-market trends and negative in down trends, and the zero-cost strategy quite clearly performs excellently. These results were previously confirmed by Cooper et al. (2003) and Griffin et al. (2002b).

Proving these results is more difficult, given that from a certain point onwards both models cease to be efficient in increasing profits. Regarding the work of Hwang and Rubesam (2007), who identify two breakpoints, one of which corresponds to 2000, median returns of the sample studied previously with those of a sub-sample began to be observed from 2000. In all three cases where it is unclear whether it is a momentum pattern, three breakpoints were also identified (return switch from positive to negative with the changing of the sample). When the test was performed on mean returns, five breakpoints were found, three of which correspond with the momentum pattern and two with the reversal pattern. In order to add to the validity of the results on the median, a double test, based on the bootstrapping method, was performed.

The existence of momentum and reversal patterns remains a controversial issue despite having been long subjected to a multitude of studies.

Notes

1. The sample includes 23 countries, nine of which are from Asia, 11 from Europe, two from North America and one from Africa. Except for Austria,

Indonesia and South Africa, the sample covers a period between January 1980 and June 1995. All indicators are converted in US dollars.

2. Analysis of portfolio betas consist only of cumulative median returns calculated by means of the weight factor (λ).
3. The analysis refers only to II5 portfolio. The first valid data for these tests dates back to 31 December 2000.

References

Aarts F. and Lehnert T. (2005). On style momentum strategies. *Applied Economic Letters* 12(13), 795–799.

Asness C.S. (1997). The interaction of value and momentum strategies. *Financial Analysts Journal* 53(2), 29–36.

Bühlmann P. (2002). Boostraps for time series. *Statistical Science* 17, 52–72.

Bianchi R., Drew M.E. and Polichronics J. (2004). *A Test of Momentum Trading Strategies in Foreign Exchange Markets: Evidence from G7.* Queensland University of Technology, Discussion Paper no. 182, July 2004.

Chan K., Hameed A. and Tong W. (2005). Profitability of momentum strategies in the international equity markets. *Journal of Financial and Quantitative Analysis* 35(2), 153–172.

Chan L.K.C. and Jegadeesh L.J. (1996). Momentum strategies. *The Journal of Finance* 51(5), 1681–1713.

Chopra N., Lakonishok J. and Ritter J.R. (1992). Measuring abnormal performance: do stock overreact?. *The Journal of financial Economics* no. 31(2), 235–268.

Cooper JM, Gutierrez Jr RC and Hammed A. (2003). *Market States and Momentum.* Working Paper.

De Bondt W.F.M. and Thaler R. (1985). Does the stock market overreact?. *The Journal of Finance* 40(3), 793–809.

De Bondt W.F.M and Thaler R. (1987). Further evidence on Investor overreaction and stock market seasonality. *The Journal of Finance* 42(3), 557–582.

Fama E. (1970). Efficient capital market. *The Journal of Finance* 25, 383–417.

Figelman I. (2007). Stock return momentum and reversal. *The Journal of Portfolio Management* 34(1), 51–70.

Griffin J.M., Harris J. and Topaloglu S. (2002a). *The Dynamics of Institutional and Individual Trading.* Working Paper.

Griffin J.M., Ji S. and Martin J.S. (2002b). *Momentum Investing and Business Cycle Risk: Evidence from Pole to Pole.* Working Paper.

Griffin J.M., Ji S. and Martin J.S. (2004). *Global Momentum Strategies: A Portfolio Perspective.* Working Paper.

Grinblatt M., Titman S. and Wermers R. (1995). Momentum investment strategies, portfolio performance, and herding: a study of mutual fund behavior. *The American Economic Review* 35(5), 1088–1106.

Hong H., Lim T. and Stein J.C. (1990). Bad news travels slowly: size, analyst coverage and the profitability of momentum strategies. *The Journal of Finance.*

Hwang S. and Rubesam A. (2007). *The Disappearance of Momentum.* Cass Business School.

Jegadeesh N. and Titman S. (1993). Return to buying winner and selling losers: implication for stock market efficiency. *The Journal of Finance* 48(1), 68–92.

Jegadeesh N. and Titman S. (2002). Cross sectional and time-series: determinants of momentum returns. *The Review of Financial Studies* 15(1), 143–158.

Lakonishok J., Shleifer A. and Vishny R.W. (1994). Contrarian investment, extrapolation, and risk. *The Journal of Finance* 49(5), 1541–1579.

Mengoli S. (2004). On the source of contrarian and momentum strategies in the Italian equity market. *International Review of Financial Analysis* 13(3), 301–332.

13
Duration Analysis: An Overview

Göran Bergendahl and Ted Lindblom

13.1 Background

Duration analysis has long been used in banking, insurance and finance [see Bierwag et al. (1978) and Ingersoll et al. (1978) for historic overviews]. Macaulay (1938) was early to use it for quantifying the length of the payment stream of a bond, defining duration as the weighted average of the time to maturity. Hicks (1939) identified Macaulay's concept of duration as the bond's price elasticity. A bond is a fixed-income security whose *yield* is determined by the interest rate (r) at which the present value of the payment stream equals its price. This makes duration a very suitable measure to calculate the interest-rate sensitivity of a bond's market value. Following Luenberger (1997, pp. 57–62), suppose that its cash flows (coupons) are received at times $t = 1, 2, \ldots, T$. As duration (D) is the time-weighted average of the present values of these cash flows $\{PV(t)\}$, it is directly related to the volatility (V) of the bond value with respect to interest changes, that is:

$$D = \frac{\sum_{t=1}^{T} PV(t) \times t}{PV} = -\frac{\mathrm{d}PV}{PV} \times \frac{1+r}{\mathrm{d}r} = -V \times \frac{1+r}{\mathrm{d}r} \qquad (1)$$

A more general analysis of the concept of duration is found in Reitano (1991). This chapter will demonstrate how duration can be applied to various types of securities for measuring their interest-rate sensitivity, and also how duration analysis can be used for determining the optimal life time (and interest-rate sensitivity) of physical assets, like production units or production processes.

Duration analysis has a direct correspondence with *survival analysis* as used in statistics, or *reliability analysis* as used in engineering. Survival analysis, as well as reliability analysis, involves modelling time to *event data* where death or production failures are considered as events. When the focus is set on death events, the main concern is the fraction of a population that will survive past a certain time t. When failures are the focus, survival analysis is mainly used to identify the time of failure for a product or a process. In both cases, predictive models use historical patterns in order to identify and assess risks and opportunities. In so doing, they relate lifetime distribution to explanatory variables (covariates). An example is how medical treatment will affect the survival of patients after a certain time period (see e.g., Bagdonavicius and Nikulin, 2004). In general terms, a survival function may be formulated as $S(t) = p(t < T)$, that is the probability p that the time t of death or failure will occur after a specified time T. As demonstrated by Cox (1972), a hazard function $\lambda(t)$, defined as the event rate at time t given a survival until time t or later, may be used to estimate duration (see also Balakrishnan and Rao (2004) for an overview of important concepts of survival analysis).

The remainder of the chapter is organized as follows: Section 13.2 gives an exposé over the traditional use of duration analysis in financial institutions and markets. In section 13.3 it is shown how this type of analysis can be adopted by non-financial firms as a tool to improve investment appraisals and pricing strategies. Section 13.4 demonstrates the high relevance of duration analysis in the energy service sector for managing production and capacity expansion under fluctuating demand. Section 13.5 concludes the overview.

13.2 Financial institutions and markets

Duration is an important concept for asset and liability management (ALM) in financial institutions. ALM constitutes the principles and the practice for controlling the economic effects on a *portfolio of various assets and liabilities* of movements in market interest rates. Traditionally, the main objective has been to protect the balance sheet, but modern ALM also focuses on how to create economic value in financial institutions.

The techniques of ALM treat the values of assets and liabilities as a set of *state variables*, which may be expanded or reduced over time. Certain contracts ('instruments') between a financial institution and its customers are based upon interest rates which are fixed over specified time periods. These fixed-rate instruments generate interest-rate risks and duration analysis is used to match the average maturity of assets and liabilities with the change in their market value given a change in market interest rates. Often banks try to utilize the concave term structure of the yield curve by lending long and borrowing short, exposing them to increases in interest rates. This exposure results in a mismatch between the aggregated durations of assets and liabilities. Depending on the magnitude of this gap management may decide on hedging actions.

Samuelson (1945) and Redington (1952) were early to discover the use of duration for *immunizing a portfolio of liabilities with a portfolio of assets*. They also disclosed the relation between volatility and duration by identifying volatility in terms of a 'modified duration' equal to the interest rate elasticity (IRE) = $-D/(1+r)$. Thereafter, duration and modified duration have been widely used (see e.g. Bergendahl, 1989 and Dermine and Bissada, 2007). Table 13.1 gives an illustration of portfolio immunization for a fictitious ABC Bank.

Table 13.1 Portfolio Immunization for the ABC Bank

		Present value (€ in mn)	**Duration (years)**
Assets	Liquid securities	200	0.5
	Investment	100	4.0
	Loans – floating rate	400	0
	Loans – fixed rate	300	1.0
Liabilities	Transaction deposits	500	0
	CD – short term	300	0.2
	CD – long term	100	2.0
Equity		100	D_E
Duration of assets (D_A)		(200 × 0.5 + 100 × 4 + 300 × 1.0)/1000 = 0.8	
Duration of liabilities (D_L)		(500 × 0 + 300 × 0.2 + 100 × 2)/900 = 0.29	
Duration of equity (D_E)		$1000 \times 0.8 - 900 \times 0.29 = 100 \times D_E$; $[A \times D_A - L \times D_L = E \times D_E]$ => $D_E = 5.39$ years	
Duration gap		$0.8 - (900/1000) \times 0.29 = 0.54$ $(DG = D_A - (L/A)\,D_L = (E/A)\,D_E)$	
Immunization		*To hedge equity for changes in interest rates:* => $dE/dr = 0$; => $D_E = 0$ and $A \times D_A = L \times D_L$	

The recent financial crises clearly demonstrate the riskiness of adopting a 'lending long-borrowing short' strategy, like that of Swedish banks financing mortgage loans with short-term debt raised on either the capital market or the inter-bank market. This made them extremely vulnerable to the drastically increased risk premiums on these markets. Without the firm intervention of the central bank the whole financial system would have been jeopardized and close to collapse. Although most banks probably wished that they had adopted an immunization strategy, a complete immunization is unrealistic in the long run. Two methods are commonly used to determine a reasonable claim for the duration of equity in banks:

(i) *Bond Method:* Treat equity as a bond with a fixed annual return over infinity.
(ii) *Residual Method:* Calculate D_E from the identity: $D_E \times E = D_A \times A - D_L \times L$

Both methods are also used in the insurance business. Here ALM and duration analysis are important instruments, particularly in life assurance. A traditional life insurance policy is the product of an activity, where the insurer sign contracts with customers, collect premiums over a long time period and pays out benefits on the death of the insured. There are also combinations of life insurances and pension savings, where the benefits are paid out to the policy-holder over time before death, or to beneficiaries on the death of the insured.

As life insurance firms collect premiums from policy-holders, they take on long-term debts to customers. The length of individual debts is uncertain for two reasons. First, the date of the customer's death is unknown. Secondly, some customers will terminate their contracts prematurely. Hence, the task for life insurance firms is to place the premiums into a *portfolio* of assets that will match their uncertain long-term liabilities. Usually, the firms invest in long-term bonds, making them vulnerable to increases in market interest rates. A major ALM objective of a life insurance firm is to match the uncertain duration of its insurance contracts with the duration of its other financial assets and liabilities. This implies a two-dimensional duration analysis, which is demonstrated by Bergendahl and Janssen (1997, p. 43) using the French life insurance firm Predica (see Table 13.2).

This analysis clearly reveals the high volatility of equity of life insurance firms, making it vital for them to reduce their share of long-term bonds in times of increasing interest rates.

Table 13.2 Two-dimensional duration analysis in a life insurance firm

		Present value	Duration (years)
A.	Property equipment	2.5	0
	Technical reserves and provisions		
	Fixed rate	84.7	4.5
	Floating rate	9.1	0.5
	Equities	3.8	10
	Loans	0.2	0
	Subsidiaries	1.8	0
	Others	6.3	0
L.	Technical provisions		
	Premiums	102.1	3.9
	Claims	0.9	0.5
	Short-term debt	1.0	0.1
	Others	0.1	0
	Income	0.5	0
Average duration of assets		(2.5 × 0 + 84.7 × 4.5 + 9.1 × 0.5 +3.8 × 10 + 8.3 × 0)/108.4 = 3.91 years	
Average duration of liabilities		(102.1 × 3.9 + 0.9 × 0.5 + 1.0 × 0.1)/104.6 = 3.81 years	
Duration of equity		(108.4 × 3.91 − 104.6 × 3.81)/3.8 = 6.66 years	

13.3 Non-financial institutions

Duration analysis is not common in non-financial institutions. Assets are traditionally managed separately from financing decisions. Working-capital management is an exception, but it is targeting liquidity gaps rather than interest-rate risk exposures. Likewise, tactical and strategic decisions are mainly production and sales oriented rather than ALM related. Pricing, volume and investment decisions emphasize profitability opportunities in the value chain rather than in the balance sheet. In investment appraisals the primary concern is that investment returns exceed the opportunity cost of capital. In a levered firm that cost corresponds to the weighted average cost of capital (WACC), which may be seen as a link between the active and passive sides of the balance sheet. Still, duration analysis could provide valuable information to decision-makers also in non-financial institutions.

Consider an investment of €1m with an expected constant annual net cash flow (a) of €0.2 m/year over an economic life time (T) of 10 years and an opportunity cost of capital (r) of 15%. That gives an expected positive net present value (NPV) of €3,754 and an internal rate of return (IRR) of 15.09%. This implies that the investment is very sensitive to an upward change in the cost of capital, which is also reflected by the duration (D) of the investment. D is 4.38 corresponding to an IRE of 3.81%. Provided that cash flows remain unchanged, NPV will change by approximately €0.04 m (IRE × NPV) if the cost of capital changes by 1% and, accordingly, by about €4,000 if it increases by 0.1%. This does not make IRR a substitute to IRE. Clearly, a higher sales volume or price margin would make the investment more profitable in terms of NPV and IRR, but IRE will be unaffected as long as annual cash flows are constant over its economic life. That follows by the duration equation:

$$D = \frac{\sum_{t=1}^{T} PV(t) \times t}{PV} = \frac{\sum_{t=1}^{T} a \times t \times (1+r)^{-t}}{\sum_{t=1}^{T} a \times (1+r)^{-t}} = \frac{a \times \sum_{t=1}^{T} t \times (1+r)^{-t}}{a \times \sum_{t=1}^{T} (1+r)^{-t}}$$

$$= \frac{\sum_{t=1}^{T} t \times (1+r)^{-t}}{\sum_{t=1}^{T} (1+r)^{-t}} \qquad (2)$$

Hence, when annual cash flows are constant, the interest-rate sensitivity of the investment is only dependent on changes in the time horizon (T) and the cost of capital (r). Assuming that the latter is exogenous to the decision-maker, there are in principle two alternative ways to actively change D and IRE. The management may either select a financing strategy adapted to the investment's current cash-flow pattern, or adopt a pricing strategy that changes this pattern.

The *financing strategy* does not directly affect the duration of the investment as long as its real cash flows are unchanged (transaction costs, like agency costs, are disregarded). However, the funding of the investment may have implications for the shareholder(s). Depending on borrowing amount, lending rate, and repayment schedule, the duration of equity

(D_E) may increase, decrease, or remain unchanged. For example, it follows by equation (2) that an annuity loan over the economic life (T) of the investment will not change D_E if the lending rate is fixed and equals the cost of capital (r). However, such a high lending rate is unlikely to be in a shareholder's interest as it allows no compensation for financial risk taking. If we instead assume a lower lending rate of 5%, the duration of the loan (D_L) would be 5.10 and, consequently, D_E would be reduced. The size of the reduction is dependent on the lending amount. For example, if the firm borrows €0.5 m (i.e., half of the investment amount), D_E = 3.67 [(4.38 × 1,003,754 – 5.10 × 500,000)/503,754].[1] Obviously, D_E would be even lower if the borrowing amount is higher and/or the loan is maintained over the economic life of the investment and not paid back until time T. Given the same lending rate and loan amount, D_E would be less than 1 (≈0.69).

In these calculations it is assumed that an interest-rate change will fully affect both the lending rate and the opportunity cost of capital. Just as for financial institutions divergences must be considered in the ALM analysis. Moreover, annual cash flows are held constant. Depending on product and market conditions, management may have opportunities to influence cash flows by adopting an appropriate pricing strategy. A *pricing strategy* may be more or less aggressive with respect to how it affects customer attraction and sales levels. An aggressive strategy, like penetration pricing, may be adopted in order to reduce the interest-rate sensitivity of the investment by 'moving' the major part of the cash flows closer to the time the investment is made. That is illustrated in Figure 13.1. In this hypothetical case, NPV is assumed to remain

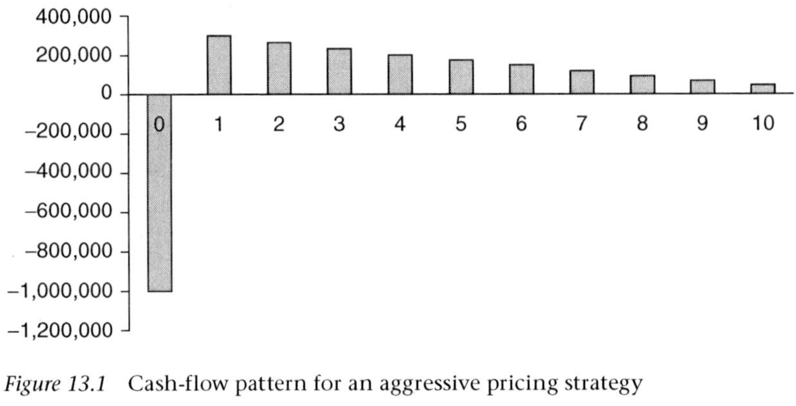

Figure 13.1 Cash-flow pattern for an aggressive pricing strategy

unchanged. With the altered cash-flow pattern, the duration would still be reduced ($D = 3.31$) and, consequently, IRE = –2.88%. This implies that the adoption of an aggressive pricing strategy makes the investment more robust to upward changes in the cost of capital. Accordingly, a less aggressive strategy, with lower initial net cash inflow but a continuous growth in annual cash flows thereafter, would result in a higher duration and an increased exposure to interest-rate risk. Hence, in the event of falling interest rates, it seems appropriate to initially adopt a price-skimming strategy that is followed by gradually lower prices.

Additional sensitivity analyses of the impact of pricing decisions as well as of changes in sales and production volume (or cost conditions), further manifest the paramount importance of the duration of an investment. In the case where the annual cash flows are fluctuating over the economic life time of the investment, it is possible to identify a cash-flow pattern where both NPV and D remain unchanged from the case with constant annual cash flows. Fluctuating cash flows are often found in service sectors since services cannot be stored but have to be provided when demanded. The demand for many energy products, such as district heating, varies over the seasons of the year, but the demand may also vary considerably between years due to natural variations in how cold or mild the winter turns out to be. This has direct implications for pricing and sales volume. However, the annual cash flows of a district heating company may also vary due to changes in input costs, such as increases or decreases in fuel prices or market prices of energy certificates.

13.4 Energy management

In many service sectors like energy, water supply and transportation it is essential for service firms to establish and maintain long-term relationships with their customers. Pfeifer and Farris (2004) analyze the importance of a satisfactory long duration for a high economic outcome and observe that 'Macaulay's duration (or Hicks' average period) is a number that equals the elasticity of ECFV (expected customer future value) with respect to retention'. Consequently, 'customer relationships with high retention elasticities are those with high durations'. Examples may be given from car manufacturing, where service and insurance programs connect customers to the producers and increase the duration of the relationship.[2] Energy management is of particular interest in large-scale technical systems (LTS) like the electricity industry and the district heating industry. The latter industry is used below to demonstrate how duration analysis can be applied to energy management. District heating is special in that different types of plants are set up to meet demand fluctuations. Plants with high fixed costs but low running costs are usually used to meet a demand of long duration, whereas peak demand with short duration is better served with low fixed cost plants despite their high running costs. In the long run it is more efficient to utilize plants with low running costs as much as possible. Price differentiation is therefore advocated for stimulating demand with longer duration.

The demand for district heating varies with the outdoor temperature, implying that the demand is (up to five times) higher in the winter than in the summer. A load diagram is a basic instrument to analyze demand variations. However, to analyze the duration of operating different plants the load diagram must be transformed into a *duration diagram* displaying the load in decreasing order over the time segments (see Figure 13.2). The diagram may either express the amount of energy demanded (in GWh) during each time segment or the average power demanded (in MW) during the same time segments.

Duration diagrams are used to determine the portfolio of different plants to serve the total demand for heat (and electricity). Plants with low running costs but high fixed costs are useful for the base load. Plants with high running costs but low fixed costs are only in operation during peak demand periods, known as 'top load'. A *normalized duration diagram* can be obtained by dividing for each time segment the amount of energy demanded by the total annual demand. Normalized duration diagrams are useful in order to compare duration diagrams

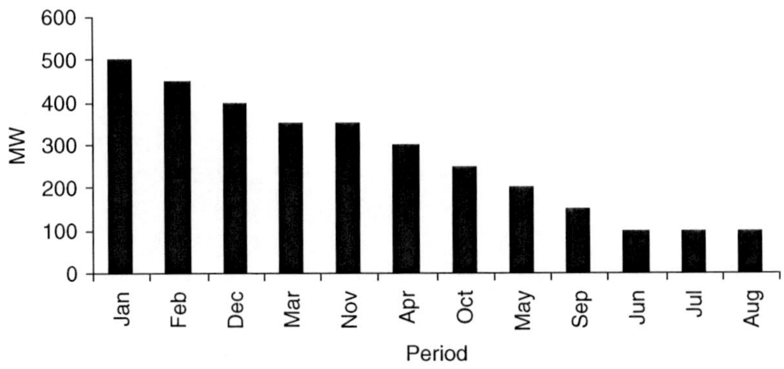

Figure 13.2 A duration diagram for heat
Source: Bergendahl (2010)

Table 13.3 A standardized distribution of the demand for heat, average capacity needed, and accumulated heat production over twelve 30-day periods of the year given a municipality with an annual demand of 1,000 GWh

30-days periods of a year	Percent of annual demand	Average capacity needed (MW)	Accumulated production of heat (GWh)
1	16	244	178
2	14	213	334
3	13	198	478
4	11	167	600
5	10	152	711
6	9	**137**	811
7	7.5	114	894
8	6	**91**	961
9	5	76	1,016
10	3.5	53	1,055
11	2.5	38	1,083
12	2.5	38	1,110

Assume that the demand for heat per hour (MWh/h) is given for each of the 7,860 hours of the year and presented in decreasing order as in a duration diagram. First, take the 30 days with the highest demand and calculate the average capacity needed for that period. With 16% of an annual demand of 1,000 GWh, this implies 0.16 × 1,000/730 = 0.2192 GWh/h or 219.2 MW. (Observe that 7,860/12 = 730). Second, assume that the firm generates 10% losses in energy, why it has to produce 219.2/0.9 = 243.5 MWh/h the first period. Then the same procedure is performed in consecutive order of the following eleven 30-days periods of the year resulting in the capacity needed in each period as well as the accumulated production of heat. Consequently, the third column states a duration diagram over the average capacity needed. Hence, the average capacity requirement of the sixth 30-days period is 137 MW, whereas it is 91 MW two periods later, i.e., the eighth one (see the bold figures in the table).

Source: Bergendahl (2010).

between different municipalities. The normalized duration diagram in Table 13.3 is taken from Bergendahl (2010, p.7) and indicates a situation, where the first time period has an average production level of 244 MW and the second one an average level of 213 MW. This implies that the *duration* for the highest average capacity requirement, i.e., 244 MW, is 30 days; the duration for the second highest (213 MW) is 60 days, and so on. Consequently, only for the period with the lowest average capacity needed, i.e., 38 MW, the duration is a whole year. Here the average duration will be 141 days of a year.[3]

Since plants with high fixed costs but low running costs are suitable for production with a long duration, and plants with low fixed costs but high running costs should only be used for shorter durations; the flatter the duration diagrams the more use there will be for the former type of plant.

A cogeneration plant is a typical representative of plants with high fixed costs but low running costs. Hence, the flatter the duration diagram the more use of cogeneration. Accordingly, existing plants fuelled by oil or coal may become suitable for a production with a shorter duration, as their running costs are high but the fixed costs low. The latter may be illustrated with an example from Bergendahl (2010, table 6):

Consider the investment and operation of a cogeneration plant fuelled by biomass with the following specifications:

- Production of heat: 533.2 GWh/yr
- Production of electricity: 296.2 GWh/yr
- Expected life: 20 years
- Investment cost: SEK 750 m
- Maintenance cost: SEK 24m/yr
- Fuel cost: SEK 121.6m/yr
- Electricity revenues: SEK 107.7m/yr
- Heat revenues: SEK 239.9m/yr

Assume further a linear depreciation schedule (i.e., 5% per year) and that the cost of capital is 5% at the beginning of its life. The fact that the duration of customer revenue is 141 days (0.4 years) implies the following duration on equity (D_E):

$$0.4 \times (107.7+239.9) - 121.6 \times 0.1 - (750/20 + 5\% \times 750) \times 1$$
$$= 127 \times D_E \Rightarrow D_E = 0.4$$

13.5 Concluding remarks

This paper has been produced in order to demonstrate that duration analysis has a use wider than for financial institutions in which duration analysis has become a vital element in the ALM of particularly banks and insurance companies. In this paper we show that duration analysis will also provide valuable information to decision-makers in non-financial institutions, where the concept of duration is not equally familiar. We illustrate the relevance of duration analysis in the appraisal of investments and put particular emphasis on the energy service sector in which investments are made in LTS. The economic life of such investments is relatively long and they are often characterized by a cash-flow pattern that fluctuates both seasonally and annually due to varying demand. In district heating, duration analysis may lay a solid foundation for developing efficient pricing and capacity expansion strategies with a special emphasis on how to identify a *portfolio of plants* in order to meet in the best way a customer demand that fluctuates over time. We show how duration diagrams can be a powerful tool in this industry for determining the need of production capacity over time. A crucial factor in the analysis is that there are customers who are willing to sign long-term contracts for prices and quantities demanded. The longer the duration of these types of contracts, the greater the risk diversification between sellers and buyers.

Notes

1. IRE (equity) ≈ –2.96% (notice that the opportunity cost of equity is higher than WACC).
2. Fader and Hardie (2007, p. 77) have notified that *"the distribution of customer life times is that of the survivor function"*. Rossat et al. (1999) have analyzed the interrelationship between customer duration, life cycle cash flow and new customer generation. Social development programs are special forms of service management programs for which the *duration of exposure* to a treatment has an important implication for the value of a program. Behrman and King (2008) have made an analysis of the importance of a satisfactory long duration for a program in order to obtain a high level of learning.
3. Computed as (0.16·1 + 0.14·2 + ... + 0.025·12)·360 = 141 days.

References

Bagdonavicius V. and Nikulin M. (2004). Statistical modeling in survival analysis and its influence on the duration analysis. *Handbook of Statistics*, vol. 23. Lavoisier.

Balakrishnan N. and Rao C.R. (2004). Advances in survival analysis. *Handbook of Statistics*, vol. 23. Lavoisier.

Behrman J. and King E. (2008). Program impact and variation in the duration of exposure. In Amin S., Das J. and Goldstein M. (eds.), *Are You being Served? New Tools for Measuring Service Delivery*. The World Bank: Washington DC.

Behrman J. and King E. (2008). Program impact and variation in the duration of exposure. In Amin S, Das J and Goldstein M (eds.), *New Tools for Measuring Service Delivery*. The World Bank, Washington, DC.

Bergendahl G. (1989). The management of assets and liabilities in banks: Principles and applications. *Revue de la Banque* (Brussels).
Bergendahl G. (2009). Investment in combined heat and power – CHP. To be published in Bjorndal E (ed.), *Energy, Natural Resource and Environmental Economics*. Springer Verlag.
Bergendahl G. Investment in Combined Heat and Power – CHP, to be published in Energy, Natural Resource and Environmental Economics (Eds. E. Bjorndal, M. Bjorndal, P. Pardalos & M. Rönnkvist), Springer Verlag, 2010.
Bergendahl G. and Janssen J. (1997). *Principles for the Control of Asset Liability Management Strategies in Banks and Insurance Companies* (Draft Report). Université Libre de Bruxelles, June.
Bierwag G.O., Kaufman GC and Khang C. (1978). Duration and bond portfolio analysis: An overview. *Journal of Financial and Quantitative Analysis* 13, 671–685.
Cox D.R. (1972). Regression models and life tables. *Journal of Royal Statistical Society, B* 34, 187–220.
Dermine J. and Bissada J.Y. (2007). Asset and Liability Management, A Banker's Guide to Value Creation and Risk Control, London, FT & Prentice Hall.
Fader P.S. and Hardie B.G. (2007). How to project Customer Retension. *Journal of Interactive Marketing* 21(1), 76–90.
Hicks J.R. (1939). *Value and Capital*. New York: Oxford University Press.
Ingersoll J., Skelton J. and Weil R. (1978). Duration forty years later. *Journal of Financial and Quantitative Analysis* 13, 627–648.
Luenberger D.G. (1997). *Investment Science*. Oxford University Press, Oxford.
Macaulay F.R. (1938). *Some Theoretical Problems Suggested by the Movements of Interest Rates, Bond Yields, and Stock Prices in the U.S. Since 1856*. New York: National Bureau of Economic Research.
Pfeifer P.F. and Farris P.W. (2004). The elasticity of customer value to retention: The duration of a customer relationship. *Journal of Interactive Marketing* 18(Spring), 20–31.
Redington F.M. (1952). Review of the principle of life office valuations. *Journal of the Institute of Actuaries* 18, 286–340.
Reitano R.R. (1991). Multivariate duration analysis. *Transactions of Society of Actuaries* 43, 393–442.
Rossat J., Larsen J., Ruta D. and Wawrzynosek M. (1999). *Customer Loyalty, a Literature Review and Analysis*. Brussels: Unipede.
Samuelson P.A. (1945). The Effect of Interest Rate Increases on the Banking System. American Economic Review 35, 1(March), 16–27.

14
Biased or Unbiased Risk Tolerance in Financial Decision Making

Caterina Lucarelli and Gianni Brighetti

14.1 Introduction

This paper focuses on the *risk tolerance* which clearly influences financial decision making. We investigated the emotional side of risk-taking behaviour, identifying subjective obstacles to the individual ability taking conscious investment and debt decisions. We used an empirical cross-disciplinary approach, combining financial competences with others from psychology and affective neuroscience. We present descriptive results from a sample of 176 individuals with different levels of financial education/competence. Some of them are traders who attended the 2008-Borsa Italiana-Trading-Expo, and some others are bank customers and bankers.

The first aim of our research is to measure the unbiased risk tolerance (UR) of individuals, in terms of uncontrolled (somatic) responses to risky choices. We employed a psychophysiological test, the Iowa Gambling Task (IGT), in order to evaluate the individual's skin conductance response (SCR) while making risky choices. Secondly, we measured the biased risk tolerance (BR) by means of a financial risk tolerance self-evaluation test. Any difference between UR and BR is crucial: it shows whether individuals are able to properly self-evaluate their risk tolerance or not, over- or undervaluing their personal capability to take a financial risk. Finally, we tried to describe the demographic socioeconomic and cultural reasons which could explain anomalies in UR and BR results.

14.2 Brief review of the existing literature

The literature about risk tolerance can be organized into five developing steps from 1970 up to now. The first stream of studies was carried out through experiments with groups of subjects whose task was to take a decision resulting in a payoff. Among these studies, Alderfer and Bierman (1970) demonstrated that, when faced with investment choices having similar mean and variance, students tend to select those options with a high positive skewness, while business managers select options with a negative skewness. This result contradicts the previous presumption of academic finance that people use only mean and variance to select investment options, and it suggests that psychological factors may affect the decision-making process.

During the 1970s, a second stream of studies enlarged the debate to an interdisciplinary level, introducing subjective reasons as determinants of one's risk perception. Baker et al. (1977) examined individual investors' risk-return preference towards common stocks. The authors carried out surveys of investing behaviour including demographic information. The authors found that age, sex, and educational level have an important influence on risk perception. In general, age and income seem to be the two main demographic determinants of risk tolerance (Hallahan et al., 2003). In particular, risk tolerance has been found to decrease with age (Wallach and Kogan, 1961; McInish, 1982; Morin and Suarez, 1983; Palsson, 1996), although some studies failed to support this result (Grable and Joo, 1997; Wang and Hanna, 1997; Grable and Lytton, 1998; Grable, 2000).

The third stream of studies, during the 1980s, introduces a behavioural approach and deepens the analysis of demographic and socio-economic factors affecting risk perception. Among these studies, Blaylock (1985) maintains that individual risk perception derives from cognitive factors, conventional risk measures, and environmental setting. The fourth group of studies began in 1990. It considers the emotional component as a further possible determinant of risk tolerance, introducing the concept of 'risk as a feeling'. As Olsen (2001) has asserted, risk always includes an emotional dimension. Grable and Joo (2000) found that psychological factors are the most significant variables of risk tolerance. Grable and Lytton (1999) found that the individual's educational level and financial knowledge are the best predictors of risk tolerance behaviour, and personal income level and occupation are also significant factors.

Up to the end of the 1990s, the main assumption was that behavioural indicators and demographic information are the most important variables of personal risk tolerance. Starting from 2000, two key innovations emerged in the risk tolerance literature – the fifth group of studies. First, Weber et al. (2002) identified conventional risk attitudes (the reported level of risk-taking) and perceived risk attitudes (the willingness to engage in a risky activity as a function of its perceived riskiness). In this context, Corter and Chen (2005) measured the difference between levels of risk revealed through traditional questionnaires used by banks, and willingness to take a real risk. They compared the results of three traditional questionnaires (their own Risk Tolerance Questionnaire, Scudder Kemper's, and the Vanguard Group's) with the 'sensation-seeking scale' introduced by Zuckerman (1994). The results show that the three questionnaires are consistent but do not correlate with the sensation -seeking measure. This suggests that any attempt to measure risk tolerance needs something more than a questionnaire. As a consequence, clinical measures were introduced to observe physical reaction to risky situations. Lo and Repin (2002), Steenbarger (2002), and Lo et al. (2005) recorded psychophysiological measures of emotional response (such as blood-volume pulse and SCR) with a sample of traders during live trading sessions. Results showed that even the most experienced traders exhibited significant emotional responses during risky market events.

14.3 Methodology: the IGT, the SCR and the questionnaire

Although originally intended to explain decision-making deficits in people with specific frontal-lobe damage, the IGT has proved effective in exploring the application of the Somatic Marker Hypothesis (Damasio, 1994) in a variety of psychiatric populations (for example Viswanath et al., 2009) and in healthy subjects (for example Franken et al., 2008).

Given that emotional responses rather than rational forces have recently begun to be considered as major factors in financial decision-making processes, it seems plausible to apply Damasio's hypothesis in the field of economics and finance. Specifically, Damasio postulates that the somato-visceral signals from the body (affective reactions) ordinarily guide individuals' decision-making and risk-engagement processes. According to this hypothesis, each behavioural option is associated with unconscious somatic responses, including neural responses, evoked by its previous consequences: responses that either encourage or discourage a certain choice. The IGT simulates real-life decision-making in conditions of uncertainty, and with consequences of reward and punishment.

In this task, participants sequentially select a card from four decks and receive a monetary outcome after each selection. Somatic reactions (for example SCR) to these rewards and punishments are generated after each card selection (posticipated SCR) so that individuals begin to trigger anticipatory reactions (anticipated SCR) that will guide their forthcoming choices. Even if gains and losses are only simulated, a similar performance pattern emerges when the nature of the incentive used is varied, for example when giving real money rather than 'facsimile reinforcers' (Bowman and Turnbull, 2003).

We used a computerized version of the task based on the original as described in Bechara et al. (1996). In this version, the subject sees the four decks of cards on a computer screen. The decks are labelled A, B, C, and D at the top end of each deck. Using the keyboard, the subject can choose a card on any of the four decks. In summary, after choosing the letter of the card, the subject receives some money (the amount is displayed on the screen). The ultimate future yield of each deck varies because the penalty amounts are higher in the high-paying decks (A and B), leading to a negative balance, and lower in the low-paying decks (C and D), leading to a final gain. Thus, decks A and B are 'disadvantageous', whereas decks C and D are 'advantageous'. The computer tracks the sequence of the cards selected from the various decks. As the subject performs the task, SCR activity is recorded continuously and collected simultaneously on a personal computer.

In addition to the psychophysiological devices, we used a traditional questionnaire with three sections. The first consists of the Grable and Lytton (1999) questionnaire, used to measure 'self-evaluated' risk tolerance; the second consists of an impulsivity test; and the third allows the collection of demographic socioeconomic information, together with personal financial choices relating to past investments and debts.

14.4 Indicators of risk

A preliminary goal of the paper was to find measures of both UR and biased self-evaluated risk tolerance (BR). At this preliminary stage of the analysis we left aside the tolerated risk (TR) measure. Bearing in mind our aim to measure any divergence between UR and BR, we needed the two measures to be metrically comparable, so we tried to find any measure of UR and BR between -1 and 1 with the following formula:

UR or BR = +1: maximum risk propensity;
UR or BR = –1: maximum risk aversion;
UR or BR = 0: indifference towards risk.

As far as BR is concerned, the measure was obtained from the global score (S), and the subject *'i'* was obtained from the Grable and Lytton test (see Grable and Lytton, 1999). Given:

S_i the score obtained by the subject *'i'*;
$S_{max} = 63$
$S_{min} = 20$
$S_{mean} = 37$

and observing an asymmetric position of S_{mean} compared to S_{max} and S_{min}, we have:

$$BR_i = \begin{cases} \dfrac{(S_i - S_{mean})}{(S_{max} - S_{mean})} & \text{if } S_i \geq S_{mean} \\ \dfrac{(S_i - S_{mean})}{(S_{mean} - S_{min})} & \text{if } S_i < S_{mean} \end{cases} \tag{1}$$

This computation returns extreme values:

- BR = +1 for individuals showing the highest level of self-evaluated risk propensity: they think of themselves as being able to afford high level of risk;
- BR = –1 for individuals showing the lowest level of self-evaluated risk propensity: they think of themselves as not being able to afford any risk;
- BR = 0 for individuals self-evaluating as neither risk-loving nor risk-adverse.

The measure for UR is more difficult to calculate because it must be a combination of two parameters: first, the IGT score, related to preference either for the disadvantageous or the advantageous decks; second, the anticipatory SCR, since we focused on the anticipated reactions that guided the financial choices. The difficulty is to obtain a global UR for subjects, considering both their anticipatory SCR to disadvantageous decks and their performance at the IGT.

In this paper we show a very preliminary hypothesis for the UR measure, being aware that the adjustment of this indicator is a focus of the overall research. At present we intend to calculate this measure for the subject *'i'* as a combination of the following two indicators:

$$UR_i = f(NP_i, NASCRD_i) \tag{2}$$

NP_i is the normalized performance in the choice of decks and NASCRD represents the measure of the anticipated SCR to the disadvantageous decks.

In particular:

$$NP_i = \frac{IGT_i - IGT_t}{IGT_{max} - IGT_t} \tag{2.1}$$

where:

- $IGT_i = D_i - A_i$ is the performance obtained as a difference between the number of disadvantageous (D_i) choices and the number of choices from advantageous (A_i) decks, during the test;
- IGT_t = number of choices made during the trial period (in this case = 20 choices);
- IGT_{max} = maximum number of choices made during the test (in this case = 100 choices).

The way NP_i was calculated made it between –1 (maximum choices of advantageous cards, which happens with risk-averse individuals) and +1 (maximum choices of disadvantageous cards, which happens with risk-loving individuals); it was equal to 0 when the subject made the same number of disadvantageous and advantageous choices. NASCRD was obtained as:

$$NASCRD_i = \frac{\overline{ASCRD_i}}{\max\left[\overline{ASCRD_{pop}}\right]} \tag{2.2}$$

In particular:

- $NASCRD_i$ is the normalized anticipatory SCR for disadvantageous choices of the individual '*i*';
- $\overline{ASCRD_i}$ is the average anticipatory SCR for disadvantageous choices shown by individual '*i*' during the test, excluding the trial period;
- $\max\left[\overline{ASCRD_{pop}}\right]$ is the maximum average anticipatory SCR for disadvantageous choices shown within the population of all the individuals.

The way $NASCRD_i$ was calculated makes it theoretically between 0 and 1: a 0 value stands for an average somatic indifference to disadvantageous decks; a 1 value stands for a strong somatic response. The choices for the function '*f*' which generates the formula (2) appear quite complex, and we are still exploring the theoretical issues related to the empirical relevance of strong anticipated skin conductance response to both disadvantageous and advantageous decks in relation to NP.

14.5 Some preliminary statistics on the somatic learning process

The following Figures and Tables show the development of negative conditioning to losses for the sample of individuals studied for this paper. Specifically, in Figure 14.1a the SCR average levels are higher when disadvantageous deck choices are compared to advantageous deck choices (on average, 0.2113 vs. 0.1992). Assuming that individuals' choices are conditioned by previous experiences, we would expect that each behavioural option becomes associated with an unconscious anticipatory somatic response that either encourages or discourages a certain choice. In fact, we find evidence of the development of a bigger anticipatory SCR for disadvantageous decks compared to advantageous decks. This is shown by Figure 14.1b which shows the average anticipatory SCR for first choices at a 0.2069 level, whereas it is 0.1969 for the second choices.

Moreover, we estimated a logit panel model where the dependent variable is the dummy *D* and the regressor is a time trend (*prog*). It is important to emphasize that we tested different models, including a trial period of 20 choices (considering only the last 80 sequential observations); a trial period of 40 choices (60 sequential observations), and finally extending the trial period to 60 choices (40 sequential observations). The logit model was as follows:

$$D_{it} = \mathrm{L}\,(\alpha_i + \phi\, prog_{it}) \qquad (3)$$

Comparing the estimates of models tested with sample of 176 subjects and shown in Table 14.1a–14.1c, we found a significant negative parameter of the time trend, increasing in absolute value from 0.0027068 in Table 14.1a (last 80 sequential observations) to 0.007479 in Table 14.1c (last 40 sequential observations). It might be expected that if the individuals understand the experiment (whether they respond rationally or somatically) and the more the choices they make, the more they will tend to refuse the disadvantageous decks. The SCR experience could thus prove to be a learning process inducing individuals to develop risk aversion, in terms of reduction of choices from the disadvantageous decks.

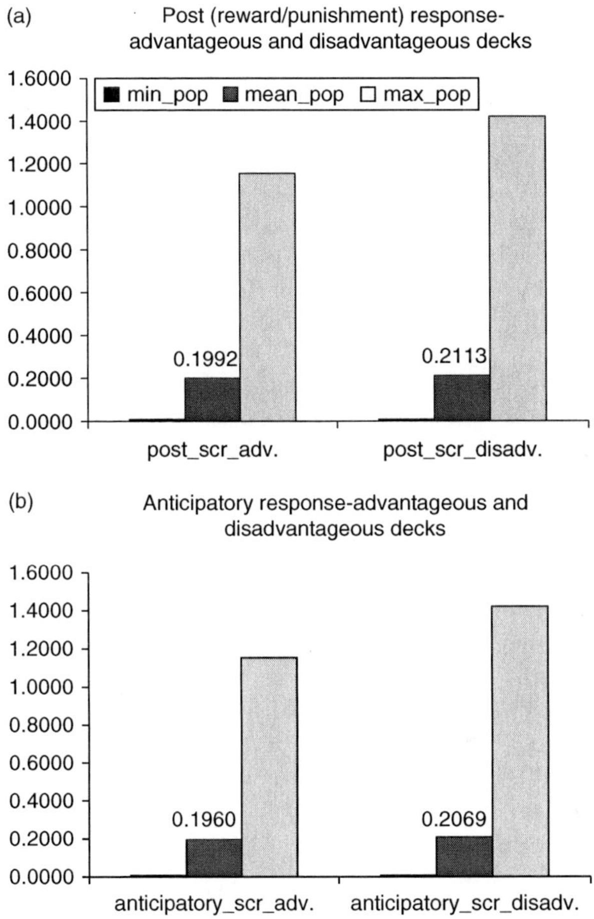

Figure 14.1 Skin conductance response (SCR) for the sample of 176 individuals

14.6 Demographic, social and cultural explanation of the results

In this section we present descriptive results of basic socioeconomic drivers which may explain differences in risk tolerance levels, both biased and unbiased, for our sample of 176 individuals. Tables 14.2 to 14.6 present, on their left, general descriptive statistics of the sample, and on their right, two-way summary statistics comparing BR computed as (1), NP computed as (2.1), and NASCRD computed as (2.2), where each line stands for the mean value and the standard deviation, respectively.

Table 14.1a The logit model including a 20-choice trial period

D_20	Coef.	Std. Err.	z	P>|z|	[95% Conf. Interval]	
prog	−.0027086	.0009235	−2.93	0.003	−.0045187	−.0008985
_cons	−1.260426	.059038	−21.35	0.000	−1.376138	−1.144713

Logistic regression
Log likelihood = −**6926.1813**

Number of obs = **14080**
LR chi2(**1**) = **8.61**
Prob > chi2 = **0.0033**
Pseudo R2 = **0.0006**

Table 14.1b The logit model including a 40-choice trial period

D_40	Coef.	Std. Err.	z	P>|z|	[95% Conf. Interval]	
prog	−.0054874	.0014306	−3.84	0.000	−.0082913	−.0026835
_cons	−1.054524	.1024371	−10.29	0.000	−1.255297	−.8537515

Logistic regression
Log likelihood = −**5154.0049**

Number of obs = **10560**
LR chi2(**1**) = **14.75**
Prob > chi2 = **0.0001**
Pseudo R2 = **0.0014**

Table 14.1c The logit model including a 60-choice trial period

D_60	Coef.	Std. Err.	z	P>|z|	[95% Conf. Interval]	
prog	−.007479	.0026596	−2.81	0.005	−.0126918	−.0022663
_cons	−.8778427	.2146363	−4.09	0.000	−1.298522	−.4571632

Logistic regression
Log likelihood = −**3375.7213**

Number of obs = **7040**
LR chi2(**1**) = **7.92**
Prob > chi2 = **0.0049**
Pseudo R2 = **0.0012**

Table 14.2 shows how the gender driver works clearly, especially as far as the BR indicator is concerned. As agreed in the literature, males tend to be more confident than females (higher average BR). Even if their performance was the same (similar NP between male and females), females showed a stronger somatic activation in relation to disadvantageous decks (higher NASCRD). That is to say, females, on average, did not evaluate themselves as risk-loving, but they made just the same risky choices of males.

Table 14.2 Gender

Gender	Freq.	Percent	BR	NP	NASCRD	
male	135	76.7	0.275666	0.052593	0.136636	*mean*
			0.223626	0.285865	0.123979	*sd*
female	41	23.3	0.075654	0.057927	0.174463	*mean*
			0.251414	0.307533	0.201439	*sd*
Total	176	100	0.229072	0.053835	0.145448	*mean*
			0.244805	0.290165	0.145951	*sd*

Table 14.3 Age

	Freq.	Percent		BR	NP	NASCRD	
Under_30	21	11.93	Under_30	0.313187	−0.02857	0.154676	*mean*
				0.185369	0.427952	0.181299	*sd*
Between_30_45	86	48.86	Between_30_45	0.19949	0.048837	0.147246	*mean*
				0.248657	0.268106	0.153413	*sd*
Between_45_60	51	28.98	Between_45_60	0.303301	0.110784	0.141018	*mean*
				0.233619	0.253143	0.131877	*sd*
Over_60	19	10.8	Over_60	0.072875	0.010526	0.137613	*mean*
				0.217194	0.280663	0.104556	*sd*
Total	176	100	Total	0.229072	0.053835	0.145448	*mean*
				0.244805	0.290165	0.145951	*sd*

Table 14.3 demonstrates that elderly people clearly evaluated themselves as more risk-averse than younger people (comparison of BR), even if the latter behaved more cautiously (negative NP) and showed a strong somatic attraction to the riskier (disadvantageous) decks. Interestingly, a life-long cycle of risk tolerance is shown in Figure 14.2.

Table 14.4 shows educational qualifications. The higher the level of education, the stronger the BR (higher average BR values). Results for NP and NASCRS are more difficult to evaluate with a multivariate analysis.

The influence of profession on risk tolerance is shown in Table 14.5. The highest BR was related to risky professions, especially entrepreneurs,

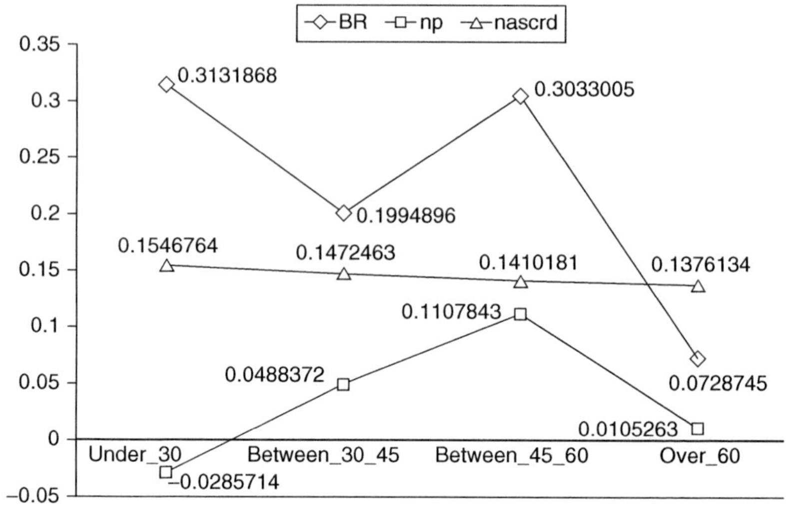

Figure 14.2 A life-long cycle of risk tolerance

Table 14.4 Educational qualifications

	Freq.	Percent		BR	NP	NASCRD	
Secondary school	11	6.25	Secondary school	0.110654	0.054546	0.129326	*mean*
				0.326044	0.294919	0.105958	*sd*
High school	88	50	High school	0.218197	0.072443	0.124702	*mean*
				0.251592	0.281979	0.119936	*sd*
University	64	36.36	University	0.247808	0.023438	0.183216	*mean*
				0.225541	0.311419	0.184137	*sd*
Master or Ph.D	13	7.39	Master or Ph.D	0.310651	0.076923	0.113587	*mean*
				0.191319	0.248425	0.08303	*sd*
Total	176	100	Total	0.229072	0.053835	0.145448	*mean*
				0.244805	0.290165	0.145951	*sd*

managers and traders. Nevertheless, the latter two showed a strong somatic activation and tended to act cautiously (negative NP), while entrepreneurs had the highest self-evaluated risk tolerance (BR), but did not react somatically (lowest NASCRD) and tended to choose more disadvantageous decks (positive NP).

Table 14.5 Profession

	Freq	Percent		BR	NP	NASCRD	
Salaried employee	74	38.54	Salaried employee	0.184083	0.061487	0.152247	*mean*
				0.245038	0.279989	0.157408	*sd*
Pensioner	19	9.90	Pensioner	0.088354	0.039474	0.168159	*mean*
				0.209351	0.274408	0.104621	*sd*
Manager	3	1.56	Manager	0.320513	-0.075	0.212301	*mean*
				0.096793	0.198431	0.244838	*sd*
Freelancer	26	13.54	Freelancer	0.205186	0.057692	0.110537	*mean*
				0.226328	0.300564	0.095002	*sd*
Entepreneur	27	14.06	Entepreneur	0.305849	0.080556	0.078265	*mean*
				0.283941	0.303769	0.096901	*sd*
Pers. Financial Advisor	7	3.65	Pers. Financial Advisor	0.296703	0.139286	0.161703	*mean*
				0.121046	0.282052	0.113352	*sd*
Trader	31	16.15	Trader	0.318859	−0.04032	0.194214	*mean*
				0.179906	0.337989	0.18142	*sd*
Unemployed	5	2.60					
Total*	192	100.00	Total	0.229072	0.053835	0.145448	*mean*
				0.244805	0.290165	0.145951	*sd*

*Multiple choices

The last aspect we considered was the influence of the knowledge of financial products on individual risk tolerance. This indicator was based on individuals' knowledge of all the following financial products or processes: bank account; bank deposit; certificate of deposit; repossession contract; postal deposit; treasury bills; stocks; bonds; mutual funds; exchange traded fund; financial management; hedge funds; structured products; derivatives; index- and unit- linked insurance policies. A general indicator was obtained, summarizing for each individual the number of known products and dividing the results by the maximum number (15). We split the sample into two classes of subject: those knowing more than 50% of the products (*high_fin_k*) and those

Table 14.6 Financial Knowledge

	Freq.	Percent		BR	NP	NASCRD	
low_fin_k	40	22.73	low_fin_k	0.104695	0.078125	0.159251	*mean*
				0.254421	0.259511	0.135321	*sd*
high_fin_k	136	77.27	high_fin_k	0.265654	0.046691	0.141388	*mean*
				0.230336	0.299101	0.149165	*sd*
Total	176	100	Total	0.229072	0.053835	0.145448	*mean*
				0.244805	0.290165	0.145951	*sd*

knowing less than 50% of the products (*low_fin_k*). In future we intend to elaborate on this to provide a more sophisticated indicator of financial knowledge. Table 14.6 shows the results.

A stronger knowledge of financial products is associated with a higher self-evaluated risk tolerance (BR), lower somatic reaction to disadvantageous decks and a lower score at the IGT (more cautious behaviour). Thus, those subjects who consider themselves as experts in this field are characterized by a lower somatic perception of risk and better performance of the task.

Concluding remarks

Any result we present in this paper must be considered preliminary because the empirical analysis is ongoing, with an enlarged sample of individuals. Nevertheless, the final study should suggest some theoretical and practical implications which are useful especially for the 'production', and also the 'distribution', of financial products. At a theoretical level, we suggest a more appropriate measure for the risk tolerance of individuals. The traditional measure, static and exogenous in the conventional portfolio theories, could be improved to become an endogenous and dynamic indicator, showing the real pattern of risk-taking during the financial decision process. At the operational level, we suggest some general behaviours that are relevant in the financial markets and could improve the reliability of both the strategic and the tactical asset allocation processes. Implications for the 'distribution' of financial products are relevant if ε_1 results are different from 0. To give an example, when the UR is higher than the BR we might have a sub-optimal situation. If an individual can unconsciously tolerate higher levels of risk, he or she receives a sub-optimal reward, so the intermediary can offer riskier products. By contrast, when the UR is lower then the BR, we have a financially hazardous situations. Individuals face a financial hazard when they engage in activities with a higher level of risk than they can really tolerate. These results appear more relevant in relation to the recent regulation of financial markets, introduced by MIFID, in terms of transparency and communication between intermediaries and customers.

Acknowledgements

This research is supported by a grant from the Italian Ministry of University and Research as a 'Progetto di Ricerca di Interesse Nazionale' – PRIN 2007 (September 2008–September 2010). We are grateful to the whole research group involved in the empirical analysis: Camilla Mazzoli, Cristina Ottaviani, Nicoletta Marinelli, Valeria Nucifora, Rosita Borlimi, Giulio Palomba, Elisa Gabbi, Arianna Rizzoli, Sara Falcioni.

We are grateful to Twice SIM – Milan and Banca Popolare di Ancona – UBI Group for their cooperation in providing an assorted sample of individuals which participated to our test. A special thank goes to the President of Assogestioni, Prof. Marcello Messori, for the opportunity to include in the analysis a relevant sample of Asset Manger. In particular, we are grateful to JPMorgan – ITALY, Pioneer, Eurizon Capital, Azimut, UbiPramerica, Arca and Prima sgr for taking part actively to our experiments. This paper is a preliminary draft referred to some initial empirical findings. The analysed database, the methodology and preliminary results have been obtained thank to the cooperation of the whole research group involved.

References

Alderfer CP and Bierman H. (1970). Choices with risk: Beyond the mean and variance. *Journal of Business* 43(3), 341–353.

Baker HK, Hargrove MB and Haslem JA. (1977). An empirical analysis of the risk-return preferences of individual investors. *Journal of Financial and Quantitative Analysis* 12(3), 377–389.

Bechara A, Tranel D, Damasio H and Damasio AR. (1996). Failure to respond autonomically to anticipated future outcomes following damage to prefrontal cortex. *Cerebral Cortex* 6, 215–225.

Blaylock BK. (1985). Risk perception: Evidence of an interactive process. *Journal of Business Research* 13(3), 207–221.

Bowman CH and Turnbull OH. (2003). Real versus facsimile reinforcers on the Iowa Gambling Task. *Brain and Cognition* 53, 207–210.

Corter JE and Chen Y. (2005). Do investment risk tolerance attitudes predict portfolio risk?. *Journal of Business and Psychology* 20(3), 369–381.

Damasio AR. (1994). *Descartes Error: Emotion, Reason and the Human Brain*. New York: Avon.

Franken IH, van Strien JW, Nijs I and Muris P. (2008). Impulsivity is associated with behavioral decision-making deficits. *Psychiatry Research* 158(2), 155–163.

Grable JE. (2000). Financial risk tolerance and additional factors that affect risk taking in everyday money matters. *Journal of Business and Psychology* 14, 625–630.

Grable JE and Joo S. (1997). Determinants of risk preference: implication for the family and consumer science professionals. *Family Economics Resource Management Biennial* 2, 19–24.

Grable J and Joo S. (2000). A cross-disciplinary examination of financial risk tolerance. *Consumer Interests Annual* 46, 151–157.

Grable J and Lytton RH. (1998). 'Investor risk tolerance: testing the efficacy of demographics as differentiating and classifying factors. *Financial Counseling and Planning* 9, 61–73.

Grable JE and Lytton RH. (1999). Assessing financial risk tolerance: Do demographic, socioeconomic, and attitudinal factors work? *Journal of FRHD/FERM Divisions of AAFCS* 3, 1–9.

Hallahan T, Faff R and McKenzie M. (2003). An explanatory investigation of the relation between risk tolerance scores and demographic characteristics. *Journal of Multinational Financial Management* 13, 483–502.

Lo A and Repin D. (2002). The psychophysiology of real-time financial risk processing. *Journal of Cognitive Neuroscience* 14, 323–339.

Lo AW, Repin D and Steenbarger BN. (2005). Fear and greed in financial markets: a clinical study of day-traders. *The American Economic Review* 95(2), 352–359.

McInish TH. (1982). Individual investors and risk-taking. *Journal of Economic Psychology* 2(2), 125–136.

Morin RA and Suarez AF. (1983). Risk aversion revisited. *Journal of Finance* 38, 1201–1216.

Olsen RA. (2001). Behavioral finance as science: Implications from the research of Paul Slovic. *The Journal of Behavioral Finance* 2(3), 157–159.

Palsson AM. (1996). Does the degree of relative risk aversion vary with household characteristics?. *Journal of Economic Psychology* 17, 771–787.

Steenbarger B. (2002). *The Psychology of Trading: Tools and Techniques for Minding the Markets*. Hoboken, New Jork: John Wiley & Sons.

Viswanath B, Janardhan Reddy YC, Kumar KJ, Kandavel T and Chandrashekar CR. (2009). Cognitive endophenotypes in OCD: a study of unaffected siblings of probands with familial OCD. *Prog Neuropsychopharmacol Biol Psychiatry* 33(4), 610–615.

Wallach MM and Kogan N. (1961). Aspects of judgment and decision making: interrelationships and changes with age. *Behavioral Science* 6, 23–26.

Wang H and Hanna S. (1997). 'Does risk tolerance decrease with age?' *Financial Counselling and Planning* 8, 27–32.

Weber EU, Blais A and Betz NE. (2002). A domain-specific risk-attitude scale: Measuring risk perceptions and risk behaviours. *Journal of Behavioural Decision Making* 15, 263–290.

Zuckerman M. (1994). *Behavioural Expressions and Biosocial Bases of Sensation Seeking*. University Press Cambridge: Cambridge.

15

Banks' Measurement of Operational Risk and the Effect on Regulatory Capital

Ted Lindblom and Magnus Willesson

15.1 Introduction

The exposure to operational risk is nothing new for banks, but as Moosa (2007:167) stresses: 'The trend towards greater dependence on technology, more intensive competition, and globalization have left the corporate world more exposed to operational risk than ever before'. For a bank the occurrence of an extreme or major 'one-off' event in its daily operations may be even more damaging than its credit losses resulting from the current collapse of the financial markets. However, the ability of the bank to properly assess and control, or hedge itself against, the negative economic consequences of such events seems to be less developed than its management of credit and market risks (Flores et al., 2006; Wold, 2006; Moosa, 2007; Bonsón et al., 2008; Wahlström, 2009). A challenge for the bank is that the main focus of its operational risk assessment must be on the distribution tail rather than on the distribution of the most frequent losses (Wei, 2007; Moosa, 2008).

Banks' assessment of risk exposures is also a concern of financial authorities. The introduction of the Basel II accord may be regarded as a regulatory attempt to encourage improvements that sharpen risk management in banks, but also to mitigate regulatory arbitrage (Aparicio and Keskiner, 2004; Calem and LaCour-Little, 2004; Lastra, 2004). Under Basel I, all banks had to comply with a rather broad and arbitrary regulation of their credit (and later also market) risks in accordance with a 'one size fits all approach' (Avery and Berger, 1991; Jones, 2000). Under Basel II that also covers operational risk-taking; the individual bank may seek and get permission to use its own sophisticated internal risk model(s) in order to reduce its capital adequacy requirement to a level where regulatory capital corresponds to economic capital. This implies that banks are 'rewarded' for having greater knowledge and better internal understanding of the magnitude of their risk exposures and how their asset portfolio should be appropriately managed in order to avoid severe losses.

According to the regulatory statutes, a bank's exposure to operational risk may be evaluated according to three measurement approaches, each with a different degree of sophistication. The most sophisticated approach – the advanced measurement approach (AMA) – develops the bank's own internal risk evaluation model. The bank can also use an approach relying on the bank's gross income as the 'relevant' operational risk exposure indicator, that is, the basic indicator approach (BIA), which is the default approach, or the standardized approach (SA), which is slightly more sophisticated from a risk perspective. Still, it seems to be a poor measurement approach for assessing the true operational risk-taking of the bank.

Lindblom et al. (2008) observe that most banks in Sweden adopted the highly unsophisticated BIA when the new accord was implemented in 2007. No bank used its own internal risk evaluation model for calculating the regulatory capital required to cover its exposure to operational risk. The obvious reason was that the AMA was not yet an option offered by the regulatory body, but it is questionable whether any bank would have chosen the AMA anyway as most banks appeared to be in a learning process. The number of banks adopting the SA was steadily increasing from one quarter to the next. However, even if the adoption of more sophisticated regulatory risk measurement approaches is giving the banks an option to set aside less capital for covering risk exposures (Moosa, 2008), this kind of incentive did not seem to matter much for the banks. Just as they held much more capital than required by the regulation during previous years under the old accord (Lindblom and Olsson, 2007), a majority of the banks continued to do likewise in 2007 despite the widening of the risk concept to also cover operational risk. As all banks used either BIA or SA in 2007, we cannot claim that Swedish banks were particularly sophisticated in their operational risk management – at least not as regards the determination of regulatory capital needed to comply with the new Basel accord. On the other hand, representatives of the banks were generally affirmative of including exposures to operational risk in the regulatory framework (cf. Wahlström, 2009, who reports a similar response from respondents in his 'pre-study' from 2004).

Lindblom et al. (2008) forecast that Swedish banks are in a continuing learning process towards the use of more advanced methods in their assessment of operational risk exposures. As shown in Table 15.1, however, the banks' implementation of more sophisticated measurement approaches has slowed down. Only one bank has yet chosen to use its internal risk model explicitly. The apparent slowdown of the learning process is unexpected considering the importance given to risk assessment by bank managers (cf. Wahlström, 2009), but also with respect to the financial crisis as more sophisticated approaches are generally expected to result in lower capital adequacy requirements.

Table 15.2 reveals that Swedish banks were generally well capitalized in 2008 as well as in 2007. The 'own funds ratio' is defined as the bank's total own funds for capital adequacy purposes[1] divided by the regulatory capital required for covering its aggregated exposure to risk. This ratio must therefore be at least equal to one. The lowest average ratio in any quarter was 2.17 (see the third quarter of 2008), implying that

Table 15.1 Swedish banks' adoption of operational risk measurement approaches in 2007–2008

	2007				2008			
Regulatory approach	Q1	Q2	Q3	Q4	Q1	Q2	Q3	Q4
BIA	76	76	76	78	68	69	69	69
SA	10	15	16	17	18	18	18	19
AMA						1	1	1
N/A	15	11	8	3	1			
Total (N)	101	102	100	98	87	88	88	89

Table 15.2 The 'own funds ratio' of Swedish banks in 2007 and 2008

	2007			**2008**		
	N	**Mean**	**Std dev.**	**N**	**Mean**	**Std dev.**
Q1	101	2.35	0.91	87	2.26	0.80
Q2	102	2.43	1.73	88	2.21	0.79
Q3	100	2.42	1.75	88	2.17	0.78
Q4	98	2.33	0.77	89	2.24	0.98

the average bank had no problem complying with Basel II despite the financial crisis and the economic recession. However, the spread is substantial between individual banks, ranging from a ratio of only 1.10 to a ratio as high as 18.08 (not shown in Table 15.2).

In this chapter Swedish banks' operational risk measurement is further examined with respect to explanatory factors for their adoption of a certain regulatory approach and how it affects the banks' regulatory capital.

15.2 Data

Apart from branches of foreign banks, all banks under Swedish supervision must comply with Basel II. Each bank is required to report its risk exposures and regulatory capital held for covering these exposures to the Swedish Financial Supervisory Authority four times a year in accordance with the document 'Capital Adequacy and Large Exposures' (FFFS, 2007:1 and FFFS, 2008:13). Our analysis is based on the banks' quarterly reporting of such data during 2007 and 2008. This means that the data covers about one and a half years of good economic conditions and half a year of recession.

Table 15.3 provides a recent overview of the Swedish banking industry, also including foreign banks' subsidiaries.

Table 15.3 The Swedish banking industry at the end of 2007 and 2008

Year / Type of bank	2007		2008	
	N	Total asset *(Msek)*	N	Total assets *(Msek)*
Commercial banks *(of which the big four)*	28	5,182,955 *(4,849,616)*	30	6,435,040 *(6,077,804)*
Foreign commercial banks	4	*	4	*
Foreign banks' subsidiaries	27	754,033	29	878,901
Independent savings banks (ISBs)	65	146,249	53	155,453
Cooperative banks	2		2	
TOTAL	**126**	**6,083,237**	**118**	**7,469,394**
Of which under Swedish supervision	99**		89	

* Total assets for foreign commercial banks are included in the commercial banks total assets.
** of which one bank got the concession during 2007, but did not start its operation until 2008 and consequently did not report anything during 2007.

Sources: Svenska Bankföreningen (2008;2009) and SCB ("Statistics Sweden").

In total 103 banks are included in the data set, but the number of banks varies across different quarters from 87 to 102 banks.[2] This is due to market consolidation through mergers and acquisition, new bank charters, and the closure of old banks. The commercial banks account for more than 85% of the Swedish banking market in terms of asset size. Four of these banks ('the big four') dominate the market with a capitalization of over 80%. The market is also characterized by a relatively large number of small independent savings banks (ISBs). More than every second bank under Swedish bank supervision is an ISB. The majority of these banks are traditional savings banks, but 13 ISBs have recently converted themselves into limited companies, fully or partly owned by a trust foundation. By definition they are now commercial banks. Six of them are partly owned by Swedbank, which is one of the big four.

15.3 Reasons for the choice of regulatory approach for measuring operational risk

As is well known, it can be a real challenge for an individual bank to measure its exposure to operational risk. Neil and Andersen (2009) report that a potential reduction of as much as 20 to 40% of the regulatory capital does not give banks sufficient incentive to adopt the AMA. Operational risk is largely seen as a residual risk, and therefore hard to define and identify (cf. Lindblom et al., 2008). Shortage of data, the context-dependent nature of operational risk, and the lack of a strongly risk-sensitive exposure indicator in risk models all make the AMA difficult to implement (Moosa, 2008). A tentative conclusion drawn by Lindblom et al. (2008) is that the choice of regulatory approach is size-dependent. This is further manifested by Wei (2007) and Bonsón et al. (2008). However, it is evident from Table 15.1 that it is not only the big banks which are using the SA, suggesting that the size of the bank is not the only explanation for banks' choice of regulatory approach.

With reference to the principal agency theory, we check whether ownership structure has an impact on the banks' adoption of regulatory risk measurement approach. As most of the banks are ISBs with no owners and we have information about the owner concentration of only a few commercial banks, the banks are categorized with respect to their association form in Table 15.4.

Table 15.4 shows that the default approach for measuring operational risk exposure (BIA) is used by the majority of the banks in each association form category, but the magnitude differs. The BIA is used by both of the cooperative banks and by almost 90% of the ISBs, whereas

Table 15.4 Operational risk measurement with respect to association form in 2008

		2008			
Association form	**Regulatory approach**	**Q1**	**Q2**	**Q3**	**Q4**
Commercial banks	AMA		1	1	1
	SA	12	13	13	13
	BIA	20	19	19	20
ISBs	SA	6	5	5	6
	BIA	46	48	48	47
Cooperative banks	BIA	2	2	2	2

two out of five commercial banks are using either the somewhat more sophisticated SA or the internally-based AMA. This difference is, however, unlikely to be explained by the association form. The commercial banks are on average significantly larger than the ISBs and the two cooperative banks, indicating that size matters more than association form. This does not mean that ownership is unimportant. A division of the banks into the following subcategories of (i) the big four, (ii) the six former savings banks (ISBs) that are now commercial banks partly owned by Swedbank, and (iii) other banks, reveals that banks in the first two categories stand out as being more sophisticated. All of these banks are either using the SA or the AMA, which suggests that institutional ownership matters. This implication becomes even more evident when considering that only one of the other seven former savings banks (not partly owned by Swedbank), and only three of the remaining commercial banks, are using the SA, that is, over 80% of the remaining commercial banks (the big four and the six banks partly owned by Swedbank excluded) are still using the default approach. This makes them similar to the ISBs and strongly suggests that ownership in combination with size affect a bank's adoption of regulatory approach for assessing its operational risk exposure.

Another size-dependent factor is related to the information systems in banks, as larger banks are likely to invest more heavily in information technology and advanced systems than smaller ones. This is suggested by Bonsón et al. (2008), who tested the impact of country origin and balance sheet intangibles as these factors were expected to be positively correlated with a bank's need for an advanced information system.

Table 15.5 The relationship between the choice of regulatory approach for measuring credit risk and operational risk

Regulatory approach		2007				2008			
Credit risk	**Operational risk**	Q1	Q2	Q3	Q4	Q1	Q2	Q3	Q4
IRB (advanced)*	AMA	1	2	2	2	2	1	1	1
	SA						2	2	2
	BIA	1	1	1	1	1			
	N/A	1							
IRB	SA	4	8	8	8	8	8	8	8
	N/A	4							
SA	SA	4	5	6	5	8	8	8	9
	BIA	60	59	60	65	67	69	69	69
	N/A								
N/A	SA	1			2				
	BIA	15	16	15	12				
	N/A	10	11	8	3				
TOTAL (N)		101	102	100	98	86	88	88	89

* All (three) banks that are using Value at Risk (VaR) models for measuring market risk exposure are assumed to be more sophisticated than other banks in their use of the internal ratings based (IRB) approach when determining the regulatory capital required for covering their credit risk exposure.

However, the authors failed to find any significant effect for either factor. In Table 15.5 the role of information systems is approached somewhat differently, displaying the relationship between the banks' choice of regulatory approach for measuring exposures to credit risk and their adoption of operational risk measurement approach.

It is evident that the assessment of credit risk exposure is vital to a bank and therefore gives it incentives to invest in improvements of its information system. As the banks have far more experience of assessing credit risk than operational risk, it is reasonable to control for whether there are any 'spillover' effects on their measurement of operational risk. Table 15.5 clearly indicates that the banks' choice of approach for measuring operational risk is strongly dependent on the credit measurement approach adopted. All banks that are using IRB, regardless of whether they are using VaR for measuring market risk exposure, had adopted SA by the end of 2008. It should be noted that the bank that initially used BIA was planning to use its own internal risk model for measuring operational risk exposure as soon as it was sanctioned by the supervisory authority. The bank reported in accordance with the AMA in the second quarter of 2008 and thereafter. The two other banks we assumed were advanced IRB users almost immediately adopted SA for measuring operational risk exposure, and according to their representatives (Jarl and Wigren, 2009) both banks may very well change to the AMA quite soon. A majority of the banks that were using the default approach (SA) for measuring credit risk exposure also maintain the default approach (BIA) for assessing operational risk exposure.

15.4 Adoption of risk measurement approach and its effect on capital adequacy requirement

Under Basel II the total capital adequacy requirement is mainly based on the bank's aggregated exposure to credit, market, and operational risks. Table 15.6 shows the total capital adequacy requirements for these three main types of risk exposures in relative terms for commercial banks, ISBs, and cooperative banks, respectively.

As expected, credit risk exposure is by far the most common risk exposure in the banks and accordingly the regulatory capital set aside to cover this exposure is many times larger than the capital held for any other risk exposure. The low market risk on average is due to the fact that few banks seem to be exposed to market risks. This risk is almost non-existent in non-commercial banks. Another difference is that commercial banks are also more exposed to operational risks in

Table 15.6 Average capital adequacy requirement with respect to risk type at the end of 2008

	Bank category			
Type of risk exposure	**Commercial**	**ISBs**	**Cooperative**	**All banks**
Credit risk exposure	79.6%	90.4%	89.5%	86.3%
Operational risk exposure	17.9%	9.5%	10.5%	12.7%
Market risk exposure	2.5%	0.1%	0%	1.0%
Number of banks	n=34	n=53	n=2	n=89

Note: Due to the transition rules, we isolate the measured risk exposure for the three main risk types when we compare their relative importance.

relative terms. In combination with the high capitalization of the banks in general (see Table 15.2), the relatively low share of regulatory capital for covering operational risk exposure may of course be a plausible explanation for the widespread use of the default approach. It does not pay off to use a more advanced approach.

When the commercial banks are divided into the three subcategories, we can observe that the big four as well as the former savings banks that are now partly owned by Swedbank display similar exposure to operational risk to banks in general. The remaining commercial banks are on average much more exposed to operational risk with respect to the capital adequacy requirement, but a closer look discloses that this additional exposure concerns only eight of the banks. As the remaining commercial banks do not differ from the average bank, these eight banks are studied in more detail. Each bank has adopted the default approaches for determining the regulatory capital to be held for their exposure to operational risk and credit risk, respectively. However, their use of the BIA can hardly be the only or even the main reason for their significantly higher regulatory capital requirement for operational risk exposure in relative terms. After all, they are using the SA for credit risk exposure. A more plausible reason lies in the fact that seven of the banks are investment banks. Generally, such banks do not have large credit portfolios and do not therefore expose themselves to high credit risks. This makes their operational risk exposure more pronounced. At the end of 2008, as much as 42.2% of their total capital adequacy requirement was held for covering unexpected losses from operational risk exposure.

The apparently high preference for using the default approach for operational risk measurement implies that the economic incentive for adopting a more advanced approach is not high enough. This demands an analysis of how the capital adequacy requirement changes when a bank upgrades to a more sophisticated approach. During the first two years of the new regulation, only seven banks have switched to another regulatory approach. One bank switched from the BIA to the AMA, whereas the other six banks moved from the BIA to the SA. Three of these six banks reported the same amount of regulatory capital as before, whereas two of them actually reported a slightly higher amount. Thus, only one of the banks that switched to SA gained in terms of a significantly lower capital adequacy requirement. (The bank that started to use its own internal measurement method, of course, also managed to decrease its regulatory capital requirement substantially.)

The relatively few upgrades of the regulatory approach and their seemingly meagre outcome, together with the widespread use of the

Table 15.7 Frequency of changes of regulatory capital for operational risk exposure, 2007 and 2008

Number of banks with...	**2007**			**2008**			
	Q2	**Q3**	**Q4**	**Q1**	**Q2**	**Q3**	**Q4**
...unchanged capital base	79	88	20	55	82	84	16
...increasing capital base	2	2	70	20	1	3	60
...decreasing capital base	4	1	0	8	3	1	12
Total (N)	85	91	90	83	86	88	88

default approach, lend support to the conclusion that capital adequacy requirement for operational risk exposures is of minor importance for the banks. This conclusion is further strengthened when we analyze the compliance reports of the banks in more detail. As Table 15.7 shows, these reports are often identical from one quarter to another. In only a small fraction of the banks does regulatory capital held change over time. Most changes or updates are made in the fourth quarter of the year, and to some extent also in the first quarter.

A more detailed analysis reveals that a majority of the banks update their reports of operational risk exposure once a year. As many as 49 banks did so in the fourth quarter of both the years, whereas eight banks made an update in the first quarter of 2008. This implies that there is a very strong link to accounting information and that these banks do not report gross income on a quarterly basis. Instead, reporting is based on historical data on an annual basis. A few of the bigger banks are updating their figures more frequently, but no bank is doing that every quarter. However, four banks made changes twice a year and two banks did actually update their figures in every quarter of 2008. It is still evident that the reports are primarily made in order to comply with the regulatory framework rather than to provide valuable information to the business units of the banks.

15.5 Conclusions

The new Basel accord forces the banks to develop and design internal risk information models and systems. This seems to have had a major impact on the risk management of banks in general, and on their assessment of operational risk exposures in particular. This chapter generates additional empirical findings on the actual adaptation of Swedish banks to the new regulations, especially by evaluating how operational risk measurement is related to the measurement of other types of risk exposure. Our analysis leads to the following conclusions:

1. The banks' compliance reports to the Swedish financial supervisory authority are accounting-based, and primarily made in order to meet regulatory demands rather than the information needs of their business units.
2. There is a strong relationship between size and the choice of regulatory approach for measuring operational risk. We observe that the four largest banks, and the banks partly owned by one of these banks, adopt more sophisticated approaches than the other banks. In addition, there is a spillover effect within banks from their credit risk measurement to their operational risk measurement. This strengthens the size-effect conclusion.
3. The economic incentives to adopt more sophisticated operational risk approaches are generally insignificant for the banks. High own funds ratios cannot be linked to the degree of sophistication in their operational risk measurement. Nor do we find that the banks that have changed their regulatory approach necessarily show lower capital requirements for operational risk exposure.

These findings show that the there is a discrepancy between the regulator's intention towards risk management and banks' risk management in practice. It is evident that reporting to the regulator is done in order to comply with the regulatory framework rather than to provide valuable information to the business unit of the bank. We can assume that either the banks are not interested in the modelling of operational risk due to the difficulties of modelling these risks formally (in other words, the benefit does not exceed the costs of adopting a more advanced regulatory approach), or the approaches provided do not cover the actual risk exposure of the banks. The latter does not exclude the possibility that the banks are using more advanced models for internal purposes. If this is true, then the implementation of the new Basel accord has succeeded in fulfilling the objective of sharpening operational risk measurement in the banks, but has failed to accomplish the important objective of making the real risk exposure of banks more transparent.

Notes

1. The total own funds for capital adequacy purposes is derived from equity capital, subordinated debt, and other near capital defined in Tier I and Tier II (and in some cases Tier III) in the Basel accord.
2. The significant difference in the number of banks that reported in the fourth quarter of 2007 and the first quarter of 2008 is mainly explained by two big mergers that in total concerned ten small savings banks. There were also two acquisitions of banks, which reduced the number of banks by two in the first quarter of 2008. One new bank was also registered in the first quarter of 2008. Although these mergers explain almost the entire drop in terms of number of banks in the first quarter of 2008, the two new banks that these mergers gave rise to do not show up in the data until the second quarter and the fourth quarter, respectively. Hence, in reality there should be two additional observations in the first quarter of 2008 and one more in the second and third quarters of 2008, where data is not provided. This also means that the number of active banks did not change during 2008, even though the number of analyzed banks changes.

References

Aparicio J. and Keskiner E. (2004). *A Review of Operational Risk Quantitative Methodologies Within the BASEL-II Framework.* Accenture Technology Labs, Sophia Antipolis, France.

Avery R.B. and Berger A. (1991). Risk-based capital and deposit insurance reform. *Journal of Banking and Finance* 15(4/5), 847–874.

Bankföreningen S. (2008). Bank och finansstatistik 2007, Juni 2008, http://www.bankforeningen.se/upload/ broschyr_bank_finansstatistik07_uppdat.pdf.

Bankföreningen S. (2009). Bank och finansstatistik 2008, April 2009, http://www.bankforeningen.se/ upload/bank_finansstatistik2008.pdf.

Bonsón T., Escobar T. and Flores F. (2008). Operational risk measurement in banking institutions and investment firms: New European evidences. *Financial Markets, Institutions and Instruments* 17(4), 287–307.

Calem P.S. and LaCour-Little M. (2004). Risk-based capital requirements for mortgage loans. *Journal of Banking and Finance* 28(3), 647–672.

FFFS. (2007). Blankett Kapitaltäckning och stora exponeringar, Bilaga 2 in *Föreskrifter och allmänna råd om kapitaltäckning och stora exponeringar,* Finansinspektionen, Stockholm.

FFFS. (2008). Blankett Kapitaltäckning och stora exponeringar, Bilaga 2 in *Föreskrifter om ändring i Finansinspektionens föreskrifter och allmänna råd (FFFS 2007:1) om kapitaltäckning och stora exponeringar,* Finansinspektionen, Stockholm.

Flores F., Bónson-Ponte E. and Escobar-Rodríguez T. (2006). Operational risk information system: a challenge for the banking sector. *Journal of Financial Regulation and Compliance* 14(4), 383–401.

Jarl H. and Wigren S. (2009). *Operativa risker: Handelsbanken, Nordea, SEB och Swedbank.* University of Gothenburg (Bachelor thesis).

Jones D. (2000). Emerging problems with the Basel Capital Accord: Regulatory capital arbitrage and related issues. *Journal of Banking and Finance* 24(1/1), 35–38.

Lastra R.M. (2004). Risk-based capital requirements and their impact upon the banking industry: Basel II and CAD III. *Journal of Financial Regulation and Compliance* 12(3), 225–239.

Lindblom T. and Olsson M. (2007). Bank capital and loan pricing: Implications of Basle II. In Molyneux P and Vallelado E (eds.), *Frontiers of Banks in a Global World*. Palgrave MacMillan, Hampshire, pp. 78–102.

Lindblom T., Olsson M. and Willesson M. (2008). Operational risk under the Basel II capital adequacy framework. Submitted to *Journal of Banking Regulation*.

Moosa A. (2008). A critique of the advance measurement approach to regulatory capital against operational risk. *Journal of Banking Regulation* 9(3), 151–164.

Moosa I.A. (2007). Operational risk: A survey. *Financial Markets, Institutions and Instruments* 16(4), 167–200.

Neil M., Häger D. and Andersen L.G. (2009). Modeling operational risk in financial institutions using hybrid dynamic Bayesian networks. *The Journal of Operational Risk* 4(1), 3–33.

Wahlström G. (2009). Risk management versus operational action: Basel II in a Swedish context. *Management Accounting Research* 20, 53–68.

Wei R. (2007). Quantification of operational losses using firm-specific information and external database. *The Journal of Operational Risk* 1(4), 3–34.

Wold M. (2006). Basel II moves operational risk into the open. *Securities Industry News* 18(33), 22.

Index